Tom Hathaway was born on 29 May 1959, at his aunt's house in Lenton, Nottingham, and spent the first ten years of his life being dragged up in the ignominious Meadows district of that city.

In 1970, following exemplary attainments in his formative education, he was invited to the prestigious Forest Fields Grammar School; therein a chance to beat the inner city traps and pursue a beckoning university placement. In 1973, the local Labour government abolished Nottingham's mainstream grammar schools and three years after that, Hathaway walked out in the middle of his English A-level class and out of the school gates for the last time, having attained little more than a seething contempt for the system which for so long had promised him the stars and then shot him down on the launch pad.

Unable to settle in a job for more than weeks, days or hours, in the summer of 1979, whilst in the employ of a major Nottingham department store (and having, unbeknown to a female colleague, got her daughter up the duff), Hathaway booked a one-week holiday in Europe. He never came back – instead embarking on a series of swashbuckling boozing and shagging adventures en route to eventually conning his way into a job at the US Armed Forces base in Berchtesgaden, Bavaria. There was to mark the beginning of a three-year period spent fine-tuning his rapidly emerging talent for being a pan-European pest.

In 1982, having squandered his late father's inheritance, having robbed two banks, having been unceremoniously dumped by two millionaires' daughters for brazen inter-infidelity, having been sacked three times from two jobs and twice deported from Switzerland (all of this in the same week), Hathaway fled back to England to take up a bar job at the then trendy News House in Nottingham's St James Street – a popular watering hole for local musicians and young poseurs of the day.

It was during a lunchtime shift here that he was introduced to and invited out for a 'bit of a sesh' by and with a notorious local rock group known as the Chimneys. Less than ten minutes into the said sesh, it became starkly apparent to Hathaway that he had hitherto been largely deluding himself as to the true meaning of the word 'misbehaviour'. When the sesh finally slumped to a close about seven years later, Hathaway was encouraged by certain entities close to the band to compile a document of at least part of their advent. This is that document.

Today a frequently published poet, Hathaway lives in London with his wife, Susan, and three quid.

Rich &
to Louise
from Tink. xxx

FULL BACON JACKET

To
Louise
Happy Trails
xx

FULL BACON JACKET

Tom Hathaway

ATHENA PRESS
LONDON

FULL BACON JACKET

ISBN 1 84401 487 8

First Published 2005 by
ATHENA PRESS
Queen's House, 2 Holly Road
Twickenham TW1 4EG
United Kingdom

Printed for Athena Press

Acknowledgements

With love, thanks and titanic appreciation to:

Andy Cope, Michael Hayden, John Barry Foster, PC Simons (not a copper*), PC Culham (a copper), Andrew Charles Dewyss, Wendy Askwith, Stevie Askwith, Robert Pollard, Stephen Taylor, Indiana Wham, Richard Evans, Christopher Charles Rolls, Pete and Pat McDonald, Andy and Cath McDonald, Stanley Maragh, Wes Edis, Georgy Porgy Pudding and Pie, Peas, Chips and Gravy twice, Dave Heron, Dave Cushley, Chris Moran, Eileen Ferguson, Michael Vermuyden Van Der Linden, Maggie O'Donnell, Mr Sulleiman's Halal, Paul Guilford for grabbing me before I left the cliff at Masada (but not for grabbing me morning wokker, having mistaken it for yer kitbag handle in Jerusalem); Referee Jidley, Ronna Didley, Amy and Erica for guarding the safety walnut all night; Raisa and Bunji, Helen Hartland, Marie Shelton, Marie Dwyer, Sophia Loren, Urko and Bones Kelly, John Blankley, Gary King, Wayne 'Mafeking' Bonser, Wayne Colley, Paul Marr, Glen Birch, Glen Musson, George 'Tapperzookie' Jarmers, Everton Outside, Les Purdy, Pete Fallon, Pete 'Hooverin' Slavonic Glasses' Stowban, Red Roy Ridgewee, Manchester Mick Mulligan, Spike Steeples and Fletch. A specially special BIG THANK YOU especially to my invaluable production team of **Mark Askwith** and **John Barnes**; and moreover, to Laura Warren and Diane Williams @ South Notts College IT wing, Clifton, for sorting out – in one last ditch onslaught – the unholy chimp's nostril created by my invaluable production team.

Well. I guess the blessed Almighty did his level best to warn and waylay me.

God bless and keep you all safely by...

Hathaway.

---

* And definitely **not** overly PC, either.

The author wishes to point out that this bloody infernal book, which was finally reluctantly embarked upon in 1996 and sodding at last completed in 1999 (I know it's now 2005 – do me a big favour: don't ask!), contains specific reference to actual events which actually took place during the mid-1980s, therefore any similarity or discord with actual events actually occurring subsequent to its year of completion can only be coincidental and unforeseen.

Most of what follows actually happened. The rest was spotted coming a mile off and nipped in the bud before it could. The names of certain of the characters have been modified, either to preserve their dignities or to enable the author to take the supreme piss with impunity.

ONE

Peel Street, Nottingham, England
8.45 p.m. Sunday, 27 October 1991

I poured out the last of the Tanqueray. Swilled it straight down. Again. Let drop bottle and glass quietly onto the carpet. American shadow twist pile. Luxury. So this is bachelorhood. Nice place I've got. Nice consolation prize. Lying next to me, her portrait photograph. Pick it up. Dust it with a sleeve. Kiss it. My little sweetheart. I'm so sorry I got you mixed up in this burnt soup. I'm so sorry I had the selfish stupidity to land you on this screwed-up planet. It's a con, and you never realise it's a con until your kids are born. Life. Life's a bus, and if you can guess which stop is yours then you sit pretty, only you've got a thousand stops to guess from and from the bus they all look identical. That's why we all cry our lungs out when we realise where we've just been born. What are you doing now, sweetheart? What are you thinking about? You're a bright little girl! Will you ever understand whyever I left you and your lovely mum for the Schizo bitch? Because I won't. You're only three. Have you met any liars yet? I was only three or four when I first met a liar. I picked up the sixpence from the gutter. Donna said it was hers. I wasn't sure. We hadn't seen him at the top of that nearby ladder, but the window cleaner came down to settle it. He knew he'd dropped the sixpence, but he gave it to me, just because Donna lied. She was never nice again after that and her ma wouldn't let me into the house anymore.

Then before you've even realised it, the second liar you've met in your life is yourself. You see it work; you see it save work and you copy – to survive. But I always felt a guilt, and that's the difference. Guilt-free liars are a different breed.

Back onto the bus. Look out for your stop. Come on, man! Pull things together! Breathe. It's a fucking nightmare. I've got to turn my head down; got to stop thinking – got to stop crying. If you give it a shot and she hears you crying, you'll get zero respect off her. Pull it together. Breathe! Look at the nice curry on the kitchen table. Toot of steam. Still hot, if you want me. Just can't face eating. Me and the curry, eh? Both active; neither actively required.

Okay! Up! Up, off your mardy, maudlin arse and make something happen! Bin the bottle, bin the curry. Dry your eyes, wash your face. Another kiss for the photograph. Got the keys; let's get out of here. Definitely go and give it a shot, but stay ice, and whatever you do, don't let her hear you cry. Women, man; so amazing. They'll say it's all right for a guy to cry – 'What's wrong with that?' Then they'll actually see him doing it and they fucking hate it, because then, in their eyes, he's just depreciated himself. Lost power. Lost value. Lost cost. Okay. I'm ice. I'll give it one last shot. Never know; the Schizo bitch might have changed personality for just long enough for you to wedge a hard-on in the doorway.

Nerves jangling still. Out to the car. Drive to Phil's old place, just around the corner. Get another drink. Wish Phil was still around. He'd take these car keys off me till tomorrow. No warmth in here anymore. Everyone moved on. Everyone moved off. Strange, analytical faces. Tacky neon promos. Mood-jarring fruit machines. Half-smiles from smooching couples, billing and cooing; littering up the postcode with smarm. I don't want to see this. Wrong frame. Two pints, two vodkas, then just get out. Back to the car. Drive. Look for a phone. Give it a shot. One last shot. Then you'll know for sure. At least you'll know. It's been two weeks now. This is the final reading. This is the forever gauge. Secluded phone box. Breathe. Again. Out. Lock the car. In. Bloody turbo; such is my luck, I've dialled four digits and there's already five or six muppets forming a queue outside. Impatient. Prying. Listening for the bye-byes. Off-putting. Bungled the number – dial again. Tut-tut outside. I'm through. It's the Schizo's voice.

'Hello, it's me. How's everything?'

'Okay.'

'Okay, or the same?'

Galling hesitation.

'Same.'

These stroppy one-worders. Annoying. Stupid. Not in the mood for incurring strop. Let's turn the heat up.

'The same today, or the same tomorrow?'

'The same for ever.'

Breathe. Remember – ice. 'So that's definitely it, then?'

'I'm sorry, Shed, just think of all the times you kicked *me* out.'

'That wasn't for my own good; that was for *our* good, and just think of all the times I took you back... no questions asked! I screwed up. I'm sorry. You enjoyed screwing up every weekend and you've never been sorry – you've never *met* sorry!'

'You've been drinking!'

'Give me something better to do!'

'Pay some more towards my bank loan.'

'*What?* You've got more chance of seeing Lord Lucan on *This Is Your Life*! You owe *me* money!'

'If you've only rung up for a row, I'm putting the phone down.'

'Yep! That sounds like you – never deal when you can run.'

'You just drink too much!'

'It seems to me that everything here comes down to bottles. Okay. I've been hitting the bottle too much. But at least I've got the bottle to admit it. I've also got the bottle to entertain a critical discussion. I've got the bottle to stand firm in a relationship through bad times as well as good times, and

I've got the bottle to stick around when the money runs out. I'll make a deal with you. I'll put my bottle down if you pick some up!'

I don't believe the spineless bitch! She's hung up. Dial again. She's going to listen to this, one way or the other. Like it or bike it.

'Helloww!'

'Hello... Look, I don't mean to upset you, but we've got to talk.'

'I'm not coming back to you, Shed.'

'Okay, okay, so that's crystal, then. It's on board. So it's just a case of natural conditions running their course, eh?'

'Yeah, I suppose that's it – I suppose it's outlived its natural conditions, eh?'

'That's not what I meant.'

'What else did you mean?'

'Well, it's simple. Your feelings for me were always naturally conditional on how much cash I'd got for the blowing of. When *that* ran out, *they* did.'

'Don't call *me* a gold-digger!'

'Your aunt's words, not mine!'

'I've had rich *and* poor boyfriends!'

Okay. So you know it's over now. Nothing to lose. Let's give it out. Like Mark Anthony always said about guts-ache. If it irritates you, neck seven pints and irritate the bastard right back. 'No, Shed, I'm not doing speed, Shed.' ... 'Okay, I *was* doing speed, Shed – had my fingers crossed behind my back while I was telling you I wasn't, Shed.' Picture *that* one for gusto.

'Yeah, and from what I've seen, the poor ones were all poor, fucking ugly bastards. The rich ones were still poor fucking ugly bastards, but less poor and unfortunately for you, less stupid.'

'Don't you worry – I'll find my happiness and settle down with someone nice!'

'Yeah, you'll find it. Then when his wallet gets bulimic, he'll be through two architraves faster than a set of squirrel's knuckles on the vinegar stroke.'

'I'm putting the phone down now until you're sober!'

'You'll never live that long!'

Bleeee... Ah, well. Let her go now. Fuck her. Dirt can't walk, but you can walk on dirt. Screaming at me like a bloody banshee like that! And she used to be so warm, sparkling, vibrant. All snuffed out. Even her sense of humour. She was always so happy and cheerful through and through. Now she's about as happy and cheerful as a jilted Dalek. Okay. That's the final reading. That's the forever gauge. Now you know for sure. Break away. Walk on, accordingly. Wonder if Mummy wrote that script for her? I know *she* didn't. Breathe. Leave them in their down spiral. Shallow trash. One day she'll finally wake up to the reality of being a closet gash-swapper, sadly devoid of the bottle to swap gash. You're not grata anymore, man. Look out through the glass. They're gawping in at you – resent you. Hurry up, pisshead; fuck your pain. I'm more important. My life's more important. It's more important that I use this phone to call the dork I'm pretending to like, to ask if the dork he's pretending to love got rid of the dork she's pretending to hate. For my important life's sake, man. Now they're tapping at the glass. I'm ice. Hyperventilating... no! *No*! Stay ice. *Tap, tap, tap*!

I'm not ice anymore. Flashpoint. Grab the receiver again.

'OKAY–LET'S–ADJUST–SOME–FUCKING–ATTITUDES!'

Six glass panels. Each one exploding outwards to a word. By receiver or boot. Now I'm a danger. Receiver trailing; still spinning, dancing. Fists bleeding. Slam the door wide open. Nobody with any important phone business anymore. They're backing away. Shock. Daren't flinch. I'll kill the first bastard that even breathes this way. Turn away. To the car. Leave them, get to the car, get away from there. Drive fast; breathe. Make towards Mount Street. Just two minutes away. You're away. There, now. Lock it. Just a quiet drink in the Hearty Good Fellow, then home.

Go in, cool it with a cool lager. Meet some people. Grin wide. Drunks laugh; they don't grin wide. They won't suspect you. Pull on the door. Walk into the buzz. Different world – hey! Neil Young on the system – good start. Last time I heard this, a problem was something so ridiculous; you laughed and just ignored it and somehow it always went away for ever. *'Hey, hey! My, my!'* Rust never sleeps. That's a bastard fact. Marie serving ale – Welsh Marie who used to sing with the Westwoods. Polite. Smiling. Nice. I like polite – so rare these days. How's it, Marie? A lager and a Bushmills, please. Great music! Keep it up! Give me twenty pound coins please; I'm going on the 'Police Pursuit and Arrest' machine. Might be a while. Coins in. This babe's fast. Low gear, now. Foot to the deck. Three – Two – One – *Green* – we're off! Where's the bad lads' car? Change gear. Heeere they come! Porsche versus Ferrari. All to be trashed. Now! Ram the bastards! Again! Again! Again! Till it blows; shit – they're away again! Get going – get them back in your sights. Adrenalin churning. This is great. Hit the turbo. Here we go. There they are. Breathing right down their necks again. Gotcha, me laddoes. Ram! Bash the gets! One! Two! Umpteen whacks and they're all done. Ferrari in flames. Excellent! Now let's go again, then again. This is a rush. Get more ale. Get two and two Bushes. Then I don't need to shift from the machine. Fifteen credits. I'm set for a fast half-hour... *No*! I don't believe it! It's the great British bell! Is it *that* time already? How time flies when you're deliriously happy and contented within yourself and life and the world. Back to the screen. Take out a black marker pen. Sheer devilment. Mark on the screen where I last sighted the felons. Arrow 'THEM'. I'm just here – arrow 'ME'. They got away under the highway bridge. I'll know just where next time, unless the marker washes off. Okay. Got to leave, but what to do with all the adrenalin?

Step outside. It's colder now. On the doorstep, looking at the car. Why not? The Schizo owns half of it and I don't care if I get killed. Death can pay the rent and take care of the bills; I can't. So it's a *real* game of pursuit before bedtime. Get in. Decide the rules. Rules are as follows: One: insufficient signals or use of mirror – fair game. Ram. Two: Loud, non-rock stereo – fair game. Ram hard. They might not hear you. Three: anyone suspected of failing the attitude exam – ram. I'm tonight's surprise package in town. Ignite. Both radios on. Let's trot. Now, let me guess – and this is merely a guess – ten to fifteen attitude failures, some without badges and being covered by downpan cab operators – will be at this precise moment in time blocking off half of Greyfriar Gate to traffic in their nefarious pursuit of black market trade or marital infidelity outside the MGM Club. Tsk, tsk. Direct contravention of rule three... yes, here they all are. Good guess! Sick of grafting and paying my way and watching them do neither. One arrogant bastard looking at me and still standing there in the road, one of his doors wide open. Today's diesels are actually a little faster off than you might suspect, my friend. Wow! My hat's off to you – never saw a man dive clean over his car before! One door, two or three side mirrors. That's a respectable haul of trophies in two seconds. Okay, that's it. Away. Cross through to the Maid Marian Way traffic. Check the mirror. They're stunned. Attitude adjustment implemented.

Away into Maid Marian Way. Find the thirty-mile-per-hour club. The drunks who stick to thirty at this time of night. Alfa doing twenty-seven. Obvious. Draw abreast. Look over. Smile. Drop into third. Ram and move. Mirror. He's shocked; pulling over – can't call the police because he's over the edge and he knows it. Okay. Don't push it. Round into Parliament Street and head home. Theatre Royal corner... oh dear! Yet more attitudes! Black and white cab just sitting in front of me on a green light while his fare walks out into the road towards him from an empty lay-by. Zounds! But how disrespect abounds! Let's have a beer and consider the forfeit. Pop a can. Take a protracted gulp. Reverse, come around... park directly in front of him and sit through eight or nine light changes... enjoy the beer. Idiot's reversing, so *I* reverse. Now he's trapped between cars, his customer can be enjoying the onset of the clock whilst going nowhere. Other traffic seems to be loving this. Okay, we're close to home, go and live there for ten hours, enough capers. Get rest.

But any rest was soon to be snatched right out of my hands. I remember taking it down South Sherwood Street. Practically home. Mission over. It had rained fairly heavily while I was in the Hearty and the surfaces were a little glassy. I was draining the can, heading down to the lights at around forty when they began to change. I was going too fast, so I booted it to go through, then I saw the front of the Traffic Granada poking out at the right hand intersection. I hit the anchors sharply and skidded sideways through the junction, can visibly in hand. Grinning right into the faces of the Granada's two occupants. Yep, starry uniforms. I swear I could briefly lip-read a double *'What the f***!'* before I righted the car, dropped it a cog and blasted on into North Sherwood, losing the can out of the drawn-back sunroof. Bloody speed retarders all the way up – just when you need to lose a twenty-nine injection four-four. I'd even swung it round into Peel Street with a view to a ditch-and-run, when fate lent a hand to smack me in the earhole with. A Sierra gunship, chasing a completely unrelated pinch, was now blocking me off in front. They'd clocked the Granada there behind me and cranked up the woo-woo and flashing blue. Okay. It's a capture. Park it. Grin. They're getting out of the Granada. Three from the gunship. *No!* I can't grip this! It's 1927 Culham – the same copper that bubbled me last Christmas when I beat the rap on a technicality. All-time record holder, Nottinghamshire Force pinch rate. Getting greater. Eats paperwork. Culham by nature more than name. He's coming over. Wind down the sidescreen, suck in some fresh air.

'Hiyer, Shed! Knew we'd be seeing you again! Have a nice Christmas, last year?'

'Not bad, thanks, Cul! I beat your pinch, I'm afraid!'

'Yer didn't!'

'Technicality, mate!'

'That's unbelievable! Frank, have you heard this?'

'Yeah! Lucky man! Until just now, Cul.'

'Yep! Tell you what, Shed! Me breathalyser went red as soon as you went past us!'

'Hey, Shed!'

What's this? Oh, luxury... another bastard's holding the beer can on a pencil.

'Look what I found rolling past! And I bet your sherbets are all over it, hey? Tell you what, lads! I was just saying to Cul as we clocked *this* one. Reminds me of that nutter back in '87 – the one that lost it in the same place and did practically the same thing. Took one of our lads' motors out on the way, then stuck his 'unter into the shuttering at Traffic's car pound and legged it. Gave himself up one hour later – you remember – mad bastard!'

I knew that'd cheer me up as I passed out in some piss-sodden cell. He's talking about the Skipper. Great. He's still famous down there. Culham's back.

'Here you go then, Shed! One nice long breath until the red bulb jumps out and the box melts, then just hand over your keys and we'll drive you to a nice cheap hotel for the night.'

Yeah, I think I've stayed there before. Sleep well, Shed; because tomorrow your feet won't touch, me ol' pal.

TWO

City Magistrates' Court, Nottingham
11.05 a.m. Monday, 28 October 1991

'We of the Bench have considered the, er... shall we say, *unusual* mitigating circumstances pertaining to this case; and to your benefit, we are inclined towards a modicum of sympathy. However. In view of the fact that you are currently on bail for a similar offence – and that you were before this Court only ten months previously, whereas *then* convicted of a similar offence... for which you... incurred a four point... endorsement... er... Clerk! Excuse me! Clerk, is this entirely correct?'

'Ahem, yes, it appears to be, sir.' Sir's eloquence foundered somewhat.

'What? He was proven to be five and a half times over the prescribed limit, yet he received only a four point penalty?'

'Yessir.' He beckoned the clerk nearer.

'Banged to rights?'

'Apparently so, sir... mitigating circumstances, sir.'

'Most unusual.'

'Most mitigating circumstances tend to be, sir.'

'Ahumph! Thank you, Clerk – ahumph! Remaining in view of the fact that you were convicted of an identical offence less than a year ago, the law would not permit this bench to prescribe anything less than a custodial sentence. Hopefully your time in prison will allow you to reflect and to contemplate a more sober alternative to this seemingly *dedicated* pursuit of drunken recklessness. You will go to prison for three months, and consider yourself a very fortunate young man. Take him down.'

That's it then. I've certainly irritated them. Turn to wave to my brother. Down the steep wooden stairs, down the corridor, through the pig pens. Handcuffed to some nicotine-oozing shitkicker, and out into the yard. Onto the wagon. Last man. Just fit in with one hand between my legs, cuffed to a bar under the seat. Other hand still handcuffed to the shitkicker, who by the way, never punched anyone, and finally my ponytail trapped in the back door – accidentally.

Dave's driving and Stan's riding shotgun. Keep your eyes on the road, fat bastard. We've gone three hundred yards and you've already done more than I was ever pinched for – sober or drunk. What if this crate crashed and went off a bridge and burned? Dave and Stan would save their dripping sandwiches and leg it. We'd all drown or fry or fry and drown. It would be impossible to get us out in time and I'd never see the kids again. All because I couldn't cope. It's time we opened up a counselling clinic for the man who 'has everything' – featuring a duty optometrist to help us to see precisely what 'everything' looks like and a 90-decibel alarm to go off and remind us to think about it twenty times a day.

Forty-five miles and not a word. Poor bastards, they're all even more stunned than me. At least I'll be out for Christmas with full remission.

Here it is; then first stop, last stop – Lincoln Prison. What a daunting-looking shit-hole. The deafening roar of crashing snowflakes; the stink of dead and decomposing dreams. November in July. Out we get. Stretch the legs; at last, a positive event.

'On remand to the left! Sentenced to the right! Strip off inside and sign for your belongings!'

'Okey-dokey, son! One set of six keys, one earring, one leather belt, three quid seventy-one pence – can I just have your autograph, please?'

Crikey, three seventy-one! One hell of a night – pity about the car keys! A cough for the doctor. Fit as a butcher's dog, eh? What a surprise.

'Okay, son, get kitted out, get some tea and I'll show you up!'

'What, you'll pull a funny face, drop your trousers and tell everybody I'm your boyfriend?'

'Ha, ha! Not bad! This place needs a good comic. No – show you up to your des res, son.'

'I'm not hungry. Let's go.'

Three floors up, seventeen doors along – *chez moi* till Christmas. Thrash of keys. Door open. Walk into the pit; pick a scratcher. Door slams. Shaft of light on my shoulder from the spyhole. Zip. Gone. Keys and footsteps move on. Pitch black.

Think. Think. Think. Has a minute passed yet? Have five? From the opposite bunk... a creak; a tiny red light. A breath. A stench of cheapest rolling baccy. Then a question.

'What you in for, mate?' What was I in for? Good fucking question.

'Nineteen eighty-seven, mate!'

'Nineteen eighty-seven? What da fuck's a nineteen eighty-seven?'

'I'm still living there.'

'I'm Bab. This is Flymo. That's Nev in your upstairs flat.'

'Call me Shed.'

'Nice to meet you, Shed.'

To be honest I hadn't noticed any of them. Lie down. Try to relax. Think. Tell yourself there's bags of room here. This is *shit*. Yep, *this* is an anagram of *shit*. Shit. We were great. Just like the Skipper always said – we were the best. The whole unsteady crew. We lived better than kings, then. Then we fell apart and now we're on our way to growing old and daft and blind and lonely and none of us will ever live up to what we did. We were *The Chimneys*. THE CHIMNEYS! How are you even supposed to begin to know how to follow that?

THREE

Ambleside Way, Gedling, Nottingham
June 1987 (a.m.)

We woke up shivering that morning, at their maisonette, sitting in two opposing armchairs with flimsy blankets over our heads, like kids playing ghosts. Twitching, fidgeting with cold.

'Vvva-brrrurrra... Shed?'

'What?'

'You awake?'

'Guess.'

'You slept?'

'Guess.'

'Me neither, mate. I think the girls switched the heating off – vvvvr!'

'Luxury. So what you doing today?'

'Facing the music, round at me mum's. You?'

'Facing Judas Priest with the London Philharmonic, round at the Dragon's. Didn't you get anywhere with Dawn?'

'Negative. Helen?'

'Negative.'

'You *do* surprise me. I thought you'd have been to Helen back!'

'I thought you'd have been up at the crack of Dawn.'

'Ha, ha – ssh! Someone's moving about!'

It was Dawn, parading through. Long red curls unwinding from last week's semi-perm. Long, gangly legs. Baggy eyes. Nightshirted morning glory. Still pretty. We risked one eyeball each to peek out and test the world for its life-sustaining potential.

'Morning, gentlemen – sleep well?'

'Yuh. Like logs. Shheeshh!'

'Excellent! Is Helen about yet?'

'She's having a lie-in. Look. I'm going into work; anyone need a lift into town?'

We slid the blankets off us. Eyes battling to keep apace with the sudden and unwelcome bombardment of daylight.

'Two, please!' We grinned across at each other with shift-alternating eyelids.

'Vic Centre be okay for you both?'

'Yeah, good.'

'Absa.'

In seconds, she was kempt, painted and slick in attire; spinning car keys around on a miniature teddy bear key ring. We stepped out into a bath of morning, then crumpled into the Mini Clubman, which fired up at first turn, surging off towards town. Sticky up front, next to Dawn. Definitely into each other. Me crouching in the back. Everyone rough as badgers' arses. Pregnant was the pause. I needed to acquire more knowledge concerning the Helen girl, like where we stood – where I stood; her movements; her plans for the weekend; what the fuck happened last night?

'So, uh, you slept okay then, Dawn? You and Helen. Like.'

'Yeah! Why, didn't *you*?' Sticky leapt right in.

'Bloody froze half to death, woman! Which bloody genius switched the fire off?'

'You should have both come and got into bed with *us*; we wouldn't have minded!'

Sticky was too shocked by this to react any further beyond the involuntary jaw-drop. I slowly keeled over out of sight until my cheek stuck to the cold PVC seat covering.

'Aaww, no! I don't believe it! Sticky, would you consider doing me a great personal favour, m'man?'

'Certainly, m'man! What might that be?'

'Well, when we get out, can you put Dawn's umbrella right

up my arse and then open it, please?' Sticky had already been grimacing fiercely.

'Me first!'

Drawing up at the Victoria Centre, we said our thanks and pecked her cheeks from either side. I clambered out over Sticky as he stroked her ear with the back of his hand and negotiated the rematch. Then we stood back with pocketed hands as the Clubman surged off again.

'Get a grip!'

'Can you grip that?'

'I can't grip that.'

'*I* can't grip that!'

'Ungrippable shit – so! We've both blown a shag! Absolutely fucking turbo result! Now what?'

'I'll buy us a coffee.'

'I'll go for a coffee.'

We shuffled woefully on. Around to the complex of open restaurants at the top end of the Centre. I slumped into a seat at the table farthest away from any possible human contact. Sticky shunted a brace of coffees carefully along the stainless steel runway up to the sweet, wrinkly old dear sentrying the till.

'Two coffees? Thank you, me duck – that's one pound twenty, please!'

'One – whoa, whoa! One what?'

'One pound twenty, please.'

'One pound twenty for two coffees? Is that with full unprotected sex, or just the two-minute hand relief with your marigolds on?'

Faced then with her utterly vacant semi-response, he slapped down the one twenty with supreme reluctance and ferried the piping hot coffees gingerly over to the table, where I was at that point, trying in vain to rub sense back into my fogged up skull with all fingers of both hands. I didn't bother to look up.

'One twenty, eh? It's rapidly turning into a day of scantily-clad beliefs!'

'One pound, twen-bastard-ty!'

That was enough. I just wanted to get home and get it over with the Dragon. I sprang to my feet.

'Where're *you* going?'

'Sod coffee! Let's just get going and take the shit!'

'Just sit down and get your coffee.'

'We might as well just go and take the shit!'

'Okay, Shed, m'man! Go and take the shit, then when you've taken the shit don't forget to tell her you're playing tonight!'

'You *what?*'

'Tonight? We're playing? At Cueball's place? Today's Friday? Pisshead?'

'Tonight?'

'Don't say you've forgotten...'

I reseated myself and deliberately forced down the scalding coffee, then licked at the blister forming over the roof of my mouth. I rubbed sense twice as hard.

'No, I just haven't remembered. Friday. Shit. I've not been home for four days. Likely as not, she'll chop me bollocks off! Aw! Shit – no!'

'Aw! Shit, yeah! You remembered last night, while you and the Skipper were in there, outbidding each other for the last bottle of vodka.'

'What on earth were me mum and dad ever thinking of?'

'Shed! Come on... look, m'man, as I see it we've got a choice here.'

'I can't wait to hear this choice. I'm agog with suspense; in fact, I'm antysiliogogogog.'

'What it is, is this. And this is what it is. I can go home and take the shit for standing me mum up at the christening and you can go home and get stormed by the Dragon for skipping the register since Tuesday. Or...'

'Is there an "or"?'

'There is an "or".'

'Name that "or".'

'Or we get a cab down to mine. Call in at Ranjit's on the way – I know it's early, but Ranjit's m'man. We take on eight four-packs and a very large wash of vodka and do it all over again – *hah*!'

'Urghh!' My head sank again. Then, gradually, two pairs of rose-coloured eyeballs found their way back to face each other.

'Yeahh!'

'Wooo!'

Sticky always said that the buzz you got on stage beat an orgasm all the way and he was dead right, although you never told the Dragon that, unless you wanted to invite some unspeakable damage. It was Sticky who'd patched things up between me and the Skipper to get me the bass job with The Chimneys. For two years, I'd wanted in; to be part of that reputation. But for two years, the Skipper had vetoed me – ever since the episode of the Indian takeaway. We'd been sitting in an Indian takeaway, waiting for an Indian takeaway. The Skipper, having stashed two pints of vodka behind his eyeballs, was acquiescent under the misplaced credence that we'd been sitting in a taxi office, waiting for a taxi. The surroundings were not entirely dissimilar; subsequently, when yer man emerged from behind the dangling beads with a package of curry in each hand, the penny finally dropped, and the Skipper went beebar and started punching me, raving on about how I'd cheated him out of twenty-five minutes' drinking time. After the waiters pulled him off, and all was calm, I banjoed him one in the mouth, and he was never too cheerful around me afterwards. For having the cheek to defend meself against a drunken lunatic, like.

On the way to Ranjit's, we reflected on some of the high points of the band's patchy five-year history – if only to make ourselves feel better and to fend off the horrors of that *other* world. There had been Jamso – Sticky's predecessor on the drums. He'd use one drumstick and a hacksaw; the only trouble being that the kit only lasted one gig, but it usually belonged to someone else anyway, so he wasn't too troubled. He was eventually sacked for losing a residency in West Bridgford, after turning up on stage with a plant generator and a road drill, with a view to 'digging the scene, man'.

There'd been the running battle between the Skipper and my predecessor, Chunky Kevin – live on stage before the lunchtime clientele at the Malt Cross. A long protracted beef concerning rights to a common girlfriend suddenly flared into a 'belt your beak with my bass/stuff this synth up your Bourneville boulevard' situation, culminating with the pair interlocked in combat, rolling downstairs and offstage, whilst diners fled and band laughed on. This was Chunky Kevin's last bout. The next we heard was that Chunky Kevin was as happy as a sandboy, living with some bloke who lectured at the university.

Then whoever could forget the highly lamentable Sunday evening talent contest at the Carlton Catholics' Conservative Club. Mark Anthony was the guitarist in those early days – meticulously hand-picked because of his immense lack of ability – but he knew how to set the ball in motion. Whilst The Chimneys thrashed it out that night, Mark was belting guitar for England and marching up and down on two lines of tables; crushing drinks, glasses and ashtrays under his boots. The middle-aged to elderly Carlton Catholics gazed motionlessly up at him from their seats, mortified by this potential threat to life. As the last note droned away, they applauded conservatively, then besieged the bar for much-needed whisky. The Chimneys were adjudged second place to the ventriloquist.

Mark was to last only a few more weeks within the bosom of The Chimneys. He was sacked for getting the band thrown out of its rehearsal room at The Fox and Crown, after the landlord had discovered him in the back garden, beating up the pub's goat which had eaten half of his guitar case. At one stage though, it must be said that the goat was enjoying the upper hand, repeatedly butting him onto a barbed wire fence after his wristwatch had become entangled on its horn and his jeans crotch on the wire.

Shortly after his departure from The Chimneys, Mark got married and went to Hong Kong for a few months' peace and quiet. All in all, not bad for a band who only began life as an idea for a one-off Christmas panto; but soon became aware that they were thoroughly incapable of memorising anything in excess of 'He's behind you!' and 'Oh no, he isn't!' Even with the benefit of a month's rehearsal.

So thus we arrived at Ranjit's, re-enriched in the Band's lofty pedigree. He'd reminded me why I was a player. Why I wanted in. What it meant to not give a shit – to go for it – to dictate your own agenda in life. Okay. Me and Joe Planet were part of it now. This was, on paper, the best line-up yet. Okay, the first few gigs had been tame, but we'd only been reformed for a couple of months. It would pick up. Stick with it. If the Skipper was chuffed with this line-up, it *had* to be okay, and he was well chuffed. He *had* to be chuffed, because nobody else in town dared play for us. It was time for celebration. We took on supplies and thanked Ranjit, and by nine o'clock we were back at Sticky's Russell Road address, making intemperate history yet again.

After several partial successes, we'd finally mastered the intricate technique of implanting one third of a gill of vodka into a freshly opened can of lager; a technique proven to be much enhanced by the preparatory measure of removing one mouthful of lager out of the can first.

By 9.45, we had no problems; by 10.15 we were rocking. The booze was getting a stiff talking to. Porn vid on the telly, with freeze frame on that *special* moment. 'Black Dog' full kick on the stereo, with Sticky singing into his can – me strumming along on guitar and doing Chuck's duckwalk. Upstairs, the first burst had practically blown Joe out of his bed, let alone his sleep. Joe lodged at Sticky's house. That particular morning he'd been anticipating a well-deserved lie-in. He sat up. Checked the clock, trying to believe his ears. That anticipation was fast evaporating. He wrapped on a blue flannel night robe and some fluffy blue socks and meandered downstairs semi-somnolently. Finding the living room door handle at the fourth attempt, he found the belief of his ears to be of secondary issue, compared to the attempted belief of his eyes. Joe was a paragon of paralysed incredulity.

'Hiyer, Joe... Get a can, m'man.'

'How is it, Joe?' Joe panned from the floorshow, to the stereo, to the video.

'Look, guys – *tup*.' Joe always made that tupping noise whenever he was pissed off.

'*Tup*.' Joe was obviously pissed off, although he couldn't ignore the telly much.

'You know we're playing at Phil's place tonight?' He'd called Cueball by his real name. He was very, very pissed off.

'Absa!'

'Yeah, m'man – absa! Let's get set!'

'Only, tup, you've both been faced all week, and it's the weekend again, tup.'

'Joe – we're set! I'm yer man, m'man!'

'We're yer man, m'man!'

'Well for God's sake slow up, tup, and get some snap down you – both of you! We're on in ten hours!'

'Sorting it now, Joe!'

'I'm yer man!'

Joe closed the door behind him without another word, and plodded back upstairs to sulk and smoke and tup. We dipped the noise slightly as a token of partial respect, and piled on into the columns of lager, purely out of a sense of duty to the band and ourselves. Joe could be moody, but when he was funny, he was fun – and all aside, a cracking guitarist. Incidentally, he got the name Joe Planet over a pool game in a pub one afternoon. He'd doubled a lucky white, which went on to pocket three balls. Some old fellah at the bar saw it and remarked, 'Cor! That were a jamstrangler of a shot, son! D'yo plan it?'

I must have passed out for an hour or two. When I woke up it was nearly four; I was upside down on Sticky's sofa, legs trailing over the back and my head in the trash bin, purple see-through toffee papers stuck over my eyes. Sticky must've hit the sack. I didn't know whether to shit, wind my watch or vote Liberal; so, with little to lose, I actually decided to pay Joe some heed for once and get out and get some snap down. After some twenty minutes, which translated closer to twenty years in my afflicted mind, I'd crossed the Forest Rec up to Mansfield Road. The vodka-induced, right-handed preferential stagger would come in useful on the way down into town, as all the snap outlets were located on the right; ergo I was bound sooner or later to fall sideways into at least one open door, free from all the inhibitions of mental and physical deliberation. Some five hundred yards and numerous painful interactions further on, the umpteenth aperture transpired to be that of the 'Alamos' chippy and kebab shoowab. I formed a type of arched buttress against the Formica counter and attempted to force my eyeballs upwards high enough to peruse the house board of fare upon the back wall. I was met with a warm smile from its highly obliging, stockily disposed Mediterranean proprietor.

'Good day to you, my friend! And what can I get for you?'

Right! So now it was up to me to see if I could still remember how to talk. My lips stole a five-second head start on my hippocampus.

'Uh! Uh! Ahah! Ha ha hah!'

'Yes, Yes! Ha hah!'

'Uh – urlo – fiss, plea.'

'A fish?'

'Yuh, yeah, asssright, a fiss!'

'And what kind of fish would my frien' like?'

'Big fiss.'

Tongs in hand, he slid aside the steamy glass door of the heated display cabinet, selected the biggest fiss and double wrapped it in all haste.

'Okay, my friend – to you that is one pounds twenty, pliss!'

'C-coi, and coi-coi!'

His lips pursed in sympathy with mine. 'Curry?'

'Yeah, yeah. Coiee!'

'One pot of curry for you!'

'Nah, nah, coie na fiss!'

'You want your curry on your fish?'

'Absa.'

He unwrapped the fish and ladled on some curry from a stainless steel pan on the range.

'Is that all, my frien'?'

'Yeah, yeah.' He began to rewrap.

'Apart from the beans.' He ceased to rewrap.

'You want beans *and* curry with your fish?'

'Psst! Psst! C'mere, psst! C'mere, attend me, citizen... Nah, come on! C'mere.'

He drew warily closer and cocked an ear.

'Nah! Now strictly between me and thee, eh? Yeah? Strilly on the QT. Ssh! Sssh! Now, then! Joe's told me I've got to get some snap down – that's *Joe Planet*, mind you! So get them peas on, sir, if you please now yes I thank you!'

'Peas? Peas or beans?'

'There is no or.'

'There is no what?'

'Or.'

'Or what?'

'Yeah! Ezackly; what or?'

'You've lost me.'

A substantial line of patrons had now begun to build up behind me. The expectancy was thicker than the grease. Just.

'Ogay, ogay, purely out of deference to your articulate disposition, citissen, I'll be economical with the crap. There iss no "or". I want both.'

'Both peas *and* beans?'

'An' a sausage.'

'I'll get a tray for this lot.' He returned from the shelving, bearing the requested trayborne delicacies.

'An' a sausage.'

'I've *given* you a sausage!'

'Want two.'

'Right then, sir, that it? One fish, curry, beans, peas, two sausages: two forty-five, please!'

'Twenty two over seven!'

'No – two forty-five!'

'No. Twenty-two over seven. Pie.'

'You wanna pie? Pies are eighty pence!'

'Eighty pence? Asseems very reasonable! Last time I looked, a pie was three point one four two eight five seven oneish!'

'Look, mate, I've got a lot of people waiting. Is there anything else you want before I wrap this lot up for thee fith times?'

'No.'

'No?'

'Yeah! Chips – nearly forgot chiss – ay! Izzisa steak and kidney twenty two over seven?'

Walking on into town, I was so faced that I couldn't see, chew and walk at the same time. Moreover; I found it physically impossible to tilt my head downwards to look at what I was about to eat. With a modicum of desperation, I glanced around the middle distance. Across Mansfield Road and seemingly in an even bigger trance than me, I clocked a weird looking bloke with a Mohican and a ponytail and a meerschaum pipe bellowing away in his gob. I shouted him over to share the snap, if he could guide my fingers to the chips for me. He didn't require a second ask; we both tucked in, and he introduced himself as 'Tinker'. His thoroughly abrasive appearance was instantly belied by his snooker commentator's whisper. He'd apparently just run out of beer money and was on his way home early, skint and hungry. He seemed a pleasant enough geezer, so I offered him a mutually beneficial alternative. I'd get him a few beers and a laugh; all he had to do was help me get safely to the gig, before I bashed my brains up a wall once too often. We shook on it.

By the time we'd shuffled down to Trinity Square, Tinker reported that we'd scoffed all but the two sausages. Neither of us wanted a sausage, so I decided on a furtively discreet jettison. Noticing a refuse bin across the square, I glanced around for any beat coppers whilst fumbling for the first sausage. Yep. No Law. Got a sausage. Just brace for the throw. Stand back, Tink! Turn and throw and whammo! I was alert to all, except the 35-foot double-decker bus which had just drawn up between me and the targeted omnium, and as its double doors jerked open, the first passenger off – a bloke meticulously dressed and scented – had zero time to react to the sausage. This, his very first vista of the city evening, exploded in the centre of his face; dribbling immediately down the front of his shirt and tweed jacket. He looked down in abject horror, then up in subjective asperity. He took a step towards the sausage launcher. The sausage launcher growled at him and Tinker advised him he was imminently likely to be eaten; whereupon he opted to abandon the arena to experience.

Now aided by a more conscious effort to be careful, I stuffed the tray and paper into another refuse receptacle, and hurled the remaining sausage up to a first floor window ledge of the *Nottingham Evening Post* building, where I'd noticed a couple of emaciated pigeons were holding court. The throw was good all the way, except that after having taken a peck apiece, the birds forced the sausage to succumb to the outward camber of the ledge. It then rolled back off and fell twenty feet directly onto the trilby hat of a newspaper vendor who was returning his unsold copies. It bounced off his hat and into the gutter. I crossed the street to him, apologising profusely, then immediately began dancing a jig for him – to make amends. He looked me up and down in sheer bewilderment as I hopped and turned and shuffled. Tinker tooted on his meerschaum, coughing out an occasional snigger. When I'd finished, I asked the newsie what he thought to that. He replied simply that he thought I was a fucking lunatic. Then he picked up the sausage, crammed it into his pocket and ran off.

FOUR

At which time, across the river, in the bed of a ground floor flat in William Road, West Bridgford, the Crocodile was busy rounding off his afternoon pre-match sex with one of the Biffers. The Clifton Biffers were essentially the main female crew of Chimney fans. They never missed a gig, and the Croc was their fave Chimney. Particularly at that moment.

'Croc? Croc? Hoooah! Croc?'

'Mmm?'

'What star sign are you, Croc?'

'Mmm!' Croc vaulted the question and concentrated on maintaining rhythm; the bed ricked on with industrial consistency.

'Croc? Croc?'

'Mm!'

'Croc, do you believe in pre-destiny?'

'Ooowah!'

Rick, rick, rick, rick, rick...

'Croc? Do you see a future for us?'

'Ooowah!'

...rick, rick, rick, rick...

'Croc?'

'Mmmm?'

...rick, rick, rick rick, rick-bang! Bang! Bang! Bang!

'Aaaah! Croc! What was that? There's somebody banging on the window!'

'Ooowah!'

She hastily snatched a pillow and covered herself, cowering at the bottom corner of Croc's bed. Croc – indifferent as indifferent could ever get, slid from the bed and, starkers as your birthday, strode serenely over to the window, hooking on his gold wire spectacles and snatching aside the flowered curtain. Standing there, clutching a prize-sized potted yucca plant was the Skipper. He motioned at the Croc to up the window. The Croc instantly obliged. His Biffer discharged a nervous shudder as her bare back brushed momentarily against the cold metal of the bedpost.

'Quick! Croc! Get this plant indoors!'

The Croc jigged the window up a little higher and carefully took the delivery, setting it down inside.

'Cheers, dear boy! See you there tonight!'

Without any questions, the Croc slammed the window back down and thrashed the curtain loosely back across. Back to the sex; the discretionary pillow was cast off, landing against the yucca; bodies slapped together and the ricking reconvened.

'Croc? Let's talk about tomorrow?'

'Mmm?'

'And the day after!'

Rick, rick, rick, rick, rick, rick...

'Ohh! And the day after the day after!'

...rick, rick, rick, rick...

'Ooh! And the... *Aarrrghh*!'

Bang! Bang! Bang!

She seized another pillow as the Croc sprang to his feet and marched back to the window to throw the curtain aside once again. The Skipper was back; this time with a slightly more concerned look on his face. And this time with WPC Farmer of the West Bridgford Police perched expectantly at his left flank. She wasted no time in fixing a gawp down at the Croc's wok handle, which was dancing angrily from leg to leg as he again jigged up the window for their better accommodation. The Skipper strained unsuccessfully to suppress a guffaw.

'Er, Croc? Mmm, can I have it back, please? Ha, ha!'

Again, the Croc nonchalantly obliged. Having kicked the first pillow aside and with the botany passed on safely out into the custody of the Law, he stormed back to his coital arena; this time leaving the curtain half-closed and the window up in order that the world please itself. Outside, in a slightly less cordial sphere, the Skipper braced himself for some face music of a much greater austerity, set against the counter-melody of the Ricking Concerto for Bedded Duet. Farmer set down the key exhibit.

'Well, the shop either won't or daren't press charges, Mr Snowis; so we'll let it go as a prank this time… but! Consider yourself warned – is that fair enough?'

Of course it was fair enough. All's fair in love and war. A gig day was both love *and* war. Even more fair enough it seemed, was the Skipper's acute insensibility.

'Okay! Yeah! Ashley, I'm vay, vay sorrindeed, Miss P-P-P – No! Hahaah! Musn't say Mss Piggy! Thass not vay nice – no! Angurn, angurn go an get my bus and you won't hear urther peep out of me, dear girl!'

'Is that a promise?'

'Proniss – homist!'

Rick, rick, rick, rick…

'Now you're not going into town, causing, are you?'

'*Au Cointreau*, dear girl. Angurna town preventing!'

'Ooooha – Croc! Croc! Huh! Hoooooaa!'

'Ooowah!'

Farmer panned from desperado to window, swallowing visibly. She squatted back down to retrieve the plant and then revisited the Skipper's swirling blue eyes.

'Well, get going, then. Remember – behaviour!'

As the Skipper loped off, relighting his roll-up, Farmer attempted another furtive peek inside, without bodily infringing the curtain. The Skipper sidled up to the city bus stop, still good to his promise. Perching at the end of a small queue of mixed patrons, he leant against a small, timber-reinforced privet hedge to reflect and roll up again.

Behind the hedge, the bus stop was overlooked by the kitchen window of a house occupied by a lady senior citizen of local upstanding. Inside the kitchen, resplendent in blue rinsed perm and sunflowers pinafore, said lady senior citizen stood at a blackened range, frying bacon and eggs in a large and even more blackened frying pan. Her attention was instantly diverted by this rustling of privet outside; whereupon to its rustler. Then, performing an exemplary impersonation of a gurning monkfish, she shed a heavily padded oven glove to hammer on the kitchen window. The Skipper, still the consummate cherubim, had no cause to suppose this dear old gorgon had attempted communication with *him*, and turned back away to continue his bushy repose. The craggy knuckles met the pane a second time. *Tap, tap, tap, tap!* The Skipper turned back to her; this time waving enthusiastically and smiling, then pointing at himself questioningly.

'Me? Oh, good evening, dear girl!'

Tap, tap.

'No, sorry – I'm not looking for business just now, thank you – I have a girlfriend already!'

Tap! The pair now held the entire bus queue's undivided attention.

'Mind you, eighteen more green deaths and you could be mine – right up until I sober up – which I would loosely estimate to be somewhere around the turn of the century!'

She partially opened the window to a fledgling crescendo of mirth amongst the queue.

'Gettoff! Get... off!'

'Beg yours, old horse?'

'Gettoff! Get... off!'

'Alright then, we'll call it 1997.'

'Offitt! I'll fetch a policeman!'

'Oooh! Get off the hedge! Sorry!' He gave a backwards leap beladen with exaggeration. 'There we are – look! I've put all the scruffy bits back in place!' He tugged at a lapel of his leather cross-zip, then sniffed hard at it. 'Here – smell that – I haven't stolen any chlorophyll!'

To the continuing chuckles, she wrenched shut the window, gave a muted admonishment and crammed the oven glove back on, concentrating once again on the pan at hand. Both she and the hot lard proceeded to tut away like ten billyed-up budgerigars, unawares that outside, in a swing of mood, the cobalt blue eyes and savage blonde mane of the Skipper were lapping from left to right, scanning the locale intently. With light-hearted conjecture, the queue conferred over his next likely gambit as he hastily vacated his post, crossed the street and disappeared into a partially obscured driveway. A few seconds later, he returned to allay all curiosities. The half-housebrick left his hand with calculated windage and elevation, exceeded the kitchen window pane with an almighty crash and to a choral gasp from his audience, successfully fulfilled its arc, landing directly into the frying pan; clean between the Danish and the Day-Lay. He gleamed triumphantly into the jagged aperture.

'Fry *that* bastard then, yer pucker-mouthed old blatherskite!'

Some four minutes later, at West Bridgford Police Station, a telephone was still burning in the hands and against the left ear lobe of Duty Sergeant Moss. Having eventually re-cradled the receiver, following tide upon tide of empathetic reassurance, he turned to his limited and overstretched and underfunded pool of staff in painful disdain.

'Farmer!' She appeared from behind some steel grey filing cabinets.

'Sir?'

'Farmer – did you interview one Paul Snowis, aka the Skipper, concerning a purloined pot plant not one hour since?'

'Yes, sir?'

'Sodding Nora! You've gotta love this manor – if *he* hasn't done it, *she*'s had it done to her. Now they're working as a bloody team!'

'Sir?'

'Go and fetch him in – he's in Bridgford Road, heavily seasoning folks' meals. Lock him up till the pubs are shut; suspected criminal damage, suspected threatening behaviour. Whatever.'

'Charge him this time, sir?'

'Not unless you want three months' paperwork and the Guvnor on your back for not pinching him already! It'll probably be Christmas Eve before you get an interview in English. No, just get the old girl's statement; see if he'll agree to pay for the window, nick him until half past ten, then caution and release him. He'll go potty when he realises he's missed drinking time, and it makes good news for the taxpayer – and a bloody good laugh for me.'

He was still loafing against the bus stop in brazen defiance as the patrol car pulled in, spewing its crew of three. One to console the hysterical chef; two to apprehend the suspect, one of which, Farmer, was advising him of his rights alongside the now lavishly entertained bus queue.

'So that's basically it, Mr Snowis. Is there anything you wish to say before we take you to the station?'

He paused. Sniffed. Sighed. 'Well. I suppose there *is* something I really ought to mention, dear girl.'

Farmer blinked uneasily at her colleague in anticipation of some deep inbound regret. She blinked at the Skipper.

'Make it brief, Paul.'

The Skipper gave a brief circumspection, ensuring the full heed of all present, then breathed deeply through his flaring nostrils and embarked upon the swansong.

'Folks? We're gonna be right back with *more* of this arrest, straight after this brief word from our sponsors... Pinched?

Captured? Banged to rights? Don't you just *hate* it when *that* happens?'

The chuckles returned to the queue. The Skipper reached inside his jacket, pulled out and popped open a can of overstrength lager.

'C'mon Paul, you know you can't...'

'I know *I* do! That's why round about this time, I usually reach for the can that *can*...' He took a protracted gulp, before it was snatched away by one of four flailing mits.

'...mm-mmm! Refreshes! And that *taste*... *torments me*!'

'Ha ha ha!'

'C'mon, Paul, let's go. Paul? Into the car...'

'So! Remember, folks! The next time the filth are about to tickle *your* ribs...'

'Ha ha *haa*!'

'Just shove him in... watch his daft head.'

With a final 'haah!' the pavement circus was shipped off to its next eagerly awaited booking. The arriving townward bus heralded an anticlimax to its boarding citygoers.

At the station, the Skipper made his statutory phone call to the Croc. The Croc called Sticky, who advised him that we were all rallying at the News House on St James Street as per, and with the exception of Joe and the jailbird and during a rare and fleeting episode of collective conscience, we had convened there some thirty-five minutes later. Tinker was introduced in an honorary standing for having kept *me* standing, and over a game of pool, we set about ironing out some of the wrinkles on this new face of the evening. The first thing we had to do was to try and reach Cueball to stall the gig for an hour. Then we had to call Joe and ask him to go directly to Cueball's place to make sure the gear was up and ready whilst convincing him we'd got some snap down. Both unenviable labours. I got the Joe job. Sticky got the Cueball job. For background authenticity, we decided to get a taxi to Bridgford Nick to make the calls – after stopping en route to take on a little viticulture at the first available offy. In the police station foyer, we collared some seating while Sticky did the dangerous with Cueball and Croc made all the relevant desk inquiries.

'Yeah, Cue... er, Phil! Yeah, yeah! But they're saying they won't let him out till at least ten, yeah? So we'll be down right after that, yeah? Yeah, well, yeah! Yeah! Start without him? Well I suppose we could, yeah! We have done before – yeah! Absa, absa! Yeah – we dragged some tramp in off the street, gave him a bottle of aftershave, a couple of roll-ups and a stylophone to play. Yeah! Yeah! A stylophone – Rolfy job – he was made up. No, no one noticed the difference, man – yeah! Yeah! No, he drank the aftershave. No. Okay. Yeah, absa; so we're giving the Skipper one hour – yeah? Yep, yep, I know, I know, Phil; I couldn't agree with you more – yeah! Yeah! I know, yeah, a right bastard, yeah! *And* that. 'Course, 'course, Phil; absa, absa, absa – everyone'll be down. Yeah – no sweat, man!'

In empathy with Sticky's *kampf*, we firstly checked that the desk receptionist was still busy at his register, then furtively revealed bottles of wine and took a rapid, though copious necksurge apiece. The Croc opting for a full-bodied red; a crisp, dry white for me, and Tinker preferring a do-it-yourself rosé kit, taking a slug on both. Then they were crammed back out of sight as the backdrop of gurgles gradually lulled Desko out of his engrossments. I was beginning to lapse into scepticism, having now practically drunk myself sober again.

'I dunno, Croc. It's got the makings of another lame one – that's if we get to play at all!'

'Oowah!'

'Let's hope Joe can sort it out from *that* end.'

Tinker had been breathing clean air ever since town. He took out the meerschaum, gave it a gentle tap against the side of his seat and blew sharply through it. Desko still had a beady on us.

'Outside if you want to smoke, Sherlock!'

Tinker grinned at us, then with slightly raised eyebrows, he stormed to his feet, muttered something unintelligible and strode past Sticky to pop out for a pipe. Sticky was still heavily embroiled in salvaging the gig over the hottest piece of cable in Nottinghamshire.

'No, no, Phil – naahh! 'Course we won't mike up the bass drum. No... what? No Phil, I never ordered the onion shampoo for you, Phil, I don't do things like that. What? Well... well, I suppose it *does* sound like one of the Shedfixman's capers, but I don't... Well, I dunno, it might have been the Skipper, yeah! What? No, Phil – nonononono – nah! We're on the wagon, man! No, not a sniff... Phil, man! This is a slammer, man! How can we be drinking? Just give us *some* credit, Phil!'

Across the foyer, the Croc and I took this as the cue for another neckrinse. Another neckrinse it was. Again, the bottles were holstered before the beadies were cast. At the phone, Sticky with his back to reception could enjoy a greater freedom to imbibe, which he did, systematically draining a third of vodka between the commentaries.

'Ahuck! Sober as a stipe, man. Yeah, yeah, I know exactly what you're saying man, Phil, man! Don't worry! It's always half-empty around this time. It'll be packed by the time we're on, man – packed! Yeah! Yeah! Great; so you'll stagger it a bit, yeah? Yep – Joe's coming down to sort it all out. Okay?'

He hung up the phone and lumbered back to the seats before the conversation had the chance to veer too far back into the negative aspect.

'Well. According to Cueball, we're in for another partial success.'

'What else would you expect from the mardy fat newark? Nothing's *ever* good enough. Anyway – what did he say?'

'What *didn't* he say? I gave him our home number. He can call Joe and save us the trouble.'

'Good. Well at least that's something – anyway, Joe can reason with him better than the rest of us. I just hope the gig's not going to be another donkey – that's all.'

'Oowah!'

Outside the station and removed from all such complexities, Tinker had been relishing a vigorous few toots on the trusty meerschaum. Arms folded, he leant a shoulder against the weathered shale blocks which ringed the doorway and let his eyes follow each billowing of smoke upwards, almost as high as the equally carefree swifts up there; darting back and forth across the dusky blue infinity. Tranquillity was lord. Companionship was prince. Summer was king, and the king, he decided, was to be hailed with a reloading of tobacco. Having emptied, then methodically restashed the bowl, he put pipe to mouth once more, presenting a silver Zippo alongside. Clicking on its flame, he drew deeply at the mouthpiece, coaxing fire onto aromatic fuel. Nothing was happening. He checked the tobacco pouch for splashes of wine. No. It was dry. At the second attempt, he billowed once more; but a sudden rush of traffic draught from the roadside wafted it, stinging, into his eyes. Holding the meerschaum aside, he dealt his eye sockets an intensive scrubbing with his knuckles. Then, refocusing through the plenitude of tears, he discerned the cumbersome lines of a small yellow tour bus across the road, preparing to disembark its itinerants – all of whom appeared to be female.

The driver, a flustered-looking nerve case, was supplementing the ailing hydraulics by tugging at the door. It finally swished open to a great clamour inside, and the driver jumped from the bus for his life as thirty-eight head of painted womanhood from the frontier town of Kirkby-in-Ashfield spilled over and around him onto the pavement. Tinker tooted on, continuing his lean-to and throwing the troupe an occasional up-and-downer. The troupe were performing a head count. One of its matriarchs had clocked this pipe-tooting odd bodd.

'Ooer! It's that detective-oojamaflip!'

'Kojak?'

'Ha ha ha!'

'Nahh! Sherlock Orms!'

'Oi! Sherlock! Can tha' tell us weeah t' Manor Club is in Bridgford?'

He understood the nouns only. 'The Manor Club? You want to get there?'

'Aye! Are you one o' t' strippers, like?'

'Haah-haha haaa!'

'I might be.'

'Well you can put yer pipe in this 'n smork it – haah!'

'Straight on over the crossroads... fifty yards down on your left.'

'Cheers, luvvy! Come on yuw lot, we're lairt as it is!'

He watched them rumble off along the pavement, then turned to scrutinise the driver's ineptitude as he shoved and slapped the door in search of the source of its inoperation. He peered again at the Kirkby women as they walked away, bouncing echoed shrieks and yelps off the buildings in the precinct. Then he turned and peered in on the three Chimneys.

'Hssst! Wait for me! I'll just be a sec!'

He turned back, tooted hard, refocused once more and marched resolutely off towards the distant undulation of Kirkby revelry.

So with less than an hour to go, the Skipper, sensing the twin onsets of sobriety and nightfall, was pacing up and down in his cell frenetically reciting a familiar, age-old mantra. 'Bastard filth! Bastard filth! Bastard filth!'

In spite of our constant harangment of the desk for the expedition of clemency, its crew stubbornly refused to budge. We'd exhausted every angle, from habeas corpus to loco parentis to a straight one-for-one trade-off of hostages, but ten o'clock repeatedly came back as the first and final offer, delivered with a clinical smugness. The smugness bugged us the most. The smugness must have bugged God too, because at around 9.45, he sent us a little cheer. Tinker had no sooner returned and retaken his seat, when all attention was suddenly drawn to a crashing open of the main entrance door.

'Leave me alone, yer bastards! Get-getchah! I'll kill yer! I'll ffkin' kill yer, yer dirty bastards! Pigs!'

The Farmer crew had seen action again, this time in the apprehension of the local drunken bagwoman who'd been setting light to billboard posters which she'd deemed offensive to women. Whether three police were enough to grapple her indoors was a matter for debate. We grinned and debated. One of the policemen had had his helmet punched askew. He paused to remove it altogether.

'Here! Just give us a hand and hold this door open would you, lads?'

'How does "bollocks" sound?'

Much less amused, they managed her gradually indoors; and she bit hands, forearms, thighs, tits – everything that range offered. She spat, snotted, gagged, swore and cursed at them until eventually, with the conscription of the desk officer, they were able to take a limb each and yet remain a safe distance from the rabid jaws and let her spit herself dry, bawl herself hoarse and thrash the last out of her scrawny unwashed limbs. Then they hoisted in unison and carried her horizontally across the foyer. Farmer puffed an immense sigh of relief. As the bearing party passed us by, its quarry's head flopped in our direction and her rolling, glazed eyes attempting to fix onto us. She was whispering something.

'See... see? ...Aww, just male pigs... see?'

Sticky winked and grinned at her as she passed by him.

'Well! So, apart from *that*, Mrs Lincoln, what did you think of the play?'

'*Ha ha haaa*!' All circus broke loose again.

'Yeraaaaabastaaaaahd! *Aaah! Aaah! Aaaaaaaah*!'

Farmer threw an exasperated scowl at Sticky as they all struggled anew to contain this fresh ignition of the president's wife all the way to the cells. Tinker peeked after them through the small wire enforced glass portal set into the security door. Then he peeked again. His eyes had registered something else.

'Is this yer man coming?'

I raced to the door. 'Lemme see.' It was indeed m'man being led out. 'Sticky! Phone a cab – fast!'

Sticky dived onto the telephone. The Croc shoved me aside to get a look.

'Oowah!'

The Skipper was paraded into the foyer by the returning desk official and nominally asked to sign for his shoelaces. We re-adjourned to the seating while he reinstated his footwear. I had to make sure he was still tickety.

'How was it for you?'

'Situation critical, dear boy!' I handed him the wine.

'Never mind – get a swig on this – *mind the natives*? An excellent choice, if I may say so, sir... I think that Sir will find that most acceptable; shall I wrap it up for Sir for later, or will Sir drink it all now?'

He downed the jolly lot without missing a stroke, and then came up, blue-faced, for air.

'Ahh! Hoo! Mmm! Thank you, sir! An impudent little bouquet – hoo! Indeed! Most acceptable. Now for some more – what's the time? What's occurring?'

Sticky sauntered over from the phone.

'M'man! What've you been up to, you ruffian? Yeah! Taxi's on its way – we'll be at Cueball's for quarter past, via the offy.'

'Of course, dear boy! And Joe?'

'Meeting us there... Oh, by the way... Skipper – Tinker, Tinker – the Skipper!' They exchanged a brief handshake.

'Marvellously pleasant evening to you, sir!'

'Skipper! Heard so many anarchisms about you!'

'I resemble that remark!'

We shared the last of the booze around, until even Desko had clocked us. He quite unsurprisingly reverted back to his 'chapter and verse' routine.

'Oi! You can't drink that in here!'

In the entranceway, Sticky spun round. 'Taxi!'

As the others made after him into the street, I gathered all the empty bottles and dumped them on the desk, right in front of Desko. He gawped at the sheer volume of disallowables.

'Well in that case, mate – you'll be needing to confiscate *these* then, won't you?' I fled, without waiting for the answer, out to the hooting taxi which was edging slowly away. Sticky hung out of a rear passenger window.

'C'mon, Shed! Hurry up and dive in!'

I fell across the others in the back seat. Someone was missing.

'Where's Tink?'

'In the boot. The car can only take four. Right! Everyone got a drink? 'Course not! No one's got a drink! Right! Central Avenue offy, then town, please, driver! You've got five minutes and we're timing you!'

Having there taken on supplies and thrown a couple of cans into the boot to the discretion of its occupant, we set off townwards, drinking furiously – apart from the Skipper, who found furious a little too sluggish.

Unbeknown to all meanwhile, at an address north of the city; a Chimneys fly poster was being scrutinised, ripped, crumpled and crammed into a garbage can, conveniently screening the freshly drained Martini bottle from view. A bowl of potato peelings was tossed in to complete the disguise. The crumpler then lit a cigarette, checked his watch, began to cough profusely and pulled out a grubby handkerchief to blow his nose. Then, leaving by the back kitchen door, he struck out for town.

At precisely 10.14, the cab, having careered over to the wrong side of the road, screeched to an abrupt halt at the doors of Cueball's emporium. None of us knew what to expect. Joe had been standing impatiently in the archway, willing on our appearance whilst tupping one of the bouncers half to death. He dashed out to us. Sticky and I drained our last cans whilst the Croc freed Tinker from the boot. The Skipper, being the sorry newark to get us into the shit in the first place, elected to pay the driver.

'For Christ's sake – what kept you? Tup, I've had to set all the gear up on me own and, tup, there's a bunch of...' The bouncer loomed over his shoulder. The Skipper was a seasoned veteran of a thousand confrontations with door sentries.

'Well, this is a *magnificent* auditorium you have here, dear boy! Any "pop" groups on tonight? We like a bit of "pop" music!'

The bouncer opened his mouth to attempt to speak. I followed the Skipper's lead. 'So long as you don't encourage those long-haired hoi-polloi with scruffy blue jeans and loud electric guitars... frankly, I can't make out half the words they're singing!'

'Haven't got a tune in their heads, they're so full of drugs!'

'Not like "Herman's Hermits" – now there *was* a good, sensible pop group. Hated beer! Wouldn't hear of drugs.'

'And girls!'

'Catchy, strumalong little numbers... bloody good tailor they had too! Every dairy in the land was proud to have their faces on the back of their milk floats! Not like today! You'd be frightened to go to work of a morning!'

'I know *I* am.'

'Ooowah!'

'Tup! Will your pair just shut up for a second? It's like fucking bedlam on acid in there!' The bouncer was finally able to get a word in wedgeways.

'Anybody invite a crew of mental women?' Tinker was already grinning, having noticed a familiar yellow tour bus, now parked neatly at the front bay of the municipal car park opposite.

'Only, Phil's going beebar! They've superglued the glasses to the tables and flushed the house cassette tapes down the bogs! Now they're chanting the place down, God knows why, I think you're crap.'

'Thanks.'

'Cheers, we appreciate that!'

'And another thing – what's all this about Sherlock Holmes is your manager and he's promised you'll be getting your cocks out?'

Now, that *did* puzzle us. For the time being, Tinker snatched out his pipe and hid it behind his back as all eyes were suddenly switched in his direction.

'Tup! Let's go and get on with it – while there's still a stage to stand on?'

He began to bundle us in. I had to declare the managerial newcomer as Joe checked us in with the door staff.

'Joe? This is Tinker – he's gonna be mmm... MC for us tonight!' The door staff were now far beyond caring.

'Just get in, you pissheads, and get playing... *Oi! You!*' The Skipper was breaking off and heading for the bar. 'Not to the bar – to the stage! *I'll* get your beers!'

He tiptoed back into line. 'Rinky, rinky, tinky, tinky! Jolly decent of you, old horse! I'll just pop off to the stage then, eh?' I'd been waiting to drag him on.

'They really *are* absolute sports, what?'

'What?'

'I've forgotten.'

'So am I!'

Halfway to the stage, I took hold of Tinker's collar as a wail of assorted profanities filled the room, courtesy of the

Kirkby Girls, incensed by this sudden pervasion of testosterone.

'What's all this "cocks out" malarky, matey?'

Joe and Sticky were equally curious. Tinker shrugged his shoulders and removed the meerschaum. 'You didn't want the gig to be a donkey, right?'

'And?'

'So I met these kife in Bridgford and I invited them down. Said you were hung like donkeys and you weren't shy about it.'

Sticky seemed horrified. He wrapped an arm around the MC and studied his watch.

'Donkeys? Tink, my man – ha, ha! Let me explain summat to yer! Not two hours ago, I made the irrevocable decision to give my hooter one beaut of a dusting with yer old original Colombian jogging powder. As a consequence of which, the aforementioned "donkey" is going to be more inclined towards the dimensions of a shaved adolescent dwarf Japanese hamster in December. So I'm hoping these women are of simple needs.'

'*Tup*. Mine's staying where it is.'

'Ahhhsoddit! Croc'll do the biz – he's not over-fussed!'

'Ooowah!'

We pushed Tinker through to the elevated stage, onto which he chirpily skipped to announce The Chimneys with an almost blasé composure, thus invoking a raucous baying which perpetuated until we were all up and ready to go. Not so bad for a chap who was skint and on his way home for beans on toast just three hours beforehand... Chants. Wails. Tribal stompings. Obviously the only thing which was going to shut them up was us. Joe turned to us to curtail all pratting about.

'Okay! Let's get ugly! Go for it! Two-three-four!' We burst into 'Let's get ugly', and the dance began. The Kirkby crew, augmented by a leather-clad line of Biffers, yelled for penis. Closer to the bar, a couple of dozen friends tapped feet, some having on occasion to parry a wayward body further waywards from the beer. Numerous new faces trying to decide whether to stay or go. Bar staff plugging ears. Cueball up and down behind the pumps, raving on about something. On we trot. Who's the silver-haired, middle-aged weirdo in the rainmac? What's Cueball's problem? As Paul McCartney once sang, 'We've got the chicken by the horns' – and for once we actually had. We sounded shit enough to make it look contrived and rehearsed. We deliberately maintained two-second gaps between numbers to drown Cueball's protestations; which seemed to make his head redder and his rage even more intense. The rest was all a polyphonic technicolour blur.

It had turned out to be, after all, a largely successful and penis-free gig. Well, we did get them out. But in deference to the 'Health and Safety at Work' notice on Cueball's kitchen door, we did it with our backs to the Kirkby Kife. It seemed to impart a certain value for money, plus it looked like we'd won over some new conscripts. Forty-five minutes. Two encores. *Off*. Back to the back room for beer. Peace and quiet, quaking with adrenalin, sweat streaming, ears buzzing loudly. Tranquillity. Unwinding inch by inch. At ease together. Icy beer cutting through the parchment. Taking the breeze at the open window. Then Cueball.

'You miked up the bastard bass drum! *I told you*! What did I fucking tell you not *one* hour ago? *Don't mike up that bastard bass drum*! You don't need it! Too bastard loud, you bastards! Why don't you listen? She's going mad! She's locked me out the flat! What did I ask you? Eh? *And* you're all pissed, you pissed up bastards! Get here an hour late – *pissed*! Then hit the piss on stage!'

'Phil' to his friends, or 'Cueball' to humans, was a former local DJ for Radio Nottingham, turned publican, turned bald and round, and turned it fast; ergo the appellation of 'Cueball'. Talk to him off the job – piece of pie. Try to deal with him busy at the shop and it's one step back, to fan his steam off you. I turned wearily to Sticky, who was hiding in a sip of beer.

'Has he finished?'

'I don't need this shit! I've got enough bastard shit! I'm locked out now, you drunken bastards! And another thing! "Cheers-goodnight-don't-get-murdered-on-the-way-home?" What kinda way is *that* to send paying customers on their way at the end of the night, you evil bastards?'

Sticky took the sip and turned wearily back. 'No! He hasn't.'

'Never again! Never again! Miking the bastard bass drum!'

'Phil?'

'And have you seen the tables and the toilets?'

'Phil?'

'And those women! Were those women with *you*? Have you seen... disgusting! Animals!'

'Phil?'

'Bitches in season! Animals! Disgusting!'

'Sod it. Talk to him, Joe.'

Joe knew Cueball better than us. We left them to their ravings and tuppings and filed quietly out into the hall for fresh air and fresh beer. Then, who was to be seen lurking about in the hall, but the Benny Hill wannalook in the rainmac, talking along the line of his hooter and revving around in his glass what smelt like a Martini on the rocks. He vacated his lurking perch alongside a long-redundant fag machine to grant us the benefit of himself. Apparently we were of interest to him. Apparently he was perchance to be an A&R man for Rough Trade Records, currently visiting Nottingham. Apparently we had something – bit rough around the edges – but apparently nothing incorrigible. He fumbled inside his coat, took out a Dunhill inkpen and scribbled down a number on a scrap of paper torn from his diary. Handed it to a diplomatically bemused Crocodile.

Apparently he'd discovered The Smiths. Croc looked at Sticky and shrugged one shoulder. Sticky looked at the Skipper. The Skipper belched for England and giggled at me. I giggled at Croc. Apparently, Mac could shove it. He seemed a little stunned if not personally downright insulted by Sticky's brash tone of inverted patronisation and the general carnival of indifference which surrounded him.

'Yeah! Well – nice one, mate! We'll let you know, eh?'

As Mac waddled off, somewhat crestfallen and vigorously revving his Martini, Croc licked the scrap of paper and patted it onto his back. At this point, that 'hang on a mo' feeling began to creep over me like dampness in your shreddies as you sleep.

'Okay. Who's darkholed the gig money *this* time?'

As if directed via some ethereal switchboard, Joe's head, under green-grey Marlowe hat, poked out of the back room doorway.

'Anyone fancy a Chinese?'

FIVE

The Mayfair. A modest, alcohol-free Chinese restaurant in Mansfield Road. The Clergyman Fig had once slept unnoticed under a corner table there for a whole Bank Holiday Monday. Sticky was first to wholly peruse the menu. He beckoned the attendance of an alarmingly dainty and immaculately turned out young waitress.

'Hi! Yeah! Okay! So, we'll take five soups in a basket, several emotional sardines in a noisy young sauce, two portions expressed as a whole of the lapin de bonk embarassée, and whatever these gentlemen would like, please!'

I poked an alcohol-weighted pair of eyes in and out of an adjacent bill of fare.

'I want five prawn smackers. If that's allowed?'

'You mean crackers?' she corrected, incorrectly.

'Absolutely crackers – but I want smackers!'

'Whaat?'

'See thirty-two. And five onion shampoos – see twenty-seven; five bottles of duelling soy – see the kitchen shelf. Thank you!'

Joe let off a tup.

'Tup, I've invited Phil, so we can discuss another gig and more money.'

'Okay, in which case we'll have five plates of chopped raw chillies – seeds in. Thank you, missus.'

The soy bottles were first to table. Sticky sent me a sideways glance. I returned one, which then fell onto his designer jacket. We raced furiously to open the soy bottles.

'Soy session!'

'Aaahsoyseshuuurn!'

'Tup. Oh no – not a soy session. Leave me out!'

'Ooowah!' The Croc cared not.

The Skipper leapt to his feet and ducked behind his chair. 'Have a care, chaps! I'm stripping off – I washed this gear yesterday and I need it tomorrow!'

Within seconds, the tops were released and Sticky and I were pumping soy showers over each other like idiots repossessed. But to his gross disadvantage, Sticky had dressed from the left side of the wardrobe that particular evening.

'Bastard! You bastard, my new jacket! At least wait till I get me jacket off – bastard! Right! Enjoy this all over your nice T-shirt!'

'That's okay, m'man, I've got loads of nice T-shirts! How many nice jackets have you bought lately?'

'Tup, behave, you newarks, she's coming back!'

'Okay, whose are the prawns? Everyone? Onions? Everyone? And rice? And raw chillies... *God*! Have you got any clothes on?'

'Just some shreddies of a rather maturish vogue, dear girl... no cares, though! All tucked safely under the table!'

'Just ignore him – he's being all practical and adult about things.'

'Your friend is practically naked!'

'Don't glorify that man with your pretty attention, sweetheart. Let's see how clever he looks with a napkin draping out of his navel! Yep! Not very!'

The Skipper had stuffed a red paper napkin deep into his umbilicus, fanning it out ceremoniously.

'There, dear girl! That's the sauce syphon safely screened off... Now! Just place the nosh before us and trust us to do the rest, there's an absolute winner!'

Sticky sighed. The echo of the sigh caught all Chimney attention for the moment.

'Well, Chims? Not a bad gig. And as for the blackguard

among us who darkholed the gig money – good luck! Good health! And damn yer eyes, you absolute bastard!'

'Hear, hear!'

'Damnable – damn his eyes!'

'Ooh – ooowah!'

'Shameless binder!'

'Ruddy scapegrace, *if* yer like!'

'Well! Being drummer, and ergo the man who counts us in, I suppose it's down to me?' Joe pulled his seat slightly back from the table. The Skipper ruffled nervously at the napkin. Sticky drew two chopsticks from the central dispenser and clicked them together.

'Ready? One-two-three-*smack*!' At this, he dropped the sticks, formed a palm and slapped it down into one of the helpings of curried prawns, showering all – particularly me. It behoved me therefore to provide the antithesis.

'Okey-chokey! Be advised, citizens! Hot random prawns at twelve o'clock!'

Smack!

'Ouch – me tit! That was bastard hot!'

'Tup, pack it in, she's coming back.'

'Pardon me, sir, can you stop smacking your food, please?'

'No!' The Skipper smacked. The Croc smacked. The prawns – bar Joe's – were by now parked all over the postcode. The waitress even bore half a crustaceous brooch, slightly to the north-east of her cleavage.

'Well, the manager has asked me to mention that if you don't stop smacking your meals, he'll be forced to ask you all to leave.'

At this juncture, I opted to play a secret ace.

'Well, in which case, you'd best explain to the manager that if *he's* forced to ask *us* to leave, then *we'll* be forced to ask the manager's wife what on earth *she* supposes the *manager* may have been forced to be doing, getting into *my* taxi from an address in Perry Road at four a.m. last Thursday. Then as a result the manager's wife could *well* be forced to ask the *manager* to leave.'

'Whoa! Played like a Trojan, Mister Shedfixman!'

'Crafty one, Shed!'

'Hey, pull yourselves together; Cueball's just walked in the door!'

As the waitress glided away with an impatient hiss and a surreptitious tit wipe, Cueball meandered over to us like an unpiloted shopping trolley. An inane grin belied the unsteadiness in his eyes.

'Join you, lads? Great gig! Look – sorry I was a bit edgy earlier. She's given me the key back... you've all ordered... What you eating – raw chillies? Skipper! Where's your kit? Joe – hiyer! Shed? Croc?'

'Oowah!'

'Sticky?'

'Yeah, ha, ha! Chillies, Phil! Great for cleaning your dirty fingers with; you just have to learn how to piss no-handed!'

'Ha, ha!' Cueball's unease broke slightly. 'Ha, ha! Yeah! I don't know! I don't know... You're ill men... ha, ha!'

'And don't you forget it, dear boy, or we may be obliged to remind you!'

'Ha ha ha!'

'Tup! So – er, Phil! Tup, it's about the money.'

'Lads! I *enjoy* having you at my place! Sod the profits at the bar! Sod the brewery directives – so long as we're all happy! Let's ride it while it lasts, eh? Wahay? Ha, ha!' He feigned an extremely poor pelvic poke to which no one was ever likely to award the faintest of chortles.

Sticky's day job was in corporate finance; he had a built-in radar system for detecting shysters. His eyebrows rose slightly.

'Yeah, absa! And we enjoy shipping in forty lager-swilling Traceys on an otherwise lukewarm evening, so they can sod your profits and sod the brewery.'

The others trickled out droplets of laughter, but I suspected that levity would bear no fruit in this particular sitcom.

'Phil. We're daft, but we're not stupid. We talk to people. We're so friendly we'll talk to anyone. We'll even talk to the Westwoods!'

'Yeah, but hang on, Shed...'

'Let me finish? And likely as not, if we talk to the Westwoods, the Westwoods'll tell us that you're sodding the profits to the tune of a hundred per gig to enjoy having *them* at your place, whereas it's a token sodding of twenty-five quid and a beer apiece for the special enjoyment of having *us*.'

He appeared somewhat aghast at the calibre of this intelligence report.

'What I'm saying is, the time's come to start enjoying having us a bit more, Philip, me ol' son.'

'Westwood crowds – Westwood money!'

'Oowah!' Cueball sucked in breath, harshly.

'Wassup, Phil? Got a mouth full of hot stew?'

'Ha, ha!'

'Lads – lads – listen! It's about the power! The lighting! Wages! Overheads!'

'All of which you'd be forking out, anyway!'

'How do you know the Westwoods aren't bulling you, anyway?'

'Because the Croc bulled Marie a week last Tuesday.'

'Ha ha ha!'

'Lads, come on! We're all reasonable men, and I can see what you're trying to say...'

'Having no trouble saying anything, dear boy!'

'...but you can appreciate my hands are tied here.'

'Wish they were.'

'I feel one of my neck-aches coming on.' We all exchanged subtle glances of resignation.

'Forget it, then – let's eat what's left, tup. Happy!'

Cueball's uneasy smirk returned as his heart jumped out of his wallet and traipsed home.

'Nah! Come on! Let's enjoy the snap! It's been a good night and, much as I hate to say it, you're a smashing bunch of lads. The bill's mine – how's that?'

'Ooowahh!' The Croc had been seated at Cueball's right, elbow on table, chin on fist, giving the immediate impression of a man hanging intently onto Cueball's every word. It provided an adequate front for Croc's other hand, which was busy beneath the table emptying a soy bottle down the nearest leg of Cueball's cream flannel chinos. The rest of us furtively massaged chillies and picked at prawns and shovelled rice about. I glanced over at Croc's half-empty soy bottle, now suddenly restored to the table from somewhere. Sticky had noticed it. He grinned at the Croc. I peeped around at Sticky.

'Make sure we save a couple of twenty-sevens for later.'

'Game on, m'man.'

We all exchanged another glance; we knew there was a jape in prospect, if not exactly what form it would take. The collective improvisation may have been in its adolescence on stage, but socially it was well in its prime. We all knew Cueball's biological dispositions. Cueball was prolific in all things. He was always prolifically esurient. Prolifically imbibitive. Prolifically unctious. He farted prolifically. He whinged prolifically. He belched prolifically, and after thirty-five minutes of inertia and fruit juices, he was going to need to piss prolifically. We picked and shovelled and bided our time. Cueball ordered last. But he always finished first, irrespective of intrusion. Then should be the moment.

Joe, sensing an impending severance of civilities and mindful of a five a.m. alarm call to the family news agency business, was first to pair the cutlery and announce his bailing out with a final shovel of rice on board.

'Well, num, that's me lot, early start the morra, num, it's

been real. Phil? Thanks for everything!' He stretched a hand over to Cueball. Cueball rose to shake it.

'Off, Joe? Okay, mate! Well – don't be a stranger, eh?'

'Chims?'

'Joe.'

'We'll be in touch.'

'With snap down us – ha, ha!'

Joe picked up his guitar case, backhanded a tip onto the table and pounded off to flag a taxi. Cueball rose again, still masticating his last mouthful. His eyes searched the restaurant for lavatorial likelihood. All around him, there was a general motion to seize either the opportunity or the set of clothes on the floor before the Skipper could.

'Lads? You're not *all* off?' I yawned loudly.

'Well, Phil – you know what they say? All play and no wok! Put it there, mate!' He shook my hand prolifically. Sticky was next to offer.

'Cheers, Philip! No rest for the wicket!'

'Ha, ha!'

'Croc?'

'Oowah!'

'Skipper? Put it there, sir!'

'Put it quickly, dear boy! I'm dropping me kit!'

Cueball waddled off towards the men's room, still blurting out an array of pretentious niceties. The Skipper danced into his trousers. Sticky accosted the waitress.

'It's never over till the fat man pays – and the fat man's paying. You got a carrier for these twenty-sevens?'

The Croc was still busy, this time tipping plates of chillies into the pockets of Cueball's jacket, which was draped around his chair back. He gave the lapels a vigorous jangling to ensure that all Cueball's loose change and belongings were thoroughly spiced. Sticky took the carrier of twenty-sevens and hoisted it on to me.

'First post, a.m.?'

'Yeah, I'll take care of it, m'man.' We were ex-Mayfair.

Inside, Cueball was prolifically relishing a prolific drainage of the bladder whilst congratulating himself on his bargaining prowess whilst prolifically picking his prolifically encrusted hooter. A five-second delay, then the first wave smote the hooter as if a sudden vengeance of the Lord was upon; and fork lightning, voodoo acupuncture and the firestorms of Dresden all happened at once in Cueball's nostrils.

'Uh? *Uhh*? Ooohyerffff! Owww! Oooh! Ah! Wha? What's...?' Cueball curtailed the pissoir, prolifically shaking and replacing his penis in order to check hooter in the toilet mirror. Nothing was obvious. Then the second wave marinated into his main man.

'Eh? Me–what–whaaat? Whatherfff? *Aah*! Aaahchaah! Eh? Oohyufff! Bastards! Bastards! Me fffftajja! I wondered why the bastards all wanted to shake me hand! Oo! Ooo! Water? Get me cock out – water! *Ooh*! No! Nose! Nose!' Leaning over the sink, Cueball ran the cold water tap full on and attempted somewhat foolishly to inhale its initial flush.

'Ulp-ulp-gnahh! Ahuck! Hucka hucka – the bastiz – whaat? Look! Look – me trousers! Croc! Croc! Croc, you *bastardooomecock*! Me cock! Me cock! Mecockmecockmecock! *Mecock – Croc*!'

SIX

Morning. Saturday – if you care; still morning. Rude, crude daylight. Loud. Pushy. Unfair. Incompatible with your mouth, your eyelids, the gnawing inside your brain. Is it morning, or is it you? Peel the tongue off the roof of your mouth. Squinting, squeezing, sleepsick senses. Lulling labouring livers. Oh no! We're back in *that* world again. Soddit. Buggerit. Gah! Get it over with, eh? Nearly Sunday. Meanwhile, bills to meet, dorks to greet and shit to eat. Come on, take it like a man. Play the game for another day. That game. *Their* bloody silly little game. *Their* bloody silly little rules. Simulate servile sensibility for the suited stupid. Purvey *plusieurs* of platitudes to the prattish plenty. In a word, work. The hearse of the thinking classes. I knew we'd all feel the same. We had to. We loved the good world too much. Still, we went to the toilet; we went through the motions. The Croc – horologist and jeweller par excellence. Running a bit late, so were the trains... Blame *them* as you face the sea of clicking Cartiers. Do you watch the clocks all day? Breathe the beer fumes sideways as you demonstrate the merchandise. Smiling Croc – are you happy to see us? Or is that a soy sauce stain story on your mind?

Joe Planet – slashing strings, pencilling on papers. Where's that, tup, bloody paper lad again?

Ding! Is it? No. Not the paper lad, it's the daft lad.

'Yes sir, what can I do you for?'

'Uh... *Shun*, *Shtar*, Shoopakingsh.'

'I'm sorry, I'm afraid the *Sun* are on strike.'

'Uh? Wuw! I'll gerrit down the road, then. I don't want that *Mirrow* – there's nowt innit!'

Ding! Great. Now it's the seventy-year-old Elvira wannabe …

'Pardon me, young man – is my copy of the *Psychic News* in yet?'

'Don't you know?'

Sticky – adjusting his tie. Slipping on the Rolex; an impulse purchase from the beach at Bodrum. Spooning down the 'Slap, Cackle 'n' Fop'. Jacket on. Away. 'Morning!' Five minutes early for once. 'Two sugars today, please! Meeting at nine, but I'll take the mail first.' … 'Very well, Mr Dickens.' … Early lunch with the buyers. Meeting at 2.15. 'I'll take it black.' Meeting at 4.30, then cut out to Jingo's wine bar and filofax transit camp. Bottle of Sin Cojones with pink grapefruit wedge, wedged in its spout. Same all round for the juniors. Jackets over shoulders at the bar. 'Love over Gold' on the juke. Yucatan yuppist's unisphere.

The Skipper – apologising for his tardiness: 'Sorry, but a horse fell on me!' Mug of tea; 9 a.m. lecture. Face the brats: 'If you'd all care to refer to module seven? We'll examine the basic principals of the semiconductor.'

Then we'll examine what the fuck inspired us to bother turning up on a Saturday, then we'll examine the basic principals of the cask conditioned bitter barrel, then adjourn to the on-site practical.

Shed. Me. Taxi driver for depressed droves. I woke up in the taxi in the garage around nine, maybe later. Freezing to death. Rough as ten badgers' arses. Deciding to give the Dragon another try, like some eight hours beforehand – before the backhand. Talk to her first, then go to work.

Okay, I tried. Off to work then, with the sweet, letterbox-filtered sound of 'fuck off back to your slut' ringing in my ears. Beautiful start. First, then: do the right thing by the Chims. Drop the packaged onion shampoo off at Cueball's doorstep. Two-minute scoot. Buzz on the intercom.

'Yuh?'

'On-eeeon shamfooce forra Missa Koobles – bye!'

'Who's that? Who is it – a taxi? Shed? Is that you? You bas—'

Run back to the car. Scoot on. Okay! I did the biz. But now I had to drink something. Definitely had to eat something. In fact, I had to do a lot of fucking things; opening the window seemed premier. Fuel looked deputy premier.

I'd tanked up at the Shell outside Radio Nottingham. I was checking the car over – poking, dipping, dusting – a token dedication of water to the camel. I was eating a Scotch egg, drinking some Ribena and scratching some hard-baked song thrush shit off the windscreen all at the same time, when a sudden glancing flat of hand whacked hard into the centre of my back, sending me sprawling over the bonnet, choking to death on the concoction of egg and juice, and I'm sure I sucked half the birdshit into the deal.

'What the huck! Huckahuck! Yer?'

I reeled around, still halfway to the hereafter. Four of them. Biker cross-zips. Brass 'Nottingham' insignia on left lapels; unopened condoms tacked onto the right lapels. Ray-Bans. Vicars' dog collars. All I needed – the Clergy. They're either just going out or just coming in.

'Sarge, ahuckahuck! You fucking nutter, you're-huck-gonna kill me doing that, one day!'

'Shed, Shed, Shed – always watch your Brookside!' He had a good chuckle as I laboured to restore respiratory par. But Sarge was okay, really. He was the guru. The philosopher. Well into yer peace, love and understanding, despite his little idiosyncrasies. He drew much pride from his Bangladeshi lineage, and much contentment from his renunciation of the material world. Yep, it smelt like they were fresh from an outstanding soirée, and by the look of them, it was ongoing. Then the ringleader, the Outlaw Tallbob Weedley, cut in. Tallbob was unfortunately my next-door neighbour at that time. Six feet five inches of skinny, blond, razor-witted bastard.

Rakish, wiry, wily and hedonistic beyond all limits.

'Shed! We're just popping out to offend dozens of people with some really appalling behaviour and alarming drinking habits, and we've decided you're coming with us. Now what d'you think of *that*, neighbour?'

'Lads, I'm supposed to be working – gimme a rest!'

Then it was the turn of Des Carson, the Small Parson. He was scarcely five feet five, but a much bigger bastard. If Hitler had made it to Nuremberg and they'd let him off, providing he lost the tache, backcombed his hair and got into some decent thread, you'd be looking at something like Des. The Parson always dipped his brow to speak.

'Shed – look, Shed! Mad, fat, drunk and stupid is no way to spend life, so come with us and lose a bit of weight, eh?' He tapped the side of his nose. 'Anyway, we've *all* got *far* too much month left at the end of the money!'

'Yeah! Look, neighbour – don't talk, just listen! We've got your monkey. Any girl business and the cash gets it, understand?'

I understood well enough. I attempted one last futile flail of resistance.

'I've already missed half the week – the Dragon's going beebar; so will the Gaffer be. What am I supposed to do for wad?'

'Shed, Shed, Shed!'

'Neighbour! You're the biggest worrier this side of the road! I've told you a thousand times – we *own* the world!'

'Some of us have *decent* jobs to lose!'

I thought about that as I coughed out the last of the egg. 'Okay, okay. Lads? I must have a dozen better things to do than piss it up with *your* shower. But right now I can't think of one – I'm too slapped!'

They gave their approval to this in the form of a few less life-threatening back-pats. Fig, the quieter one, mumbled his customary, 'Ay up, sport!' with a hiccup in the middle. As we got into the taxi, Tallbob advised me not to engage Fig in conversation if I could at all help it, as they'd been slipping garlic salt into his beer all night. Fig often preferred deep, personal conversations with himself anyway. By trade, he was a roofer. God alone knew how he managed to stay on the buggers; he was on a completely different set of tiles every night.

Before I parked the taxi, I thought it would be wise to do the decent thing and radio the base to call in sick. Again. I clicked the set on.

'Okay, shut up for a minute, you reprobates... Thirty-nine to base?'

The hard-pressed, arid wit of the controller crackled back at me. 'Well, Thirty-nine! I don't believe it! What's up, can't you sleep? Or is it another day with a glass wedged over your head?'

'Hey, Poley! That's very kind of you, mate – see you Monday, then!'

'Whoa, whoa, just a minute, Thirty-nine! Now we've got you, we've just called back on a complaint from a lady passenger! You picked her up at Babel's Club on Tuesday night – remember?'

'Vaguely.'

'She says you were very rude.'

'Time of the month, mate!'

'Watch your mouth, she's on the phone at the moment!'

'I meant *my* time of the month, mate!'

'She can hear you on the radio – she's going crackers! Now she wants an apology off you, to begin with!'

The Clergy were biting their lips and rumbling. I couldn't hold them off for ever.

'Okay, okay... Listen, I'll tell you what, Poley – and I can't be fairer than this – tell her I'm very sorry, unreservedly so, and just to make things all square, tell her if she buys me ten or eleven beers, I'll sleep with her.'

The Clergy guffawed aloud as I waved in vain for silence and order.

'Right, that's it, Thirty-nine! See the Gaffer on Monday morning! You're bang out of—'

'Thirty-nine, out!' Click. 'Right. Let's adjust some attitudes.' There were grins all round to that particular suggestion. Not that it varied from the agenda anyway.

So that was that. I was out with the Clergy on a Saturday. Having sneaked the taxi home, Tallbob decided we had to be manly about the hangovers and irritate them back, by opening the show with a plateful of greasy shit at the Elbow.

Now if you considered Claridges to be the top of the tree, then the Elbow, in relation, would be somewhere not far from the earth's core. The Elbow was always meticulously cleaned, decorated and painted whenever England won the World Cup – ready or not. Table manners, payment by banknote or inspecting your food during or after purchase, consumption or ejection, were all frowned upon intensely. It was an alarming prospect, but we voted for, and cheerfully piled in, removing the Raybans just in case.

He was in a back booth, trying to duck out of our line of sight, but the Sergeant had spotted him straight off.

'Noakes, Noakes, Noakes!'

'It's Nil-nil Noakes!'

'Nil-nil, nil-nil, nil-nil!'

'Noakes, yer bastard!'

Nil-nil Noakes was a good laugh, and a basically sound, intelligent, good-looking lad, if a touch on the corpulent side. But Noakes possessed this very annoying mating habit, which made you want to do the twist on his head for a bit. Noakes would fish around to learn whether one of us had been recently shagging around, then if so, he'd 'accidentally' call up or bump into your dragon. Tell her all about it, then try to persuade *her* to do the same on *you* with *him,* since *you'd* already done it on *her*. Of course, *he* was invariably invited to fuck off; but then *you* could be. That's why we called him Nil-nil. In the very recent past he'd cost Sticky his dragon. He'd tried to do it to Mark Anthony and his wife, Wendy. He'd even tried it on me and the Dragon before we were even thirty seconds into Mark and Wendy's wedding reception. I hadn't got him back yet, but he knew fucking well I'd still got it on board.

Fig ambled over to Noakes' table. Fig may have been as sensible as a rubber bell, but he was perennially polite.

'We'll join you, if we may, sport!'

Whilst the Parson ordered up the grease, the rest of us crowded in around Noakes to examine what we were about to receive. He was halfway through a Full English with considerably less prospect of relishing the second half.

''Allo, lairds!' Noakes had moved up from London some years ago, but the South had stayed in the mouth. I decided to put him on his back foot straight away.

There'd been a reputable rumour circulating that his flatmate, 'Bones' Kelly, once caught him bollock naked in the bathroom, listening to the football results over the radio whilst wanking off rather heartily.

'So, Noakes! How's the classified pools check?'

Tallbob picked up on it, toying with a ketchup bottle. 'Many late flick – er, I mean, kick-offs?'

'*Oooh*! Bolton Wandererzzahh!'

'Noakey-Coakey!'

'Aw, leave it aht, lairds – I'm eating me grab!' The Sergeant stole a handful of chips from Noakes' plate. 'Oi! Do you mind? This'll be the larst meal I'm gonna git today!'

'No, I don't mind at all... I'm just concerned about your health, Noakes. I wouldn't want you to become an even fatter bastard, you fat bastard!'

'Ha, ha!'

'Oi! Mind the language, lairds. I 'appen to use this place orften!'

'We can tell *that*, you fat bastard!'

'Ha ha ha!'

Noakes was kitted out in a pristine and previously unseen light brown suede blouson jacket. The Parson had had his eye on it for a while.

'I say! Look! Noakes is sporting a rather super-duper looking crowd-pleaser of a jacket here. No doubt set you back a quid or two hundred and eighty?'

'Actually, two andred 'n fifty, mate.' Which probably meant £29.99... Now he was rushing his food, in case. He was more than heavily out-gunned and preparing for a rubbishing. Our five plates of grease arrived and we began a cursory inspection to make sure everything on the table was dead. As the cutlery was thrown around, I perused Noakes' jacket, feeling the quality of the hide.

'Yes, that's quite a vestment, my friend.'

Tallbob quickly concurred – in total disearnesty. 'It's the best one I've seen this side of beef!'

'Nope, you just don't see that class of jacket in a top-notch restaurant anymore, Tallbob!'

Fig had begun to chortle to himself. His face had broken out into that look of impending contribution. He didn't contribute much or often, but when he did, you could guarantee it would make all the difference to the day. His eyes fixed on near-distant space.

'I saw a disgusting thing in a café last week...'

Now there was disgusting, and Fig's disgusting. Disgusting, you forget on the way home. Fig's disgusting, you carry around like herpes for the rest of your life. With a 'meal' in prospect, I knew I wasn't going to need to hear this anecdote, so I met it at the door with, 'Fig. After, eh?'

The Sergeant coiled slightly. 'Fig, we're eating.'

Even Noakes put a forkful of egg and chips on temporary hold. 'Don't wanna 'ear it, Fig!'

But, however sadly for peace and propriety, Tallbob, by his

very nature always seemed to feel compelled to play Lord Harry's advocate. 'It's alright, Fig. Go on – *I* want to listen!'

The Parson too, sensing Noakes' queasiness, couldn't overlook this platinum opportunity for a fast shitmix. If he'd been a Muslim, he'd probably have prayed in the exact opposite direction to the rest of the temple, then argue that if Mecca was south-east, it had to be north-west too, eventually. He nudged Fig hard.

'Give it to us, Fig. Ignore *them*.'

I braced my ears. 'Then shit and off we go again.'

The Sergeant looked three-quarters away, surrendering knife and fork to plate. 'I'll kill you, Fig!' But Fig had decided anyway.

'Well, there was this geezer at the next table to me, scoffing a bacon sandwich, and after he'd finished, he took his false teeth out and sat licking bits of bacon off them…' *Uproar*. And then some. Fig was slapped half to death by everyone's bacon rashers. His head and face were awash with grease.

'You dirty facking barstard!' Noakes slammed down his fork and changed colour a little.

The Parson now seemed a little dazed for his sins. 'Yes, yes, I'm sorry I spoke.'

The Sergeant held out a palm. 'You owe me for this fucking breakfast!'

Tallbob slapped Fig once more with his rasher for luck. 'You're as much use as Van Gogh's glasses, you simple peasant girl!'

Well, they'd asked for it. I couldn't think of much to say, other than it seemed like I wasn't destined to finish a meal that day. At this point, I noticed Tallbob and the Parson trying to quietly catch my attention. They'd moved in either side of Noakes, who was now ruefully slumped forward with tears in his eyes and a hand over his mouth, swallowing hard. They both covertly held rashers of bacon in hand. Tallbob winked and assumed a patronising tone.

'I'm dead impressed with this jacket, Noakes – is it real suede, you say?'

'Yeah – the best, mate... *urb*!'

'I can't get over it! Mind if I have a quick feel?'

'Do what you like... Just don't make me talk anymore – I'll fuck-hick-ing puke!'

Tallbob and the Parson both reached around to the back of his shoulders, to sample and relish the outstanding hide.

'Well, you've got a bargain there, Noakes!'

'I'm impressed; get up and get yourself a drink if you're feeling a bit Uncle Dickey, matey!'

'Uh – yuh!' Noakes excused himself and shuffled off to the counter.

Tallbob and the Parson broke into a wide grin as they watched him. I knitted my eyebrows at them in curiosity. Then the Parson's head bowed at me slightly. He hissed through his teeth. 'The jacket!'

I looked up at the errant Noakes, then at the jacket. Across its shoulder blades, the cut bore a generous horizontal pleat of suede. The pleat was conveniently deep enough to poke something inside. To poke, for instance, a bacon rasher or two inside – and they had. Four or five rashers hung out of the pleat, somewhat akin to fringing on a Salvador Dali biker jacket. It was time to leave before he bubbled it – or someone else did. Tallbob sprang to his feet.

'Well! It's nearly eleven; there's this *place* I know, not far away, where you can pay eighty-four pence and someone fills a big glass up with beer and lets you drink it all as quickly as you like!'

I'd still got two rashers left, so had the Sergeant. As we all filed out past the heavily disgruntled Nil-nil, we offered him a consolatory pat on the back, wishing speed to his recovery and, of course, insidiously adding more rashers to the effect.

'Take it easy, Noakes. Plenty of deep breaths!'

'Noakes, Noakes, Noakes.'

'So long, sport.'

As we jockeyed for an exit, Tallbob wheeled around towards the counter.

'By the way, Noakes, if you're hungry later, there's a pub down the road that does a nice jacket potato with a choice of fillings *and* does a lovely drop of wine – or you can take your own. Your own filling, that is!'

'*Uuurbip*!'

'Ha ha ha!'

'We recommend the bacon filling!'

'Ha ha ha!' He still hadn't bubbled it, nor had anyone else, yet. I hung back to let the Clergy leave first. Then, before I followed them out, I turned to throw him one last clue.

'Go there, Noakes – treat yourself! Get a full bacon jacket!'

SEVEN

By the time we'd bowled down Mansfield Road to the Yorker, Fig had wiped most of the grease from his hair, face and shoulders – or so we'd told him numerous times, before inviting him to shut very up. The Yorker – an archetypal legacy of Watson Fothergill's headiest Victoriana – offered a lavishly ornate array of architectural elegance to all from its bustle-derailing frontispiece without; whilst within affording ample wooden-boarded floor space to cater for one's singularly inimitable predisposition for saloon monkey business. On the yin, the establishment was at the time being overseen by a long-suffering Celtic cosmopolitan who'd never even considered his strong resemblance to comedian Eric Sykes until we'd first very obligingly pointed it out to him.

Upon entering, Tallbob removed his leather cross-zip and instinctively lanced it across the room to land flatly upon the table at which he'd decided we were all about to sit; thereon swiftly and incontestably dissuading a brace of students who were poised to realise a similar ambition. Two more jackets met with the first and we stormed the massively set oaken bar, waiting upon Eric. In the jading back-wall mirror we all reviewed the cosmetic penalties incurred at yestereve's ravages and permitted ourselves a token grooming. Fig gyrated his shoulders, cranking his head up and down and around to try to view the bald patch at the back from the front. The small Parson took out a comb. The Sergeant glanced once, then did nothing. Tallbob stooped and gave his scalp a fast, furious scrubbing. My attention was then drawn via the mirror to the two toothbrushes parked in the breast pocket of his sleeveless, open-necked Army shirt. One blue toothbrush, one pink. The banter had been centred on last night's capery – in mind of which we had begun to count up and stack loose change on the bar – when Eric emerged from the cellar door, metal bucket in hand. His eyes goggled widely upon clocking us, and in his softly concerned western Irish brogue, he let slip, 'Aww, naww! Not you lot – not first thing in the day!'

'Eric, Eric, Eric!'

'Look – keep the noise down, Eric – you'll stampede the beer!'

'Five large ones and less of your language, matey!'

'Chop-chop, sport! We're gagging rather!'

Eric lost the bucket for the moment, then slowly sidled up to us, chin on chest. The dog collars were never to his taste.

'Yezz'll all be lucky to be served at *all*, after last night's horseplay, lads!'

The Parson was in first. 'Horseplay? What channel was it on?'

'He means Black Beauty.'

'Can't be *us*, sport! We don't drink in here.'

Eric half-opened his mouth to speak, but Tallbob sharply pre-empted him.

'I know exactly what you're about to say, Eric – and that's what we've come about. We all feel thoroughly ashamed of ourselves, and we've decided that we'd like to come down and apologise for our behaviour last night.'

'Well then, lads, that's very civil of yez, er...'

'We'd also like to apologise for our behaviour for tonight and for tomorrow night.'

Eric's placatory grin subsided. 'You'll bluddy behave or get out, yer buggers! I mean it, now!'

Fig leant aside to me and murmured quietly, 'We can always go over the road.'

But Eric had caught his remark. His face flushed again as he resettled the glasses directly back upon the shelf. 'Okay!

I'll stand so much...'

Faced with a looming drought, Tallbob and I had to act fast to save face for all. We were as one.

'No Eric, he means go *over* the road.'

'Not go *over* the road.'

'Whaaat?'

'He doesn't mean go *over* the road to the Peacock...'

'He means literally what he says: "go *over*" the road!'

'Uh?'

'Check it.'

'Yeah – inspect it!'

'Look for little cracks!'

'See if there's any of them potholes. Bloody nuisances!'

'Repaint the white lines!'

'You've lost me, now!'

'That's Fig's trade – he's a roadworker. You with us now, Eric?'

He re-fetched the glasses, shaking his head as if the roof leaked nonsense. 'Alright, come on! What d'yer want? But it's your last chance!'

We were cramping up, agonised, trying poorly not to guffaw. Tallbob composed himself.

'Five pints of bitter please, Eric.'

Eric swung on the pump.

'That's four quid twenty – and I've fucking *told* yez – the name's Pete!'

'Sorry, sorry! Five pints of Pete, please, Eric.'

That was it. The Parson and I had to get away from the bar or laugh us all out of the Yorker for good. The others joined us, and Fig received another slap in the ear from Tallbob for his trouble. As we settled down to business, Tallbob – himself a more than competent blues guitarist – insisted on a detailed report on yesterday's events at Cueball's and then, more importantly, a blow-by-blow account of both the ambiance and culinary status at the Mayfair these days.

Within two minutes, Fig got up to take orders for round two. As he left to play the ferryman, quietly – inmanifestly – out was drawn a fresh pot of garlic salt.

By the time Fig had retaken his place, their tactics had been decided. Tallbob would play the 'deeply concerned for your well-being' and place the distracting questions, whilst the Parson furtively sprinkled from the 'pot' to the Fig beer.

'So, Fig, when are you seeing the Trapper again?'

'I haven't got a clue.'

'We know that, but when are you seeing the Trapper again?'

'Ha ha ha!'

'Is this the sweet young thing I've seen him courting?'

'He's courting disaster!'

'Fig, Fig, Fig!'

Fig rushed to his belle's defence. 'Hey, her name's Dianne, and she just *happens* to be very sophisticated and intelligent, if you *must* know.'

'Oh shit! Where've we been since home-made tattoos got sophisticated?'

'Anyway, Fig, you appeared to be having a little lovers' tiff last night. What sophisticatedly intelligent topic was *that* all about? Don't answer if you're nervous – take your time – hey! We're *all* nervous!'

'She keeps accusing me of wasting money on curries. I told her I haven't been near a curry for weeks, but she keeps going on about how I reek of garlic. I haven't *touched* the bloody stuff!'

'Pfff – ha ha ha ha!'

Tallbob raised a clenched fist. 'So did you give her a stiff talking-to, later?'

'Well, not really, no!'

'Oh no! So what you're saying is that you passed out again and she gave you the Spanish Archer; so it was a trot back home to reliable old Fenella the Fist – *yet* again?'

'None of your business, sport!'

'Ha ha ha.'

'Fig, Fig, Fig!'

'He's only done the bashful tortoise again – oh no!'

'Fig, you're better off without that kind of relationship. Forget her! What kind of woman throws a man out in the middle of the night, anyway, forbidding him to ever darken her bed sheets again?'

'Ha ha ha!'

'Fig, it's no use just falling asleep at the drop of a hat... and it's even less use at the drop of a skirt.'

'Ha ha ha!'

'Fig, look, it's high time you learned the difference betwixt a-wooing and a-wowing.'

'Fig, I remember when you used to be such a light sleeper – you used to sleep with a light on. Now you're such a hard sleeper...'

'Ha ha ha ha ha!'

Fig reached for his cigarette papers and tobacco and began to construct a comforting roll-up. This sounded the retreat into one of his moody, indignant silences – which often happened when he was caught without valid answers in a Clergy crossfire. But Tallbob was unremitting.

'And don't think you can try and smoke your way out of *this* one, mateyboy, m'laddo!'

'He's ignoring us... how childish!'

'Don't worry, Fig. Get engaged to your fist. Look, sex is fine, but you can't beat the *real* thing!'

'Yeah, anyway, sooner or later some girl's going to want to know why you're always walking around with two elastic bands, a sawn off chopstick and a can of hairspray.'

'Ha ha ha ha!' The ice was broken. A detectable smirk began to bloom in Fig's well-weathered juff as he took a final deep draw on the roll-up, dropped it at his feet and stooped to tread it out on the floorboards. As he did, the Parson was sprinkling the umpteenth whack of garlic salt into his beer. Fig sat up again, raising his nose in the air to accentuate a loud sniff.

'You're all sick bastards.'

'You've got it in one, Fig! We're sick. Sick to death of shagging every night with these large extendable penises of ours!'

'Ha ha ha!'

'Don't you worry, you sick bastards, I've shagged plenty this year!'

'How do you know? You have to get undressed to count to twenty-one!'

'Ha ha ha!'

'Fig, Fig, Fig, you're taking this far too personally. I'm sure there's lots of women who fancy you, matey!'

'Thank you, Sarge! Hear that, you sick gets?'

'Trouble is, they're all sitting in a bar in Bangkok!'

'Ha ha ha.'

Fig's index finger wagged at us all in turn. 'You can scoff. You can *all* scoff as much as you want. You won't be scoffing when I'm rich – hah!'

Tallbob gawped vacantly at Fig. Then towards us. Then back to Fig.

'When you're rich?'

'Yep, when I'm rich. Hah! That's done you! Hah!'

The Parson resisted the all-consuming urge to crack his poker face and leaned forward to address the garlic cloud. 'And, er, exactly *how* were we proposing to *attain* this sudden state of, er, affluence?'

'Hah!'

'Come on!'

'Hah!'

'Come on! You know you want to!'

'Hah!'

'Fig – either piss or get off the pot!'

'Dark bulb!'

'Dark bulb?'

'Dark bulb. Hah!'

'No, I'm sorry – I think I misheard. Did he say *dark* bulb?'

'That's what *I* thought I heard him say.' The Sergeant's jaw fell, as he turned back to Fig. 'Did you say "*dark*" bulb?'

'That's right. Dark bulb!'

'A dark bulb. Right. Can somebody do what I'm frightened to do, and ask him precisely what the fuck he's chuntering on about?'

The Sergeant risked the inquiry. 'Come on then, Fig, sport. What's the *dark* bulb?'

'Dead simple. Money-spinner. You've all been to discos at night-time... dozens of coloured flashing lights, lighting the gaff up... *Now*! You've never been to a disco in the daytime, right?'

'I have.'

'So have I.'

'Thousands.'

'No, you're just trying to be funny. Okay – listen. Why don't you see so many daytime discos? Eh?'

'Passing.'

'Shitty advertising?'

'Because people tend to be at work?'

'I think he's on one. I think he's on a dozen.'

'I think he's barking in the wrong forest again.'

'I think he's barking!'

'Go on then, Fig. We'll wear it. Why don't we see... *discos* in the daytime?'

'Yeah! Now then, it's because it's too light...'

'Oh, for *ffffff*!'

'Oh dear! It appears he's knitting with one needle again!'

'...no, wait a minute! If you can control the light...'

'Fig, Fig, Fig!'

'Don't do it, Fig. You're still young. There's the whole of your pensionerhood to get skeewappadooley in.'

'Fig, Fig, Fig. Look, sport. At the risk of sounding somewhat gauche here – if not a little zany – may I, just for a second, drag a completely wacky, untoward concept into this conversation? Fig. Have you ever heard of... curtains? As in curtains for *your* credibility? They're long, soft things that hang either side of most windows – on the inside, usually. To make a room darker, the general consensus of opinion dictates that you grab them both then put your hands together. This tends to darken most rooms with dramatic effect.'

'Yeah but if you had a dark...'

'No, Fig, no. Curtains, Fig. Curtains. Just pull them together. Just like we're hoping you'll do with your senses one day.'

'...if – just listen! If you could switch a bulb on and darken your room, curtains would be obsolete!'

'Lord, please take me today – or him!'

'Fig, do you realise we're talking about negative energy here?'

We attempted, each in turn, to nurse Fig's ailing mind back to the unfamiliar perimeters of reason.

'I'll suss it... I'll knock one together!'

'Negative energy, Fig. You'll knock it together?'

'Piece of piss!'

'Oh, like black holes "piece of piss"? Like cosmic phenomena, only partially understood by the greatest scientific brains on earth "piece of piss"?'

'Like a mass so dense that it can bend light – widely only believed to occur in distant galaxies – *those* dark bulbs?'

'Hey, *larfing boy*! I did physics too, you know!'

'Tell you what, then, Fig! I wish I'd met your physics teacher! He must have been a bottomless pit of information and class "A" narcotics.'

'Ha ha ha!'

'So let's just get it straight, then. For the record. You'll just craftily hop the gun on NASA by, say half a millennium, and pop off out there the odd billion light years or so and collar the first star that appears to be decaying a bit. Then hang about with a packet of fags and a newspaper while it implodes, then nip back with a piece or non-piece of it and shove it in the light socket – or is it the dark socket? Or should every self-respecting gaff have both? Then you'll plod about in a truck, offering ready cash for everyone's completely obsolete curtains and blinds to recycle... for padding the walls and floors and ceilings of your new home, right?'

'I know what I'm talking about. I knew I could expect this kind of derision from you peasants.'

'Peasants? Smack him, Tallbob! No – strangle him, while I smack him! The rest of you, kick him a lot!'

'Was *that* all a dream or did I actually live through what Fig just said?'

The Parson sighed almost interminably. The Sergeant looked away. He squinted hard, then began painfully to recall Fig's previous offer.

'He's done it again! Last week, it was the foldaway canal barges.'

'Whaaat?' Tallbob had evidently missed that particular one.

'The portable foldaway canal barges that he's working on to alleviate the current housing shortage. They sleep twelve people out on the canal and then they can fold down to fit in your rucksack.'

'You're wanking my crank, of course?'

'Ask him! This was last week's money-raker.'

'Go on! Scoff! I know what I'm doing.'

'I can't grip this.'

'Don't even try.'

'We know what you're doing too, Fig. And what you're doing is talking your way directly into the Big House.'

'And as I recall, the weekend before the barges, it was the sand in bus roofs to stop them keeling over. The sand automatically jumps the opposite way to the bus as it goes round a bend – and I believe that's the key phrase here.'

'Hey! I got that straight up from a bus driver!'

'And did he have wet trousers by the time you got it, Fig?'

'Fig, Fig, Fig.'

'Fig, take this good advice from a genuinely concerned friend. Finish that beer and start running as fast as those little legs will go and get some help, because – believe me – you're very, very poorly.'

'Listen to me, Mr Smart Shit Taxi Driver! You might own a smart new taxi, but you're still a peasant!'

'Fig, I'd be happy to enter into a duel of wits with you, but I refuse to fight an unarmed man...'

'Ha ha ha ha!'

'And call me a peasant again and you'll risk the full incurrence of my rampant displeasure.'

'Hey, shut up! The entertainment's just arrived!'

Tallbob's attention had been immediately aroused by the hormone-jangling rhythm orchestrated by two pairs of high heels rapping across the wooden floor. Fig and his wonderful world were suddenly relegated to the back burner as we observed priority and evaluated the footwear's occupants, now at the bar. The occupants themselves weren't exactly vestal visions of the classical genre. Their faces had been pleasantly vandalised by thirty years of council estate crap-taking. Hair long and dulled by repeat prescriptions of pregnancy. Their dresses probably cost less than the night's ale they were about to swill down, but they fitted snugly and they were short enough to short circuit all your shortcomings. The legs. The legs awaited a good summer, but they were pretty, and the dresses... were short. Well – they looked okay to *me*.

'Excuse me, would you, gentlemen?' The Parson began to descend vertically until he was completely out of sight beneath the table.

'What's *his* game?'

He then reappeared flat on his back, sliding away from the table by using alternate feet to shunt himself inches at a time across the floor, until his face came to stare directly up the girls' dresses. Eric was chatting away to them, pouring their lagers and playing his own part in the comedy of ignorance. For at least two minutes, tears rolled down our cheeks as the Parson lay unnoticed, gawping up in constructive comparison between the twin vistas. Then one of them dug into her handbag for payment and clocked his grinning dial just beyond focus.

'Oooeerr! Yo dirty little bastard! Were yo looking up our frocks?'

The dirty little bastard froze. 'Actually no, I was here first! I thought you two were just showing off.'

'Ha ha ha ha!' Two freshly poured lagers slopped loudly into his face. He stayed put no more, jumping up, spluttering, shaking his frothy head, wiping his eyes.

He loped haphazardly back to the table.

'Ugh! Ugh! Lager without lime! Ugh!'

'Ha ha ha.'

'How's the view today?'

'You're an ill man!'

'Sparkling, Martin! What news from Carthage, Desmond?'

The Parson retook his seat, still brushing off his shoulders.

'Gwwuuth! Square crotch? She could sit down twelve times and *still* miss a slice of wedding cake!'

'Ha ha ha ha!'

Then he began to fumble around in the pockets of his leather cross-zip. 'Okay! Let's adjust some attitudes.' He was still aflush with mission adrenalin.

From one of the pockets he produced a small blue bottle.

'Okay! Look. Who fancies a nice blue pint?'

'Hey-ho!'

'Let's go!'

'Now *that's* the ticket!' He began adding a few measured

drops of the blue food colouring to each of our beers in turn, lending them a rather striking oceanic presentation; and for the next two hours, Eric's life was made a greater misery by sporadic droves of students appearing at the bar at frequent intervals, asking for pints of blue beer – 'like the blokes had over there'. By then he'd given up trying to nag at us. He was even daft enough to ask Tallbob why he had the two toothbrushes, whilst serving his umpteenth beer.

'Well, Eric, you see – I use the *blue* one for my top set of teeth and the *pink* one for my bottom... by the way, is there any paper in the toilets?'

'Sure there is, why?'

'Good. I won't need the pink one, then!'

Leaving Eric motionless in traumatic calculation over this, Tallbob spun round, beer in hand, narrowly avoiding a clash of elbows with one of the two lovelies. They both jumped aback with guarded disrelish of this unconventional specimen, slopping their latest lagers again in the process. Tallbob, stoically weathering this latest jettison, cast them the most bemoanful of expressions.

'It's alright! It's alright! Don't panic, ladies! I wasn't trying to chip your make-up!'

The afternoon was racing by and we'd swilled down buckets of blue beer. Fig was becoming progressively and irretrievably daft, as per passing out upright on a stool in his garlic-gassed stupor. And the crew drank on. Then later, amidst healthier conversation, Fig began to snore. He still held a half-drunk beer in his hand, which was gradually subsiding and threatening to soak his trousers and/or crash onto the floor at some close point in time. The Sergeant reached over and tactfully screwed the glass out of his brick-battered fingers and placed it on the adjacent table. We acknowledged the consequentially frosty glances being thrown at us from behind the bar by giving the air two or three placatory pats and pouting knowingly, as if things were well under control.

Eventually, in some dire need of a sabbatical from Fig's ozone-sucking rasp, we'd adjourned to the pool alcove for a while, to aimlessly knock some dulled and dented sphericals around the raggy, sun-bleached baize, when it happened. Boy, did it. Some seventy or eighty co-patrons were all at once smitten mute. This sudden quiet was punctuated only by a random gasp or two, followed by some strange and anonymous clattering; almost as if another – but this time, more orchestrated – cataract of fluid was gushing down onto the floorboards. Rife was the bemusement as we collectively peered out from the alcove toward stage centre.

'Oh, shit!'

'What the *fff*–?'

'Fig, Fig, Fig!'

'Go, Fig, go!'

'Ahaa, hahaaaa!'

'I just can't grip this – ha, ha!'

Not that he could hear any of us. He'd really played his ace this time. Head hanging and still deep in somnus, he'd risen to his feet, and in full view of the aggregate Saturday evening staff and clientele, he'd snored some obscure annunciation, extracted his member and with full pep set about emblazoning his total capacity upon the postcode. Eric, whooping all the way, took nearly a whole second to hurdle the bar, lay mit to his nape and shake it like a fat cruet.

'Fwake up! Fwake up! Yer dorty bastard, yer!'

Wake up he did, and some awakening in front of seven dozen people, with your busy cock in your hand. Fig looked up. Fig looked down. Fig looked around.

'Wha? Wha? Wassup?' The house roared.

'You're bluddy thrunk! C'mon on! *Out*!'

Fig sorely attempted to fine focus on this harsh, dream-bursting assailant. 'I think you'd better let *me* be the judge of that, sport!'

Roar!

'Judge all yer loike! Yer goin' out!'

'On whose authority?'

'Ha ha ha!'

'Why, yer cheeky bastard! C'mon! Get movin', yer dorty little shoite!'

'I challenge you to say that in the presence of my absence.'

Roarrr!

It was the Fig show. He'd got the whole house in his pocket and, sensing the glorious infamy, he played to the gods all the way to the door, as they clumsily grappled for a strategic grip-hold on each other.

'Yer bluddy barred – *barred* this toime, mate – bluddy right you are!'

'Well, everybody? Apparently, I'm being ejected. As to why? I haven't got an iguana!'

'Ha ha ha!'

'Ouch! No need for *that*, sport! I'm going, I'm going… I'll just finish me beer first!'

'No, yer bluddy well won't! *Out*!'

'Ha ha ha ha!'

'Hah! He thinks I'm bothered. As a matter of fact, I don't give a parrot's fart!'

'Ha ha ha!'

'Ouch! So long then, everybody! That's one iguana and one parrot! Don't you worry, I'll be back – byeeee!'

He was finally out. Gone. Eric turned back to the bar, sweeping his thick, grey hair clumsily back into place, sighing, 'No yer bluddy well won't, mate!'

There was an uneasy lull as fourteen dozen eyes fixed on the door. Two or three murmurs and the ambient buzz of conversation began to escalate again. Then suddenly, up went the highest roar yet, at the unforeseen realisation that Fig was still crouched behind Eric, following him back in. Eric rounded on him again, but too late. This time Fig had flown for sure.

We saved Eric the trouble of looking for us, and had already bailed out of the side door by the time he was stalking the alcoves. Across the road, in a disused shop doorway, Fig was redressing his attire from the skirmish. We dodged the volleys of townbound headlamps and rallied at the doorway. Tallbob tossed him his jacket.

'Well, Fig? I think you'll have to agree. That was a performance of *impeccable* sophistication.'

'Compelling! One of your premium exhibitions, sport.'

'Mere words befail me at this time.'

'No wonder the Trapper booted him out. How would *you* like to share your bed with the fucking Trevi Fountain?'

The awakened prince donned his enchanted jacket, licked his teeth, smacked his chops and gave a grunt. But didn't give a fig.

'Right, sports! Where's next, then?'

'What? With *you*? Jail, probably.'

'We'll try and find you a singles' bar for unattached marine mammals.' The Parson patted Fig's back cheerily.

'Well after *that* little floorshow, I'd say it was your call, Fig! We'd quite cheerfully follow you to the ends of the earth, just for the chance to witness some impromptu slapstick of *that* calibre!'

Fig shrugged off the Parson's arm and sneered.

'All right, all right – don't rub it in. I don't mind where we go, as long as we don't go up the Green. I don't fancy ending up on my own, playing pool with some thick Touareg who's pretending to be friendly all the way up to mugging me outside.'

We rolled our eyes in abandonment afresh. The Sergeant was even less impressed; sighing copiously at this latest raving.

'Fig, Fig, Fig! I'm disappointed in you! Deeply

disappointed! You ought to know by now – fools, thieves and liars come in all colours!'

'Look. Me and Tallbob are off down to Trinity Square to powder our noses – who's with us?'

The old Colombian jogging powder. I wasn't into that cack. I'd got a feel for home, anyway. The day had been poetry and nothing less, and from here on it was heading nowhere other than down. Tallbob could see I wasn't a taker. He checked the toothbrushes, checked his wallet and his change pocket. He curled his finger ends and gave his scalp another good pummelling. He held out a huge friendly hand to me.

'The pleasure was all yours. Don't forget. Bob's your neighbour.'

We exchanged the customary four position handshake, culminating in the rising bird, accompanied by a duet of whistled tweets.

'I'll pop round tomorrow. I'll probably need to.'

'Be there or be safe. Don't worry about the Westwoods – we'll talk to Pilkington – he'll fix it.'

'Tight lines!'

I shook the remaining palms and bailed out homewards, replete with the Sergeant's parting lesson still jangling in my ears. Home. Aye – there's the rubbishing in prospect. From the Council of Drunken Cavalier Poets to the Council of War in a mere twenty minutes... but how lies the land?

EIGHT

Inch the key gently into the Yale. Gently, gently. Now the gentle shove. Gentle. Is she? Isn't she? It isn't bolted, it's... open. She's either out or she's still in the mood for conducting interviews. Or not. Tower calling battle stations... Anything can happen in the next half-hour. Lights are all on. Sod this creeping around. One big breath, then slam the door and march right in: you're a Chimney, you own the world, you soft bastard! So, just get in there and take the flack. Marching down the stairs into the hallway. Okay. Where's it going to hit me from? Bedroom? Bathroom? Living room? Living room's favourite. I nudged the door open a few inches and peered in with a smug, sickly, jovial grimace. Telly's on. *Bang*! My head launched the door wide open. I was ever so slightly concussed and partially orientated as she stormed past me into the room. But as the sight of her unfolded before me, I realised the stunning had hardly begun. My heart swapped seats with my Adam's apple; my blood bubbled and my legs went numb and half-buckled. *Now* I was stunned. She stood fixing a large, gold gypsy earring in front of the mirror. Selina. The Dragon. On her tiptoes.

'What the fuck do *you* want?'

I tried to answer but my gob was well and truly smacked, I couldn't peel the tongue off the roof of my mouth. All I could do was gawp and exhale a couple of dry, whiney tones.

In front of me was every red-blooded male's fantasy; probably a few red-blooded females', too. Light-killing long black hair, glistening aura, dancing curls luring you on to the dark, piercing Arabian eyes – meticulously lined. Flushed high cheekbones sweeping down to the voluptuous damson lips, painted to model precision. The heady redolence of her scent filled the room. Then her clothes. Tightly cut black double-breasted leather tunic and ultra-streamlined black leather pencil skirt. She pulled on black leather gloves to complete the effect. Black tights? No: schoolmistress seams neatly dividing the backs of her racehorse calves, obviously black nylon stockings. She stepped into the five-inch black patent stilettos which had been waiting neatly together by the coffee table. She clearly had some lucky bastard in mind for a 20-ton bombshell. My voicebox finally jump-started.

'I, I, tried to... ahem!'

'You tried to what? Telephone? Well *this* fucker must be *broken*, then!' She seized the phone from its cradle on the coffee table. Even that briefly accessorised the black leather before she launched it towards my face. I dodged to feel it brush my ear at about seventy miles an hour before hitting a framed print, knocking it wonky and slightly chafing the pale green wallpaper into the deal. Either the miss or the wallpaper made her seethe even more intensely.

'Four days? *Four fucking days*? You must think I'm fucking stupid! No one treats me like this – like a piece of shit!'

'You locked me out last night!'

'Oh, what a *bastard* I am to you! Okay – *three* days! So which slag have you been poking *this* time, eh?'

'I haven't been near anyone!' Which was a lie. 'I haven't touched anyone else!' Which was sadly true.

'Well, I don't know when I'll be back, so now you can go and enjoy yourself as much as you want!'

'Where are you going?'

'Out.'

'Out where?'

'My business.'

'Who with?'

'Someone.'

'Someone who?'

'Someone who appreciates me... Get out of the fucking way!'

I picked up the telephone and listened for signs of life. It had survived. I put it back on its cradle and followed her round to the kitchen as she lit a cigarette on one of the cooker rings.

'I appreciate you.'

She flew at me again.

'You fucking *what?*'

I retreated backwards into the living room.

'*Don't* you take the fucking piss, you bastard!'

I had to vault the back of the sofa as the phone came looking for me again. This time it glanced off the back of my head and bounced into the soil base of the rubber plant.

'Selina, look, just stop this shit! All I've done is booze and play bass. Ring around! Ask who you like! Just calm it! I'll take you out whenever you want, if you think something's going off. I'll take you out *now* if you like – anywhere! Let's just have a good night out together! I'll do anything to make it up to you, if you just let me!'

God, I was *begging*! My balls had commandeered my brain and now they were overriding every bodily function; I was feverish – hyper – crazy – possessed – repossessed.

'Too late, I told you. I'm meeting someone. Anyway, no doubt your *mates* will all've been briefed on how to cover for you!'

'Okay, look the phone's... yep, it's still working – call him! *Or* her! I know I'm bang out of order, but just give me one last chance – just for us! Whoever it is, just put it off for two hours. I'll take you out for a meal. We can talk!'

She sat down impatiently, set down the cigarette and began fiddling with the earring again. There was barely enough room in the leather skirt for her to cross her gorgeous legs. She wriggled her ankle, menacingly tapping the air with her stiletto. She knew she had control. She picked up the cigarette, took a long draw and blew the smoke out slowly towards me.

'No.' With the rebuff issued, she licked the damson lips tantalisingly. That was it. She was enjoying the command. She was enjoying watching me squirm on the hook; but I knew at that point that I'd won... and I was going to get it. The next move was to make sure she wasn't going to leave the flat.

'Oh, come on, Selina! Just one chance? I always come back to you, don't I?' I didn't want her in two hours; I wanted her that second. It had occurred to me that a restaurant wouldn't be the best of uses, as you get arrested for shagging in restaurants.

'Look...' Look? Fuck! I was beginning to sound like the Parson. 'At least we've started to talk. Tell you what? Let me just get us a takeaway – it'll take just twenty minutes in the car if I phone the order through first!' Bollocks to the legal limit; the adrenalin surge had probably massacred half the booze, anyway. 'We can eat something nice – then I'll do whatever you want. Stay in, go out – whatever!'

She just stared quietly and coldly into my eyes. The silence was galling.

'If you've got a phone call to make, you can do it while I'm at the takeaway – if it's private! Just to postpone things?'

Longer silence. Still staring at me. Is she goading me? Daring me? Three long draws on the cigarette – the last one blown slowly into my face with three calculated instalments. That was it. Flashpoint. Detonation. A surging deluge of raw, unrefinable voracity came powering through me from head to toe. My balls crackled off, Van Der Graaf-fashion, making me jolt towards her with the most guttural growl I'd ever given out in my life. In the sudden embarkation, I could feel the soaking wetness in my pants and down one leg. My cock was straining, raging – champing to get released – digging its spurs into my balls – recrackle! I rammed hard against her upper thigh as I straddled her, trying to kiss her evasive mouth. My hands were on autopilot, incapable of deciding where to grope next. She jerked her face rigorously from side to side to resist the vicious attempts to part her lips with my mouth, and tongue for to drill inside.

'Fuck off! Just... fuck-off! Don't touch me! I've told you, I'm meeting someone else... *Geddoff*! Don't touch my make-up!'

'Who?'

'My business... I've told you... aaah!'

I worked one of my dirty mits inside the leather tunic and onto one of her magnificent tits, which I massaged greedily before giving it a good shake through her lacy black bra, chafing the nipple. She couldn't suppress the moan. She was adoring this.

'Who?'

'My business.'

'Who? Is it the bloke who's been after you at work?'

'Might be.'

I unbuttoned the tunic and seized the other tit, kneading them both less harshly and breathing down the side of her neck. Her head was still turned rigidly aside.

'The one with the really big cock who had you up against a wall at the Halloween dance a few years back?' I drilled her ear with my tongue, as if I was drilling for an answer.

'Yesss!'

'Is it really? Honest?'

'Yeasss!'

'Call him, while I get the meal. Tell him "some other time". If I don't satisfy you in *every* way tonight – *and* do anything and everything your dirty little heart desires – then you can fuck him tomorrow – deal?'

For a full minute, there was a nervy, silent carnival of uncertainty, orchestrated by the TV, the rustle of lace, the creak of leather and the opulence of osculation upon neck flesh. Then she let the cigarette tip and fall into the rubber plant soil. She stared me directly in the eyes. For a while, I watched my hands kneading. Then, looking up, my eyes gazed deeply back into hers. Her lips parted. I felt the sudden and long awaited fleeting of tension from her coiled muscles. Her head rose slightly.

'Do you love me?' God, at last. The final fence.

'Selina, I love you – I need you – I want you. Honestly! You should know better than to ask.'

She gave me a doubtful sideways look with half-closed eyelids. 'You're not just saying this?'

'I promise.'

She moved her lips forwards to kiss mine. Then with both hands, she shoved me backwards onto the carpet as she sprang to her heels, dusting off and hitching down her skirt, and rebuttoning the tunic.

'Good, because it's your last fucking chance! I want King Prawn Ceylon, two chapattis, no rice – and you've got twenty minutes before I change my mind!'

'Great! It's done! I'll give the Raj a call! But what if we're having to wait? It's Saturday night... they could be busy.'

'Well, then I hope you enjoy yourself, sitting here alone having a good wank, thinking of me getting shafted in the back of his car.'

'I'm away – I'm there – I'm back – twenty minutes it *is*!' I dived at the phone. Dialled the Raj. Come on, come on, come on, come on, you gets! Selina stalked around, pretending to adjust cushions, ornaments, pot plants, her clothes, her attitudes, whilst throwing me the occasional over-the-shoulder and down-the-nose leer.

It seemed more akin to half an hour – but I'd managed to get the order through in a minute or so. Then, slamming the phone down haphazardly, I turned to Selina – still troubling over her presentation – smoothing down the seat of her skirt, checking the line of her stocking seams from reverse angle in the mirror and juggling her tits back into the optimum position of comfort within their lacy black hammock.

'Okay, I'm away. Please don't go out – wait for me!'

'Eighteen minutes – clock's ticking!'

I was out of the flat like fury's kick and down to the car. I needed both hands to get the key into the ignition; I was shaking uncontrollably. King Prawn Ceylon? She's really in the mood for some heat; that's usually *way* above her station. The motor fired up nicely for once, and I leaned forwards, shoving the wheel as much as turning it – as if it would push the car faster off the mark. Mission underway. All I could think about was Selina as my fingers drummed at the wheel and gear stick, and my balls beat time against the seat. Please God, let me, let me, let me, let me, let me...

At the Raj, I was soon forging the beginnings of a track into the carpet, pacing up and down it like a freshly quarantined puma. Raffi looked deeply concerned.

'Please, Mr Shed, take a seat for a while!'

'What? Is it nearly ready?'

'A few minutes...'

'You said that a few minutes ago! Come on, Raffi m'man! This is life and death, matey!'

'Anyway! Where is the missus tonight?'

'Raffiman! If I'm late, I daren't tell you where she'll be! Can you just have another look?'

Raffi beamed his Raffi beam, and winked and nodded and scuffed his starchy white shirt and brisk, black velvet bow tie along the edge of the door as he low-tailed obligingly off to the epicentre of the pong. I'd just bitten my last nail to the quick, when he returned – mercifully this time, laden with goods.

'Here we are, Mr Shed! Two King Prawn Ceylon, four chapatti, one chips, that's—'

'That's ten quid – get yourself a pint, Raffi – *bye*!'

We're off on three and a half minutes. That's what I've got, anyway. Dump the carrier next to me. Sod the grease patch; first two or three arses will soak it up nicely tomorrow. Screech off into Mansfield Road and head back to the love nest. Lights. Come on, lights; less than two, now. Come on, you little green bastards! Come on, come on, come on, come on, come on – yes! Fast illegal right turn – no choice – that stops a couple of oncomers in their tracks; soz! Second right, sweep down the ramper. Tightly parked, and only width enough for one. Dangerous – but no headlamps forthcoming, so boot it. Yank on the anchors in front of the main gate. Now I can see my door at all times. Shit – I'm late! Twenty-one plus, in all! I can't see her anywhere in the street... *surely* she's in! Leave the car out here for a while. If it gets nobbled or twocked, so let it be. My balls have spaken; if she hasn't gone yet, she can't go.

I'm through the outer gate, racing up the concourse. No sound of slamming doors, ten seconds up the stairwell, now I can see the flat again. I'm twenty seconds away from either paradise or a double Prawn Ceylon, a poxy film and a redundant wok handle.

Is she? Is she? Come on, babe – you know it makes sense! Again, I carefully turned the key and flitted swiftly inside. But this time, no lights. Eh? Trepidation beginning to wash over me. Step out of my shoes. Downstairs in two leaps. Hesitant. Not a sound from anywhere. Don't say it, please don't say it! At the bedroom door. Blackened inside. Over to the living room door. Gentle nudge. Creak of hinges. Blackness again. No lights, no telly, no sound. Bastard! Bitch! Come on – tell her, God, please! I nudged the door further ajar. Silence. The scent still lingering on. Get some lights on, to examine the scene... perhaps find her note or some other clue. Click. Empty room. Bastard. I'm alone. Am I?

'Shit! Selina? Shit!' I dropped the carrier and flopped into an armchair.

'Bollocks, shit and bollocks!' Then alarm. Four or five lazy, languorous echoes from high heels hacking across the kitchen linoleum. Swishing of garments. Thank you! Thank you, God... maybe?

'I make that twenty-three minutes – wanker.'

My sinking heart began to soar again. 'You're here, babe! Thank God! Sorry! I tried my best!'

'Doesn't seem good enough, does it?'

'Where are you? I can't see you... did you make the call?'

'I'm in here, and no I didn't – yet. Maybe.'

I bundled into the blacked out enclave of the kitchen, aware only of her dusky silhouette seated on a high stool at the far end. I was frantically fumbling for a light switch and a worktop to land the carrier on, but then the subtle click of a cheap stick lighter brought all necessary illumination to the prospect. The carrier fell from my curled fingers again, but this time involuntarily. I could almost hear my pulse banging at the insides of my temples. My lungs jumped out of sequence, invoking a double sigh. I froze to the spot, the only bodily movement coming from a torridly squirming penis. Now I could see the light switch too. I popped on more light. God! The window! The neighbours! She doesn't care! I slashed the curtains to, picked up the slightly askew carrier and stood facing her again. God help me! This scene... If there was any way to preserve for ever this scene in my mind and nothing else, I'd never get bored, I'd never need alcohol and I'd never leave the garden again. Carve this in rock, weave it into tapestry, laser it into a hologram: Aphrodite, 2000 AD.

'You look... beautiful... you're gorgeous! You're my dream!'

'Do you think so?' She edged forward on the stool. Apart from the gloves, the leather had all been shed. The make-up had been liberally reinforced. The seductive smile was less cold. I knew I'd pleased her – for once. As she drew on the latest cigarette, her beautiful mounds heaved, straining against the black lace. She crossed her long legs, making the black knickers, suspenders and nylon stockings follow every bodily alignment with feline acquiescence. A shiny heel slowly twisted and squeaked against the foot rung of the stool. She was the most alluring thing in creation.

'Well, wanker? Why were you late?'

'I'm sorry.'

'Sorry's your middle name.'

'I'm sorry. I love you. Please let's fuck. You know fucking well no one can do what you do to me! Are we still in this deal?'

'Is *that* supposed to be an explanation?'

'I'll do anything to fuck you, Selina.'

'Will you?'

'Yes, anything... Did you make the call?'

'Who to?'

'Your friend.'

'What friend?' She drew on the cigarette, smiling coyly.

'Your nine-inch friend.'

'Ha ha, I'm not spoiling *anything* yet! I can still meet him, if I like.'

'What? Tonight?'

'Whenever I like. Strip.'

'Pardon?'

'Strip. Just down to your pants.' I didn't need asking three times.

'So you'll do anything to please me, will you? Wanker?'

'Anything you want – *anything*! Is the heating on? I'm freezing!'

'Are you supposed to be a man? Just shut up whinging and get your kit off – no, *not* your pants – there, that's better.'

Either through cold, or excitement, I was shivering visibly now. Throughout all the tease talk, she'd been rattling something at the side of the stool, taking care not to let me see what it was. I'd assumed that it would have been one of her bangles or bracelets. As it happened, I wasn't too far off the money.

'Open the food!'

'Are we eating first?'

'We'll see… just shut up and open it!'

I carefully prised open the steaming hot foil containers, setting them systematically out on the worktop alongside us, then grabbed a clutch of cutlery from the drawer and two dinner plates from the wall cupboard, then turned to face the throne again.

'Where do you want to eat?'

'Put that down.'

I sat the plates next to the food, piling the cutlery on top of them. 'You want to eat it here? Shall I serve the food out?'

'Shut up and come here.'

My cock was now twitching with expectancy. I stood directly in front of her. I was millimetres from her leg. She placed the cigarette down on the worktop edge.

'Come closer… stop. That's it! Now turn around for a minute.'

I was at a total loss trying to guess this game's name, but as long as she wanted to keep me suspended in this hypnotic euphoria, the last thing to enter my head was disobedience – or further pointless questions, which might impede the onset of the master plan. I complied in an instant… and in the very next instant, I was to learn the source of the rattling as soon as my back was turned. All at once in a single motion, she had grabbed my wrists behind me and snapped on a set of heavy steel handcuffs. My hands well and truly imprisoned. She then spun me back around to face her again. Her eyes scrutinised my bulge, scarcely contained by the briefs. I shivered again, profusely.

'Now what, Selina?' She studied my eyes, then the bulge.

'Now? Now this.' She reached inside my briefs, taking my balls in a clenched leather fist.

'Now you pay for treating me like garbage – bastard!' She squeezed, slowly, more and more intensely until I flinched and gasped. The dull, morbose ache was unbearable to both receptacles and brain. My thoughts were cast for a moment back to the good old days when sex was safe and coal mining was dangerous.

'Oww – ooooh! Selina – please! That really hurts! Please!'

'It's supposed to! Who've you been shagging?'

'*Owch*! Nobody, honest! Oww! I promise, nobody – nobody can compete with you, I swear to God – *yahhh*!'

'Okay!' She released slightly. 'If I ever find out otherwise... I'll just have to cut these bastards off – okay?' She released a bit more.

'Yes, yes, okay!'

Finally she relaxed her grip. 'Okay?'

'Okay.'

Suddenly, she bared her gritted teeth and gave it the hardest squeeze yet, making me yelp and twitch and dance. Now the intense ache was making me sweat in the coldness of the kitchen. I was beginning to feel sick.

'I swear – aahh! Nobody else!'

She removed her hand just as swiftly. I immediately moaned aloud in relief.

'Right! Hopefully that's settled then. Now we'll eat something!' The smooth, leather-gloved palm returned to caress the bulge back from its pain-induced flaccidity. Then leaning forwards, she slowly lowered my briefs, letting them fall around my ankles. I began to lift a leg to cast them off. Quickly she grabbed my erection.

'Uh-uh! Stay still! Who gave you permission to move?'

'Sorry.'

She slid down from the stool, dragging it to one side, then, strutting back over, she squared up to me, nose to nose – arrogantly, provocatively. Her stilettos bestowing her an equal standing. For a while she stood, her eyes exploring, examining, fathoming. Her soft body brushing against me in measured doses. As the examination began to torrify, she slid a heavenly smooth, sleek thigh between my legs, inching it slowly... tantalisingly... up... down... in... out. I needed badly to return her caresses, but damn the handcuffs! The ecstasy was frustratingly incomplete. She pulled away a touch, and her wanton leer turned to the foil container. I attempted movement to allow her passage, then it became suddenly apparent that she'd worked her foot slyly through one of the leg holes of my briefs. Now, in conjunction with her metal cuffs, a firmly planted high heel between my ankles implied that I was going nowhere without injury. I resisted all urges to move.

'I was going to ask, why did you order Ceylon sauce?'

'You're asking a lot of questions for someone who'll do anything to please me!' She took a dessert spoon and immersed it in one of the curries.

'Here! Try a bit!' Before I'd had chance to back away, she'd grabbed my chin and force-shovelled the spoonful of Ceylon sauce briskly between my teeth, before vertically extracting the spoon to ensure maximum delivery.

'Tell me if it's hot.' I was struggling desperately to hang on to this hasty development as it was, without the complication of speech. It took a while to restore enough manoeuvring space for my tongue to utter its futile, half-cocked protestations; but by then all chilli had broken loose, searing it from corner to corner – inducing a fierce suction of breath, followed by another, followed by a flood tide of saliva rushing into combat for the sake of any surviving taste buds. Selina giggled gleefully at the sight of the naked, red-faced prisoner's erection falling flop as he tried to suck, blow, swallow, eat and talk without banging his tongue against anything – all at the same time. Meanwhile, the final two prawns, having held hands to dive down whole, left my mouth finally clear – apart from the burst saliva main. Now I could ingest some cool air to further quell the inferno.

'Hoo! Hah, hooo! That *is* some hot gear – you'd – *ullp*!' In came a supplementary gobful on the now attendant dessert spoon. It was by this time occurring to me that I'd given the bitch four whole days to concoct these little diversions. Hopefully she might have run out of ideas after this one. Now, whether I had two mouthfuls or twenty-two, the outcome would be the same: human blowtorch. This in mind, I resigned myself to chew on and dispatch the beast till the fun be done. But surprisingly, after two feeds she set the dessert spoon aside on a dinner plate.

I revelled in the respite, as all her postulations now seemed to be gradually refining to the nearness of an intense sexual outcome. Turning away from the food, her eyes reverted back to the subject in hand; in *her* hand. She resumed charge of the subject's object. Cool leather, making hot flesh flush fully. Once again, the compass began to point north. She watched it happen for a while, then she looked into each of my eyes in turn – once again baring her gritted teeth. No. Not the look of a woman deficient in ideas. I made another attempt at dialogue.

'As I was trying to say…' I had to swallow again… 'you'll never get near *that* stuff, it's much too hot for you. I'll make you something else if…'

'Well, you'd better *hope* I can get near it, mate!'

'Why? What?'

Without failing in her attentions to the object, she reached for the untouched portion of the curry and brought it over to the focal point of activity. No. There were ideas yet.

'How long's this going on for… *whaa?*'

Totally impervious to the consequences, she plunged my cock deep down into the Ceylon sauce, using the extent of my facial distortion as thermometer for the upper limit.

'Holy Moly, Selina! This isn't funny anymore!' She hauled it out… curried.

'Hmm! Not as long as a chopstick, but it can wear more than a spoon – ha, ha!'

'Fucking hilarious! I'm running out of ribs! For fff-sake, get this off me, Selina! Please?'

'Ha ha ha!' Her whole body was laughing.

'Will you please take this off?'

The laughing abated. She paused. Smiled. Chuckled. Then, setting down the food, she slid into a squat position, taking my cock fully into her delicate, pretty mouth.

'*Oooohh*!' The pleasant shocks can be the biggest ones. Wow! Now we were getting somewhere. But not. She grabbed for the Ceylon sauce and plunged it in again, in joyful pursuance of this bloody obscure feeding ritual. It was time, I thought, to list the blessings. One. Give thanks that the cock's been round the block a few times. Two. Give thanks that Raffi burns a dull Ceylon compared to Ab's or the Bengal. Three. The power of Ale abideth within me. Four. So what? Peace is back among us. She's enjoying herself – so am I, in truth. We've both got what we want – we're just a little more avant garde in expressing and celebrating it. I'm really lucky to have this.

View, if you will, the big picture. There are twerps throughout the land staggering home to nought save their attendant fists tonight. One last can in the fridge to escort them upstairs for a good J Arthur at a pair of 2D tits across Page Three; then pass out and wake up alone, when the dawn wok handle pokes them in the belly button to inform them they're about to piss the bed. I've got Selina. This is going to happen all night; we've got four days' worth to catch up on, so what's the point in griping over a glowing cock? Another plunge, another serving, now *she* was appreciating the temperature. Resuming the upright posture against the stool, she ditched the foil container and its Indo-aquatic contents into the sink, took her leg out of my briefs, and with a hand to my chest, began shunting me backwards towards the living room.

'What now, Cockfeaster?'

'Now shut up!'

'Whatever!' I shuffled backwards as proficiently as the expanding briefs would allow. Selina, half-smiling, loped onto me with catlike stealth, still in government. With a delicately timed nudge, I was dumped horizontally backwards onto the sofa. There I stayed put, eagerly awaiting the next instalment, watching her delve into her handbag and take out a condom. A black one? Now, there was a greater urgency to her movements. She tore the wrapper apart and flapped the sheath on me in an instant. I studied her procedure.

'Why the bag?'

'Just shut up!'

'You are beautiful and I feel great, but if we're about to have the fuck of a lifetime, are you sure you want a bag in the way?'

The leer returned. 'I don't know where it's been! Anyway, we don't want *both* of us to get burned – do we?'

'I love you.'

She yanked her knickers down to the floor and stepped briskly out of them. 'If you love me – you'd better keep it good and stiff, because I want it all night!'

'Let's go.'

Bless the girl; she mounted – jamming it clean up in one, without mess or messing – and set off at a hard, fast gallop. I was desperate to slip the handcuffs and pull her further onto the grind, if that could have been possible.

'Do, do you think, I, I could take, these cuffs – mmmmph!'

She was concerned neither for my comfort nor my pleasure, nor would she now stoop to hinder her concentration with talk. She clamped the leather gloves one on top of the other over my mouth and thrashed her damnedest against me, growling, gasping, intoxicated with turbulent passion. Twelve or thirteen more thrashes, then the irresistible, the unharnessable shudder and the desperate scramble to preserve it. Longer, longer, her hair thrashing wildly, nails gouging at me, jaw clenched, breath hissing, cursing, swearing, blaspheming, head reeling. Then slower, slower, slowly back down to earth. Back to the verity of the room and its contents. Back in command of breath and senses.

We exchanged smiles, a brief kiss, then she ploughed on. This time around forty thrashes; the next, maybe eighty. Then, having finally negotiated for the elimination of the handcuffs, I ditched the sheath and we dog-fashioned it, whilst crawling off to the bedroom to eventually call time just after dawn and pass out in the anyhow position. Shit. Forgot the flowers again.

NINEY, NINEY, NINEY

Breep-breep.

'Uh? Awww!'

Breep-breep.

'Ffffkit – get that, babe. Please.'

'Eh? Wha?'

Breep-breep.

'The phone, babe – you're nearest.' With her eyelids still glued together, she fumbled for the receiver, clasping it awkwardly to her ear and dragging its base off the dresser and onto the floor in the process.

'Yuh? Ello?'

'Haaahahaaa! Darling – I want you *now*! This very second! I'm hot, I'm damp, I'm sweaty, I'm baby-oiled up and ready! I've got a pan-handle just listening to your dirty voice! I want you. I want you in school uniform – navy blue knickers – pleated skirt – gym plimsolls; don't forget the white socks, pull them up just over your knees, then I can pull them down again with my teeth and lick your kneecaps. Then what about a frantic tit-wank and...' She dumped the receiver on my back and rolled over. 'Here, it's Sticky.'

'Stick?'

'Hooo, Shedfixman! Dragon still hate you? Should I call you back, later on?'

'No, you can't call me back later, and stop calling me Ron!'

'So she's still speaking to you, then?'

'Yeah! She's still speaking – she says "fuck off!"'

'Ha, haa! She's speaking to *me*! She's just been chatting me up with a load of filth! Anyway, have a good night?'

'Clergy night, mate! Fig ran amok.'

'So I've been hearing. So, to cut to the chase – the green's booked for eleven. There's going to be an announcement, then it's choir practice. All shall attend!'

'Eleven, okay. See you there.'

'Go on! Give her one...'

I reached around her to drop the receiver. Checked the LED clock. Ten zero two. Not much in the way of forewarning, but at least I'd touched base overnight. Made a generous deposit at the lovebank.

'So you're out again?'

'Ess, I won't do another night out on you.'

'I've heard...' So I pulled her over, climbed on top of her.

'Okay, okay, I know – don't speak, don't argue – just kiss me!'

I kissed. She kissed me back, but wasn't convinced.

'Come on, Ess! Take that as your guarantee.'

'Okay, and this is *your* guarantee: I'm spending tonight with *someone*. It's up to you if it's *you*.'

'It's *me*, alright! I won't be late!' I left her to flop back over, while I rooted the cupboards for some clean jeans.

The Skipper appeared mortified; he was hoping he'd misheard.

'*In* the curry?' The others now paid sudden heed.

'In a *Ceylon*?'

'*In* the curry?'

'Choc up to the back wheels, sirree!' Sticky winced. The Croc oowahed. The Skipper chuckled at their facial contortions.

'Ignore them, dear boy; they're as green as the turf beneath our tootsies!'

'Have I clocked this right? Which curry shop did you get it from, Shed?'

'Ceylon? Ruddy Nora!'

'Got it from the Raj – excellent wood, sir!'

'Thank you, sir! And thank heavens you had the sense not to fetch it from the Bengal; ruddy weapons grade kit at that shop – oh! Top drawer wood yourself, sir!'

'Thank you, sir!'

'And by the way, you're a sick man, sir!'

'Thank you once again, sir!'

Sticky's mind still couldn't rest.

'This is legit? In the Ceylon?'

The Croc perished the very thought. 'Hoo-hoowah!'

'*Ignore* them, dear boy, *ignore;* for your life is your own.'

'So, Shed – er, she didn't mistake it for a prawn, then.'

'Ha ha ha.'

'Ha ha! Ey! That's *king* prawn to you, mate, and as it happened, she found an emperor – nice wood!'

'Emperor? Bollocks! Shed, m'man, get right out of town if you're telling us it didn't blast your trawlerman to kingdom come!'

'Not nearly as much as it blasted her garden after I'd got the sheath off.'

'Ha ha ha!'

The Croc's eyes narrowed again behind his specs. 'Ooowah!'

'So where's Joe? Oh, thoroughly pukka wood, sir!'

'You know Joe. Sunday nuptials with his *fiancée* – he's meeting us at choir practice.'

'You know Joe!'

'Joe you know!'

There had traditionally been a game of bowls prior to any rehearsal or team talk. Today the sun had chosen to blaze particularly brightly down upon the lush, well-nurtured greens of the Forest Rec, accentuating *their* supreme verdancy. The circumjacent flower beds boasted aloud their fiery multiplicity of colours. There for us. There for the whole of mankind – but not for Joe. Joe became possessed of an almost vampirical terror at the very mention of the unholy prospect of exposure to fresh air and sunshine. But we knew Joe.

The greens attendant, a slightly built, white-haired, placid sort of chap who took pride in his own presentation equally to that of his greens, seemed ever happy to greet and assist us. He remained ever unperturbed at our little eccentricities, ever deaf to our profanities and ever at hand to clear the storm gullies of whatever spent booze flagons we could clutter them with. The Skipper chished open the latest one and gave the announcement.

'So then, chaps! Rumour would have it that we're playing the Mardi Gras next Saturday with the Mclads, no less and no more! Sticky will – er – enlighten!'

'Next Saturday?'

'Naturally, dear boy.'

'It's all been arranged. Any problems?'

'Hey ho, let's go!' The Croc compressed his lips, chished on an older one with less gaseous a chish and partook, copiously.

'Oowulp-aahh!'

'How many ends left here?'

'Four. We're waiting for Curly... Yeah, here he is now!'

You could spot Curly Ashmore's wicket-toothed grin in a crowd half a mile away, set in its pallid, wrinkly dial beneath the ludicrously loud brown Afro hair. Curly was the Skipper's flatmate, a legend for his complete lack of respect for a pint of beer. He'd once evacuated twenty-eight of them to his solar plexus in four hours. He was loyal and conscientious at his job at the travel agents', and a loyal and vociferous Chimney fan, attending every gig. By day, he would often express this loyalty by turning in to work in, for instance, suit, shirt and tie with a reverse Mohican hairdo. That's an Afro with a 1½-inch path through the middle. At the gigs he'd express loyalty by standing right at the front to barrack us off for the entirety, whilst demanding that we play something by either Kate Bush, or the Bonzo Dog Doo Dah Band. Curly was the people's choice, the well-loved favourite, the textbook example of our creed, and as he approached along the cinder path, it appeared that the drunken, obnoxious bastard had brought a guest along, hanging at his shoulder and on his words. The stranger's morosely dowdy clobber had seen better times – probably wrapped around another body. He exuded a windborne stench of solicitors' chairs and care placement orders. His skin, eyes, teeth and mousy, unkempt mop were all in dire need of a cosmetic benediction. I felt a rare and instant dislike coming on.

'Who's the dole office doormat with Curly?'

The Skipper was poised to launch a wood. He aborted his concentration to turn and focus on the arrivals.

'Oh, that's All Night Billy – tagging along again, by the look of it.'

Sticky hadn't quite caught the answer. 'Who?'

'All Night Billy – he's just moved in at our place, from some halfway house up in Liverpool. He's doing the twilighter at the all-night garage in Bobbersmill. Bit of an odd fish, but always wakes us with a cuppa, always brings the milk and in any case, we need the extra rent, dear boy!'

Sticky and I chished, in stark apprehension.

'So how did he get the job? Nick it?'

'He's *okay*; he's a doofer – just looking for a crew to run with.'

'Looks more like he's looking for a concurrent sentence to run with.'

'Okay, Paul, I'll wear it. Just keep him away from my gear or I'll do for the doofer!'

'Let's not be too harsh on the boy. Smile... ooze nice! Curls, m'lad! How the devil's own blue blazes are you, dear boy?'

'Curly-Wurly! Hi, guy!'

'Morning, Chims! Okay! Sticky – Croc – Shedfixman – meet Billy. He's got the back pigeonhole at our gaff.'

The doormat's eyes flickered as he began to swing his shoulders.

'Aright, Sticky! Croc! Shed! Ay up, mace! Owza gaiwn?' He grabbed for my hand and shook it unilaterally. I'd always hated shaking hands with strangers, dunno why. I hated it even more when they still had a stinking fag wedged between their fingers. But to be fair to Billy, all he had to do to earn dislike was to appear at a band rehearsal. In the Chimney biosphere, there existed three classifications of fellowship. Firstly, the faces. People you smiled at, or chatted with, or said 'hello' to on the bus or down the boozer. Then the inner circle. Friends you didn't see as often, or folk who had done you a major or minor favour, or with whom you may have had steady tradings. Then finally, those long or reasonably long-proven through deed or definable quality of character. Those most kindred of spirit. Those known as the Frozen Chu. These were perfectly at liberty to turn up anywhere and say and do whatever they wished and help themselves. Curly was the Chu's flagship. Billy wasn't even a face. I instinctively turned to shake Curly's hand to quell the unease as Sticky rolled his penultimate wood and reviewed the details for next Saturday.

'So we're all tickety-boo for the Mclads gig, yeah?'

'Looks like it! What's the deal on the door?'

'Splitting it thirty-seventy with them.'

Curly jeered. 'What? The real, live Mclads? As in the big swillin', curry crunchin', lost me watch in yer wife's knickers so you'll have to hang on a tick, Mclads?'

'Yep, Accrington's finest!'

'So who's thirty and who's seventy, dear boy?'

'Come on, Skip, they're a big name – it *is* a break for us; nice wood by the way!'

'Thank you, sir; in that case, might one propose that they might consider apportioning the spoils in direct relation to everyone's individual ability to drink?'

'We could nominate two road crew and field Curly!'
'Yuh! I'll drink the bastards out of seventy per cent!'
'We'll do that anyway!'
'Ooowah!'
'And bag their bags!'
'This is assuming their bags aren't all blokes, dear boy!'
'Or satchels, ha ha!'

The Skipper laid down his wood. Pursed his lips. The hazed, cobalt blue eyes met with the haze of the high summer ethos. He smiled knowingly, nodding contentedly to himself. He turned to the gully and swooped again upon the restless flagon, which was now ailing in ale.

'Gentlemen! Financial aspects aside, let us charge our gullets and then let us remind ourselves – we are the *best*!'
'The *best*!'
'The *very*!'
'The *absa*!'
'Hoo-hoowah!'

Four dead flagons did a Barnes Wallis into and around the gully. Curly impatiently fanned his hands at Billy, who was lending as much of his flagon as possible. Billy finally conceded, belched socially, then began to embark upon some thread of semi-pertinent babble. The Skipper wagged a finger of intercession, delving into a kitbag.

'Now! Round about this time – whether it be a special occasion, or just with friends in mind – one often prefers to unwind with yet another cider syphon... mmmm!' He chished the final flagon and drank and offered it on. Billy, already becoming impatient with his apparent exclusion from the offer, snatched it on the second circuit, took a painfully long swill and then began to scan around, weighing up the green as if perfectly au fait with the sitcom. The white-haired greens attendant appeared cheerfully on cue to evacuate the spent flagons from the gully. Upon handing him the final casualty, we opted to abort the game and press on. Not least because

Billy had now decided to snatch anyone's wood and trundle it over anyone's lane and generally impersonate anyone's prat. As the attendant was now returning equipped with trusty wood bucket, the Skipper envisioned making his collection easier, with Billy in mind.

'So then, gentlemen. Might one suggest that we adjourn homewards via the offy, if – and *only* if – we are requiring a supplementary of beverage?'

So far, Billy had been a drinker, but not a bringer. The Skipper's statement was succinctly designed to remind us all that if Billy was tagging further on, then his fingers were going to be meeting his pocket fluff into the bargain.

Unusually enough, the offy in question was in situ only some five or six doors up the street from the Skipper-Curly residence, and within minutes the party of six was marching through its frontal architraves with military aplomb; therein to peruse its variegation of cans and bottles. Its licensee, a small, pleasantly-disposed Punjabi lady whose chin was seemingly staging a pitched battle for ubiquity between hairy tufts and warts, appeared a little concerned that day; likely as not concerned, as we *all* were with the surly, furtive demeanour displayed by Billy. Or perhaps, it was his subtly expressed interest in the chin. We attempted to put her at greater ease with diction which had been long since considered extinct in Hyson Green: 'Good day' ... 'Thank you' ... 'Please', even. I'd been in the process of choosing my poison when I suddenly felt eyes upon me, prying for my attention. Looking across my shoulder, I noticed Billy, nodding firstly at me, then at a stack of beer and lightly patting the side of his jacket. I ignored him for the moment, turning back to my selection.

'Curly?'

'Shed?'

'Would you kindly advise your new housemate that any covert liberation of the produce in here will be frowned upon intensely? Thank you, sir.'

'Billy? Don't covertly liberate the produce – it's frowned upon. Intensely.'

The *Captain* approached the counter to weigh in his groceries. He beamed cordially, politely restricting his stare to the super nasal vicinity.

'I think that'll be all, dear girl. I say! Being one of your most frequent visitors, I don't suppose I qualify for a smidgeon of a reduction. For bulk?'

Her insecurity melted, she grinned warmly. 'I'm sorry, it's already on special offer.'

'Would it help if I told you I was really a Viscount?'

'Pardon?'

'Well, I've often wondered – should Viscounts receive diecounts or should Visscounts receive discounts?'

She shook her head in total departure, gazing up to the heavens. Sticky sighed with a grotesque smirk, then briskly changed the subject.

'You think we ought to get something for Joe?'

'What? After the way he pounced on *our* cases, last time we were faced?'

'Er, actually, it's a resoundingly definite bollocks to *that* suggestion, dear boy!'

'*Do* cover your ears, my dear... I suppose he can share mine, if he comes the glum chum – Billy! Just take those fucking cans out of your rag, get them onto this counter then get your fucking wad out! You've been told!'

'Uh? Ah! Yeah, cool, Shed. I was just going to, mace! Ha, ha!'

''Course you were. Okay, are we all done then?'

We filed out as one, marching Billy on in front for safety. Down the street, outside the house, Joe was perched on the front gate, looking a little irked on account of his being forced to wear an incessant tirade of inquiry from the local urchinry *au sujet de* 'Wot's in the case, mister?' The consequent tups were clearly audible from seventy paces. Firstly, we all greeted

Joe – whose angst was then able to change horses from the children onto Billy. Then, accompanied all the way by a lug-ringing, tup-embellished recount of another weekend's worth of woe and catastrophe, we stamped into the weather-worn, mid-terraced property and on up to the second floor and its rehearsal suite, which doubled as the Skipper's boudoir.

As per normal, there ensued the mandatory fifteen-minute period to ensconce and take refreshments. Then, with Billy still popping about like a pea on a drum, offering to do everything doable whilst reciting hairy-arsed rhinoceros shit for beginners, we set up the modicum of equipment necessary for choir practice and began the business in hand. Over the following couple of hours, we were to enjoy a constructive and convivial practice session. A racier version of the Drifters' 'Save the last dance', rewritten as 'Save a damp cloth' was tried out, but sensibly shelved for later, given the six-day deadline. By mid-afternoon, the Skipper's voracious thirst had seized the controls and he was suddenly taken very drunk; moreover, things had generally taken a turn for the abstract.

I'd just enjoyed a heavily overdue rinse of the prince at the rather Spartan downstairs facility, whereupon stepping back into the darkened landing, I was instantly confronted by the stealthily tiptoeing figure of a drummer in his mid-twenties.

'What's your...?'

'Shhh! Shed!' Pointing upwards, he motioned us to whisper.

'Wha?'

'Ssst! Quiet! There's been a change to the advertised programme – except for those viewers served by the Hyson Green transmitter – yeah?' He threw an extravagant wink.

'What d'you...?'

'Shhh! It's gone quiet upstairs! Flush the bog again!'

Convinced he'd either spun his lid or surpassed the Skipper, I stepped back into the cack cave and pumped the chain. After a few thirsty wheezes, the water crashed down again to provide the desired backdrop of racket. Sticky beckoned me to listen closer.

'Hsst! Right! What it is is this. These desperadoes are going to be going into town in an hour or so. You and me, on the other hand, are meeting Helen and Dawn for a bit of a barby in Redhill. I just called them from the offy. They're picking us up from the New Inn, Carrington! Forty-five minutes. Sound right to you?'

'Sounds tickety-boo and three quarters, me old Buckaroonio!'

'Right! Let's get back up there, come up with some right old tosh for the others, and ditch the sitch!'

'You're me man, m'man – go, go!' We charged back upstairs, chuckling and punching each other in the shoulders. At the Skipper's door, we paused to face one another, grunting austerely. The grins faded.

'Poker?'

'Ahem! Poker.'

As Sticky made for the door handle, a sensible question suddenly announced itself to me. I grabbed his arm away, motioning him back out of earshot to the far end of the corridor. This time Sticky cocked the intrigued one.

'Why...?'

'Shhh!'

'Why the...'

'Shhh! They'll hear!'

I lowered my voice as far as humanly feasible but it was impossible to strike the balance. 'Why do...?'

'Pardon?'

'Fuck this lark! I think we need another piss.' I gripped his forearm again and lunged downstairs, causing his head to flail back in the catch up. Stumbling back into the most splendid room of the house, I gave the chain another umpteen cranks before the flush kicked back in, under dire protest. The conversation could reopen.

'So what's the problem?'

'I was wondering – er – why *exactly* are we whispering about this?'

'Work it out, king prawn prick, Your Majesty: Billy?'

'Billy? Oh no! Not fucking Billy, again! Now what, Billy? Don't tell me – he wants to jump into my sack as *well* as my town, my band, my beer glass, my bowling green and my benefit queue!'

'Shed. Dear friend, trusted confidant, fellow musician and dork. Let's put it this way. Billy's tagging along with the crew tonight. Noakes will also be out tonight. Billy's never *met* Noakes. Nobody's likely to *warn* Billy about Noakes. Both of them are known to thoroughly excel in the art of *discreet* conversation – *with* a view to keeping all mankind generously informed... Any of this begun to percolate, yet?'

'I'm, er, acquiring the picture.'

'Acquire this one, then. For worst of all: Billy's never met the dragons, and we don't know where or when he's likely to. So if he *does*? How's he then likely to know who's whose?'

'Crikey dick, Stick! You're bang on, m'man. Just think – at the very best, another nil-nil scoreline! At ultimate worst? We could finish up with *two* full bacon jackets out there!'

'Yep; Noakes...'

'And All Night Noakes.'

'...working shifts.'

'Can you grip that?'

'I can't grip that. Ungrippable. Right! Back upstairs! Let's hogwash and go!'

'You're me man, m'man!'

With all objectives now on board and understood, we strolled back up to the fart-filled funhouse, where the Sunday chapter of Alcoholics Unanimous was now swinging away with full pep. Sticky fed them some sort of old hokum about leaving behind an important client's business number on a card in a wallet on a shelf up a duck's arse in a corner of a room at Tallbob's place – and since I lived next door, it seemed practical that – blah, floof, blaller. I grabbed my bass to add a little authenticity to both now and later. Then, having exchanged the usual parting pleasantries, we were gone. We trotted perkily down to the street, up to the offy, around the corner and then, abounding in spirit and the chirpy banter, which Sticky and I always reciprocated, we marched onwards, diagonally across the football pitches towards Carrington and its expectant tinsel.

We pitched up at the New Inn some twenty-five minutes late, but relieved to find Dawn's Mini Clubman still in the car park, sitting neatly abreast of the usual Happy Shopper turbos – or was it Dawn's? We made a brief cursory. The girlabilia strewn haphazardly around inside provided the confirmation. We had company. At the double doors, we grasped a brass handle apiece, hauling them decisively aside in full compliance with the auspices of the dramatic entrance.

We scanned the overbodied, smoke-pothered room as the doors returned to nudge us on a pace, then we forged a pathway along the epidermis of the resident garbage in order to hold a broader circumspection. At the bar, there they were. Perched on high stools, proudly shining on. Unassailable pearls at a swine fair. Dawn's 'come home soon' smile escaping through the cataract of red curls, Helen's twin electric sapphires blazing out from beneath an ash blonde valance. Dawn glanced up at the bar clock and sighed; Helen raised her eyebrows and tapped at the face of her wristwatch in token protest. To restore some levity, I used my bass as an improvised paddle to negotiate the sea of bodies while Stick followed on with one hand on my shoulder and the other pinching his nose all the way to the girls, who were now giggling and sparkling ever keener and sweeter. There had to be the remonstrations. The gentle jostling for elbow room, the feigned disgust; but then the more intimate eye contact and a peck for each cheek to confirm that we were all truly, pleasantly, immodestly relieved to be back together again, somewhere amid life's corybantic carnival.

'Well! Thanks for keeping our seats! You can have the floor back, now!'

'How does "bollocks" sound, you cheeky pair of bastards? You're lucky we've not pissed off by now!'

'Er, Mr Sticks, m'man?'

'Yes, Mr Shedfixman, m'man?'

'This young lady aside you appears to have a very dirty mouth, am I not mistaken?'

'Indeed she does, sir, and may I remark what a great pity it has been that she never once brought it into the bedroom with her!' A set of cherry-painted fingernails thrashed Sticky's ear. I parked the bass against the bar. Sticky fished out a fiver.

'Right! So what'll it be, m'man?'

'Oi! We're late – you haven't got time!'

'Utter pish, madam! Sticky, m'man, indulge me. Have we *ever* been given to passage into an hostelry which clearly emblazons a man's name and business above point of admittance and yet *failed* to imbibe of the barley therein – whether by default or by lack of whim?'

'I can neither recount nor conceive of such a folly, Mr Shedfixman!'

'Then pay ye small heed to this brace of demireps and hie ye forth without let or Hindenberg to point of sale and fob us fastly off with the fruits of these Fultronics!'

'Are you two on drugs? I said we're late!'

'Helen – dearest. Ish. Pardon me if this sounds all overly romantic and soppy, but would you consider perhaps shoving that glass of swill in your kisser and starting to behave?'

'Shed! I really don't know why I bother with you – you're the absolute limit!'

'Well, I'll have to remind you why, then! You love the rough, and *this* rough says and does all the right things... Oh yeah! I nearly forgot – *and* I'm pretty damn good-looking into the bargain.'

'Go on then, Shed! Give her the damn good tongue-lashing that she's been howling after!' Once again, Dawn's backhander found its mark.

'Whoa-ho! Violence! Brutality! Come on, Shed! We'd best get the beer down and get these women home before they go off the boil!'

'Come on guys – really – we'll miss all the grub!'

That was a valid point. We'd been enjoying the day so much that it had slipped our minds that we were actually starving somewhat. We bombed the beers – except Helen, who gave me hers to expedite the departure, then fell out into the car park and made for Redhill–Clubman class.

The Hamlet of Redhill, consisting as it did of two pubs, one garage, one graveyard and a perceivable polarity of social standing, gave rise to avid speculation on the way as to whether we were set for a society bash or just a cram-in at a cabin on its council crescent. Having passed by the latter, it became palpable that we were in for a shindy at a not inconsiderable gaff. The Clubman subsequently buzzed off the main road and into a broad and gravelled driveway, lined by groves of large rhododendrons. At the end of the groves, a vast, pink pebble-dashed country manse loomed above landscaped shrubberies, rockeries and blooming beds of practically everything capable of sucking at soil. Upon stowing the Clubman, we were beckoned over to the house by a rather swarthy, emaciated odd fish with a black bouffant barnet and a seemingly incurable hop, skip and frolic.

Having issued Dawn and Helen with a brief peck on the cheek, he then led us all into the reception area and issued the four of us with laden punch glasses, in keeping with his self-appointment as duty sycophant. He bade Sticky and me introduce ourselves at our own leisure, and began to usher the girls away to inspect the newly decorated hallways. Before setting off, Helen cast an over-the-shoulder glance.

'You two be alright?'

'Tickety!'

'Turbo!' What she actually meant was, 'Behave, you bastards, or we'll all be having your balls for bhajis.' So, suitably admonished, we drained cup and returned to the nucleus of popular insensibility for a second dunk into the punch.

Above an hour's worth of dunking and introducing later, Sticky and I were well immersed in doing the party things. The 'haven't we mets?' The 'can I offer yous?' The 'do you really? That's very interestings!' The concurring, the food prodding, the jokes that wouldn't upset anyone's mum's psychiatrist, the general stuff for which the Chu would have cheerfully shot us, if they'd only seen us at it.

Then, halfway into the occasion and halfway into the drawing room, as I was halfway into some twaddle-laden platitude or other, the flap happened. Suddenly, out of nowhere, I was taken ever so very drunk. I had become progressively inert to the point where the can of ice-cold pale ale had suddenly, seemingly, with a mind of its own, shot off from my misaligned grip. It then ditched over four pairs of shoes and rolled off into the hall, spiralling out its contents over and around the newly laid and pristine Chinese carpet. Silence. Above the silence, the unmistakeable clang of two vaginas slamming shut for the night. The pale had taken me beyond the pale. Twin sapphires drilling into me from somewhere – I could feel it. Quick! *Think fast*!

'I'm dreffly soz... let me clean that... do you have a clov?'

Ouch! I sounded worse than the pale ale. Another silence. Then all at once, some twelve or fifteen slightly better-acquitted party-goers bleeped into life; buzzing, burrowing – almost bumping into one another in the stampede to acquire the now much-coveted information which may have led to the placement of a clov. It was evident that the residence with *everything* had been musefully devised without the savagery of human error in mind; and as the beer sank slowly into the deck, the scene became somewhat reminiscent of the effect produced by farting down an anthole. In dread of the potential consequences to all this, I attempted to be seen to be taking some initiative.

'Bloody Nora! Don't worry, I'll use me sleeve... honiss! I don't mind, iss an old shirt!' The Black Bouffant swished in, hands and arms akimbo.

'Ooo! Oh no, Shed! Don't you *dare* get yourself mucky! The man's here! He fitted it for us – he'll know best what to do!'

'But ah'll do it – honiss – I don't mah...'

'Okay! Right! Let me see! Let's have a look!' They weren't kidding. The guy who fitted it *was* there.

'Right! No! Don't touch it! Don't touch it! No! Don't scrub it! You'll ruffle the nap... you'll scatter the weft! Then you'll notice it every time you come home! The weft has to run towards the front door, not the stairs! You'll darken the woodwork! I'll deal with it – leave it to me! Come on! Shoo, all of you!'

Helen was standing beside me, shaking her head at the stain and then at me.

'Helen – I'm soz. Issa genuine poe fart.'

'Just mingle, will you both? Everyone'll think you're being loutish.' The only person grinning throughout had been Sticky, for likely as not, he'd probably been taken fabulously drunk himself.

'Okay, Shed! Me? I'm taking the front parlour and mingling.'

Helen remained unimpressed with the sarcasm. I kissed her hair. Unimpressed.

'Okay, okay, I'm going! Consider me Doctor J Mingler! You can expect to find me in either Latin America or sulking in the kitchen – whichever's the nearest! Bye-bye, Sticky! See you after the war!'

'Bye-bye, Shed, old chap! Be brave! Don't worry, it'll soon be over, then Johnny can sleep in his own little room again!'

'Chin-ho!'

'Kam Fong!'

'Steve and Danno!'

With that, I was barged cleanly into the kitchen by an intolerant seven-stone vexling with sapphire eyes ablaze. Sticky escaped to the parlour to invest precious breath on nothing constructive; I paused against the dishwasher until Helen had drifted on, then sneaked a replacement pale ale from the fridge and adjourned to the sunny outdoors... to a white wrought-iron bench overlooking the pond, where a solitary toad cheerfully thrashed around, inspiring the departure of all care, and eclipsing all ambient clatter and claptrap with his plishy-ploshy repertoire. We watched each other; him drifting in his pool, me drifting in mine. We watched.

Clunk. I'd lost the satellite link with the trance, which had concluded abruptly courtesy of Sticky parking his rump further along the bench and clunking a beer can down beside him.

'Hey! It's a Mister Toady!'

'So we missed the food after all, eh?'

'There's one sausage left on the barby.'

'*That's* what it is? I thought someone had been vulcanising ravens.'

Toady showed off his very best plash, then spread out his limbs, fingers and toes to sway gently in the returning ripples.

'Stick, m'man, is it just me, or are they all on the other bus?'

'I'm afraid it's the other bus, m'man.'

'What's the other bus? You haven't been upsetting our friends again, have you?'

Helen and Dawn had suddenly manifested behind to inspect the quality of our behaviour – and obviously to do a quick Gibraltar on the conversation. I reached behind me for Helen's arms. She yielded and stooped forwards, wrapping them around my chest. Someone had to ask.

'Helen, sweety? Who actually invited you – and us – to this bash?'

'A workmate of Dawn's. Why?'

Sticky looked somewhat jiggered by this. 'Dawn, would this workmate be the lady presently ensconced in the captain's chair in the parlour, by any chance?'

'I think so, why?'

'The one in the comfy, sensible shoes?'

'I've never looked. Why, what do you mean?'

Sticky exhaled forcefully. 'Sheesh! That's a relief, then.'

Helen, more than anything, hated to be kept in the dark over matters. Consequently, she dug a craggy elbow into my ribs. 'Tell me what he means!'

'Ouch, bitch!'

'So tell me!'

'She wears comfy shoes? No? She's a woman who wears comfy, sensible, flat shoes?' She just stared back even more vacantly.

'Stick, help me out here; she's beginning to wank my crank – let's just throw them some clues until the ninepenny coin drops? Sheesh!'

'Comfy, comfy, practical on the tootsies? No? Shed.'

'A G-Woman?'

'Whaa?'

'Okay – bull?' At this, Dawn shrugged her shoulders; Helen looked on, shaking her head. Their corporate naivety was nothing short of staggering.

'Okay what about... gash-swapper?'

'Spunk-shunner?'

'Well, fuck me, you two...'

'No, Stick, don't fluster; they *will* understand this today, or, as God is my worst fan, I will perform a carnally gratifying act of the grossest indecency with that amphibian over there. Helen! You can do this. Come on, babe! Bull! G-Woman! Comfy shoes! The parlour is replete with half of dykedom –

busily negotiating the swapping of gash – whereas the lounge and hallways are happily blessed with sandboys?'

The coin stayed put. 'Sandboys?'

'Yep! Them! Sandboys!'

'Fudge-nudgers!'

'Bourneville boulevard browsers!'

'Rump-stokers!'

'The A-Team?'

'Funny as fish fur!'

'Bottles of chips... Oh, for heaven's sake, gals! Is this or is this not a bit of a rum do?'

Dawn periled a vague guess. 'Do you mean that our friends might be gay?'

'Waaay!'

'Whoah!'

'Wooo, release the toad! I'm going home for Christmas after all!'

'Yep! He was beginning to panic, m'man – look! He's broken out in warts!'

'Har, har!'

'Ooh look! A frog! Near your foot, Shed!' The black bouffant had emerged from the kitchen with two or three more guests. He'd shown them the punch, he'd shown them the halls, he'd shown them his best side. Now, obviously, it was the turn of the wildlife in, on and around the pond.

'I told you! There – look! Near Shed's foot!' They all grouped round to wondrously behold the three-ounce wart warehouse, which shied timidly away closer to my shoe in a last ditch bid for anonymity.

'Ooh! Pick it up for us, Shed! Go on – dares you!'

'Leave it alone.' I felt an excuse to leave coming on.

'Come on, Shed! Pick the frog up!'

'I can't see any frogs.'

'At your foot! Look! Be careful!'

'This is not a frog. It crawls... it has warts. Let me introduce you: *Bufo Bufo*, meet Homo sapiens – with less of the sapiens.'

Helen glared me a dagger. At least I'd resisted the more obvious 'meet Puffo Puffo'. Sticky was becoming equally restless.

'Come on guys, let's leave the poor little bugger alone to his pond and his sexual preferences.'

This provoked a little more thought amongst the guys, if not more daggers from the girls. I was now concerned that one or more of the great learned present was about to panic and drop a silly big hoof on the toad. So, to a choral gasp, I scooped it up in my fist and set it back down on a pond lily at the furthest extent of my reach. Then, wiping its shit down the side of my jeans, I trotted over to the griddle, fetched the raven sausage and chucked it onto the next lily to that of the toad's.

'There you are, matey! Now neither you nor your frog can say you haven't got a sausage.'

Sticky laughed heartily. The girls frowned on, as two impending storm clouds might. The guys sipped uncomfortably. Sticky loped stealthily past everyone to place an arm on my shoulder and usher me away for a brief word at distance.

'Shed. They're nice people. They've offered beer and hospitality, now it's time to shoo the boo.'

'Yeah, bang on, m'man. Time to speak to the girls and ditch the sitch; if we stay, we'll end up pissing someone off.'

'We piss someone off – we piss the girls off.'

'We piss the girls off, we blow another shag.'

'We blow *another* shag, we've got to beat ourselves up. Brutally. And if the *Chu* ever gets wind...'

'Brutally...' Helen was nudging her way over, ever intolerant of exclusion, so I offered, 'Go for Dawn, Stick. I'll push from this end.'

But before she could get the quiz started, I laid a span of fingers lightly between her shoulder blades and guided her discreetly away from the other bus. I opted for the more macho 'it gives me little choice in the matter' gambit, supported by the twin flankers of 'just as unhappy as you about this' and a large bucket of puréed gooey romantics.

Questioning and distraught, the sapphires blazed quietly up at me as if I was about to blow the whistle for the assault on Leningrad. I gently propelled her around the corner.

'Come here, you.' I pushed a full kiss onto her mouth. She was half-responsive, half-trusting.

'What is it, Shed? Has someone offended you? Have I offended you? Shouldn't we have...?'

'Shush!' I kissed her again.

'No one's going to upset anyone. Helen. They're lovely people. But we play for The Chimneys, Helen. We cannot be turning up at gay costume dramas – the image doctors would crucify us. Surely you understand that?'

'That's crap.'

I called in 'B' flank. 'I know, but look, babe, it's not just that. I've shared you with everyone for over two hours. Am I being so unreasonable by wanting you to myself for the rest of the day? There's a lot of things I wanted us to talk over. I thought we could spend today getting closer, but we're running out of today. Come on, babe! Let's go somewhere?'

For a few seconds she searched my eyes. 'That's crap too.'

I kissed her again, but harder, rougher. Pulling her dainty little arse onto me with both hands.

'Look, Helen. Don't worry about upsetting anyone. I wouldn't be surprised if Sticky and Dawny are having the same conversation.' I bloody well knew they were. 'He thinks a hell of a lot about Dawn, you know.' Her arms shifted wrap from my waist to up around my neck. She smiled with some reserve, then she shook her blonde waves and the sapphires began to weigh me up from sideways on. Then suddenly, she grabbed my head jerking it towards her face.

'You're fucking impossible, you creep! Come on. We'll

speak to Dawn – she's the driver.'

'That's the spirit! Lead on, Lulu!'

She took my hand and we wandered back to the pond – where by now even more of the other bus were congregated. The toad, mercifully, had had the sense to submerge out of it, and Sticky and Dawn were lovingly entwined, at oneness with the goo pot. That warm, enamouring smile had returned to her face. Noticing Helen and me, she took a break from the smouldering passions to address the other half of the Clubman contingent.

'We fancy blowing to the Penny! You two coming?'

'Oh, go on then, if we must – *ouchabass!*' The craggy elbow slammed into my ribs again, but it couldn't suppress the gleeful smirk that I was casting back at Sticky's gleeful smirk. The 'Inn for a Penny' was in the girls' neighbourhood. We weren't even going to stop on the way. M'man had done it again.

In an afternoon seemingly fraught with excuses, the girls delivered theirs to their hostess and the little camel-coloured Clubman chugged away from the pink palazzo, with all on board waving at the happy minions behind, who were now free to enjoy a closed shop.

Over at the Penny, the Sunday ambiance was buoyant as per expected, but luckily we managed to secure some sprawling space in a vacant corner. The girls, being close to home, could now relax, let some hair down and drink a little bit more seriously. They wasted no time whatsoever – opening with V 'n' Ts and then larger V 'n' Ts, then the heavens have opened V 'n' Ts, after which the evening became a general crescendo of vodka, light music and heavy petting. Everything was part of one and the same big racing blur.

Lord knows how we got back, but in the next scene, I was kneeling in Helen's living room alongside Helen. Snogging. Playing vinyl LPs on a rickety old system. Sticky and Dawn had gone to bed. We'd begun to roll around on the floor together, but she wouldn't hit the sack with me until she'd played her favourite song – some old Elvis Costello shite. But it didn't sound too bad at the time. Then another gap. Then a dying sun was wishing its last through the half-turned Venetians against her bedroom window, throwing an exotic slatted shadow over her petite naked form as she knelt on the bed, ready to surrender. The sapphires burned and sparkled more beautifully than ever. I wanted to relish that picture of Helen for ever. I sat for as long as art could defy the beast, just melting in front of her eyes, branding her onto my memory. Then beast. She fell with a counterfeit squeal and we kissed deeply and rolled and loved. I remember that she nagged a little over the lack of foreplay, but unfinished business can nag harder than women. Then the beautiful day was complete. Everything serene, quiet, still, Helen sleeping. I felt the softness of Helen's summerblanched body just once more, all over. I pulled the sheets over it in case the night grew cold. I kissed the side of her mouth and left her to dream. In another world she was my wife. I stroked my fingers through her blonde waves. Thank you, Helen. In the bathroom, I found the cheapest soap she had – to wash away her scent. I dressed in the living room in order not to disturb anyone. Headlamps flashed twice against the window from the driveway. I grabbed my bass from behind an armchair, then gently clicking shut the glass panel door after me, I quietly slid into the taxi and was home in bed beside Selina just before she awoke at around 12.30 to coil an arm and a leg around me and ask what time I'd got in. She fell back to sleep before I could answer.

Bye-bye, beautiful day.

TEN

Five dire days of brash, orthodox conformity in the harsh world of knuckle-under soon subsided into another heavily pregnant Saturday morning. I woke up at around six, fizzing over with pep, ready to rock 'n' roll. I leapt out of the sack and trooped immediately to the bathroom to brush my teeth, piss endlessly and run a hand under the cold tap all at the same time. Sneaking back to bed, I then slid the cold hand inside the sheets and on to Selina's piping hot back.

'Ooyerbastard!' Having successfully coerced her into facing the ceiling, I climbed in, climbed on and shagged away for England. Fifteen minutes suited us fine. Then a five-minute commercial break. Then just the one more – to burn off the last of the pep. All pep so dispatched, we fell back into a doze under a tangled sea of linen.

The next call to consciousness was delivered by a husky, fag-stained voice over the intercom. Selina came striding into the room.

'That's my taxi – I'll see you tonight, then.'

I'd forgotten that she'd decided to go into work. 'Tonight? Where?'

'I won't come if you don't want.'

I'd forgotten that too. She'd been nudging at coming to the gig all week, whether it was about keeping tabs or checking to what depths I'd sunk, or just out of plain old interest. I just said 'okay'. After all, it was at a gig that we first met and she fell in love, so who knew? Maybe it might rekindle a few little sparks between us – love's fragile flame – summat daft like that.

'Yeah! Of course, sweetheart! Meet me inside the Queen's

Hotel at eight! Get a cab...' I grabbed her denim-wrapped arse and pulled her down onto me.

'Come on, the meter's running and I'm late!'

'Just needed a kiss, mmmwap!'

'Okay, see you at eight then, loveyerbye!'

'Love yer, tek care!'

She lent her customary ham-fisted crash to the front door and she was off. I lay still, listening to her hurried footsteps fade, then fanned out in sub-duvetial splendour and began to recount the format for the day in prospect. A format which quickly convinced me beyond all doubt that I had no business whatsoever being awake yet, and that a further deposit at the sleep bank plc was sensible. I set the radio alarm for high noon.

The second rude awakening, when it came, ambushed me some two hours ahead of the alarm. It came in the form of a chirruping telephone.

'Uh?'

'Shedguy! Ready to rock, m'man?' It was Sticky's unhealthy, unnatural, bouncy, happy, let's get snappy, morning clarion routine. Sticky was a morning bod. Sticky was an evening bod; Sticky was a bod for all seasons – yeuchh!

'Whaa? Uh, yeah. Where we meeting... again?'

'Malt Cross, between twelve and one, and a bad attitude is compulsory, I'm afraid.'

'Don't be afraid – it's only me. Wassa time?'

'About ten past ten. You still in the sack, you shitkicker?'

'We can't *all* be Mr Weetabix – what time are you pitching?'

'Does duck shit drop downwards? Twelve. Hey, are we safe to talk? Is the Dragon about?'

'She's gone to work, why?'

'We're getting a visit – we'll be in for some later!'

'How d'yer mean "getting a visit"? In for some what?'

'I rang Dawn in the week – they're both down tonight.'

'You did what? Oh, fucking turbo! Oh no no no no no no no, Sticky man, no! Tell me I'm dreaming this, would you?'

'What's up with you?'

'Well you better ring Dawn clean back then, because the Dragon's only f'kin coming on down tonight too, also, as well as, plus, but!'

'*Whaat*? You never bring the Dragon – none of us do! What are you playing at, soft newark?'

'You smouldering great shit slice! Just get it sorted, will you?'

'I can't.'

'What d'yer mean, "can't"? Can't? Never heard the word. You must mean "can"!'

'I mean *can't* – they're both out of town today. They're coming straight to the gig after work.'

'Oh, fucking luxury!' And so was Selina. I could've yelled at Sticky until the cows evolved, but I knew most of the blame was mine for this one. He was only looking after us, all said and done. Rekindle a few little sparks? The bastards were going to *fly*, and nothing few or little about it! Very far from rekindling love's fragile flame, I was about to sling a chromium-dipped bouquet of spanners into its injurious works.

'Holy bastard Moly! I think I'd better start drinking – what's the list of options for a 10.30 commencement?'

'In town? The Bell, the Toll Bar or the Newky Arms on North Sherwood street.'

'Sweet. How very poignant – well the Bell's certainly tolling for *my* fucking newky at the moment!'

'Ha ha ha ha! Look, I'll be right out. I'll meet you at the Newky – we'll discuss this sensibly.'

'No, we won't – we'll get cannoned.'

'Sparklin', Martin! Wait if I'm late.'

'Wait? I'm thinking of checking in!'

'See you forthwith.'

I got dressed, got money and got going; I always thought more clearly on the move. In ten minutes flat I was in the Newcastle Arms, biting the tiger's bollocks. I was draining the second Pils as the door flapped open for its second time that morning. In skulked a head-hung, repentant-looking young man, with mournful grey eyes which peered woefully up at me through long chestnut curls. He hadn't even put a comb through them as part of the penance. He sidled towards me, scuffing his toes, like a child reluctant to go to school. I chuckled loudly at him.

'Come on, m'man, bollocks to 'em! I'll get you a beer. Whatever goes up, we've got each other; we've got a bloody good band and we both know that playing live's better than any orgasm!'

'Shed, soz m'man, I tried to get hold of...'

'Sticky, just fuck it – really! So what if the propeller's in for a direct shit hit – it might *even* be a laugh! Come on... *'Scuse me*! Barkeeper, sir! M'man would like a drink, please!'

'Pils? You're drinking Pils at 10.45 in the morning? You'd better get me one too, one-too, testing!'

'Yeah, apparently the place is full of beer at the moment.'

'Yeah? What I'd also like would be if you could turn down the music, please bartender, because I've still got to ring in sick; I said I'd be in this morning. Got any coins, Shed?'

'Can you grip this? He's just trashed my love life – *twice*! Now he's mugging me! The beat goes on.'

'Come on, m'man, first things first. Get the excuses over and done with – what d'yer say?'

'Yeah, I suppose it's got to be done.' I handed him some coins for his call. I wasn't too chuffed about the jukebox though, as it was *my* quid powering it.

'Hurry up then, Stick – I want to hear these records.'

We wandered into the passage, Pilses in hand for moral comfort. At this point an impish little morsel of bedevilment was occurring to me.

'Stick, let me bat first. I've got to ring in myself, but I know exactly what I'm going to say. I'll be ten seconds, m'man.'

'Go for it.'

I fumbled for more change, stood my Pils on the floor and proceeded to dial my favourite radio operator. I was through immediately.

'Hi! Hello! Whozat? Poley? Yeah, it's me – how d'yer guess? How are we all today? Shit, thanks! Look, I can't make it today – there's been an accident! No, seriously, it's not funny! I've been involved in a nasty accident! No, really! Yeah! What? What happened? Well, I've accidentally superglued all my loyalties to the three major breweries... hello?'

Sticky spat his Pils all over the wallpaper, then gulped furiously for air.

'Ha, ha – ahick, ahick!'

'Hello? Oh, no! Poley's hung up on me – ha ha ha!'

Sticky took up the receiver and beckoned for me to guard his Pils as he pumped in some coins.

'Grab this a sec – shhsh! I'm through! Yeah, can I have the buying department, please? Superglued, you prat! Hello? Alan? Yeah, It's me – yeah! No, I can't get in; the dog's got out again! Yeah, he's a little bugger... okay... okay, mate... until Monday... yeah, why?'

I took both beers and motioned to Sticky that I was going back to the bar. He nodded whilst heaping on the horse shit. From the bar stool I could hear the dialogue lapse into the expected esoteric claptrap. Now a little bedevilment could be loosed.

'Er, barkeep?'

'Yes, sir?'

'He's finished now; you can crank it back up. Don't spare the horsepower!' The barman did alike, almost rattling the speakers free from their mountings before re-adjusting the dial to a more convivial settlement of racket.

'Ha ha ha ha!' It would only be a question of seconds before Sticky was talking his way out of shit. He soon stormed back to the bar, a smidgeon miffy.

'You bastard! That was my boss! I had to give *that* one some hard explanatory!'

'Well, Stick, m'man? Now we're about even – cheers!'

'Cheers, m'man!'

'Anyway, what's all that "dog" rubbish you were expecting your boss to wear? You've never owned a dog! Mind, you've woken up with a few, I s'pose.'

'They think I've got a Dalmatian.'

'Dalmatian? Why on earth a Dalmatian?'

'Don't you know? One in ten Dalmatians is born stone deaf.'

'So?'

'So, how do you shout a deaf dog back if it gets out?'

'Master of an excuse, m'man – you'll do for me – cheers!'

'Cheers! I got that one from Flesq Evans – he had a deaf Dalmatian once – you remember Flesq?'

'The only taxi driver in Nottingham to drive a dead man around all day having a lovely one-way conversation, then get out of the taxi at the hospital, having forgotten the handbrake, and become the only taxi driver in the world to run himself over, ha ha ha ha!'

'That's the man – cheers to Flesq!'

'To Flesq!'

It was always special, passing time with Sticky; the man took some cack for being the yuppy, but the man was never boring, never down, never idle, never negative. Always the contributor, always the motivator, always full of pep, always the dirty, shag-happy, tart-sniffing mongrel I could easily relate to. You could never tire of Sticky. To keep our minds away from the prospective trouble ahead, we swilled and harped on about times gone by. How we'd come to be mates back in '76, when as the result of a chance conversation at

Moor Farm's Sunday rock night, it transpired that the girl I'd recently taken up with had recently dumped him. The next time I saw her, I dumped *her* for having such crap taste, and this set the code between us for ever. Needle, but respect. Outrage, but tact. Abuse, but first aid.

On we swilled, recalling the nefarious Saturday morning in '84, when Sticky was preparing to move into a room at the Small Parson's house. He'd brought his mum round to see the place, blissfully unaware that the Parson was walking around stark naked, crying his eyes out. The Skipper was standing singing in a sea of beer cans whilst playing the pinball machine. I was peeled off and taking my turn rocking in Sticky's prospective nest with Juicy Lucy – a fruity little deal we'd bagged the previous night. Sticky had to save his mother's life by throwing her back downstairs and into his car. For revenge, over the next couple of weeks he answered the door wearing Lucy's discarded knickers over his head whenever he was expecting me to call. Until he did it once too often and encountered two policemen investigating a noise complaint in conjunction with a note received by two female neighbours, inquiring as to their immediate availability for a tit wank.

Five or six Pils further on, we were mindful of moving it. We'd exhausted the jukebox and the barman really had to do some work. Sticky patted his stomach as we stood to depart. Obviously no slap, cackle and fop on board.

'Shed, I'm hungry – you hungry? We should eat something, m'man, there's a big day coming – hey! We don't want Uncle Joe shouting.'

'It'll be "get some snap down", then we'll get tupped to death!'

'Ha ha ha!'

'The credits have finished anyway – fancy a kebab? I'll buy us a kebab.'

'I can put up with a kebab – Kismet?'

'Kismet, Hardy!'

We drained the bottles and scooted the couple of hundred yards down to the Kismet; there to spend some fifteen to twenty minutes wrestling with various goujons of marinated sheep-rump, prior to the traditional farce of attempting to arrest three pounds of shredded cabbage within a soggy, disintegrating bread purse as the streams of chilli sauce and yoghurt sneak through your fingers and off up your sleeves. With the whittling away of the keebabs, we turned to view the swarming shoppers through the painted-on window lettering. The Croc's constrained countenance was periodically sighted at his shop window opposite, pawing and fussing over various lustrous displays. We eventually caught his attention, exchanging a thumbs-up. According to the world, it seemed, Saturday would proceed as normal. Then the world changed its mind.

'Hey, Shed! Feast your eyes on this shit!'

'This shit-nice anagram!'

'No – here, look!' Tottering. Teetering. Boistering. Bad-mouthing. The Skipper and Curly, staggering along in the middle lane of Parliament Street – in traffic, pretending to be in a car. Curly adjusting his invisible seat, winding down the imaginary window to eject his cigarette, whereas seated alongside, the Skipper playing it cool with one hand on the presumed steering wheel, the other arm resting over an absent doorframe, to the high delight of the following vehicles. He waved to us and gave the fuel gauge a tap as they passed by the Kismet.

'Shit, Sticky – what's the time?'

'Oh, all of about ten past one!'

'And they're both stratospheric!'

'At least All Night Billy isn't in the back seat!'

'That's something. It's another beautiful evening we're set for!'

'At this point, I feel it's only kindness to warn you about Fig – or should I say "not" Fig.'

'The list goes on. Okay, what is it *this* week?'

'Grip this. He says he's sick of taking shit off us, so he's bought some book of wrestling moves, changed his name to "The Iron Gherkin" and he's challenging us all to come out tonight for some punishment – that's *if* we're men enough.'

'Excuse me?'

'Apparently tonight's "fight night". Tag team time. A bill of catchweight bouts – one fall, one submission or a knockout to decide the winner, and Fig wants the blue corner because he's the "Gherkin".'

Twice I looked away. Twice I looked back, expecting his smile to crack and him to say he was kidding. Twice, he just nodded in resigned affirmation of this; this latest disharmonium to ravage Fig's mind. He wasn't kidding at all.

'Yep! He's back on the "believe and you will be" circuit!'

'Okay, that's me. Ready for the Malt Cross?'

'Let's do it.'

Having borrowed the food prep sink to cleanse mouths, fingers and sleeves, we thanked Kemal the proprietor for this indulgence and struck out for the Malt Cross and whatever it held in store for us; at which round about time, less than two miles away, another empty Martini bottle was being wedged inside an empty cereal box and thrust down into an outside wheelie bin. A Chimneys/Mclads fly poster was then ripped cleanly in half and laid methodically on top before the lid was closed. The thruster then lit up a cigarette, gave a hard, gutsy cough and struck out for town.

A supplementary order of beer was being delivered at the Malt Cross as we rounded the brewery truck, pausing at the entrance door. I turned to consult m'man.

'Cassidy and Sundance?'

M'man concurred with a nod.

'With a bit of Rik and Viv – ready? Two-three-four...'

We tore the door aside, leaping simultaneously into the bar, arms flailing wildly.

'...*Pils frenzeee!*' But we passed largely unnoticed, when matched with the farrago already taking place therein. The usually well-received Saturday lunchtime crooner was today having to raise his stakes to remain even remotely audible above the chaos, whilst the chaos was mutating by the minute, in order to head him off at the chorus. A visiting crew of Royal Marines were heckling mercilessly, egged keenly on by the Parson and Mark Anthony. In the centre ground, Tallbob had the Iron Gherkin's head firmly secured in an armlock; meanwhile a hidden sniper strafed the room with promotional beer mats from one of the balconies. Over in the dining section, the honest, decent, Janet and John patrons of the real world were striving hard to shovel down their luncheons and get out as fast as humanly possible, geed alarmingly on by the sudden crash of crockery and utensils provided by Curly's lifeless body keeling over into someone's lasagne. The marines howled with laughter. The owner of the lasagne howled nose to nose at the Skipper, who'd gone to claim the body and a bit of salad.

As we surveyed the devastation in sheer, stark bewilderment, a peach of an opportunity presented itself. For there, standing at the bar, rolling a fag with his back to us, was the Sergeant. We had the bounder unawares. We exchanged a wink and stalked towards him.

'After three?'

'Three!'

Whaaak! Two prime flat-handers landed clean and keen between Sarge's shoulder blades, showering a barman with tobacco, and shunting Sarge's specs an inch further down his hooter. *His* socks were well and truly rocked for a change.

'Hey, Sarge – watch yer back, m'man! Ha ha ha!'

'Shhit! Shed, Shed, Shed! Sticky, Sticky, Sticky! You pair of f'kin bandits! Fancy me getting caught off-guard by two of the worst musicians in Nottingham.'

'Sarge, Sarge, Sarge – musicians? We deeply resent that allegation!'

'Yes, and we demand to know the name of the alligator!'

'So how the hell are you both? You've joined us at a particularly choice moment in time. The Iron Gherkin's treating us to another masterclass of applied stupidity.'

As Sarge shepherded the scattered tobacco back into a collective tuft upon the bar, we treated ourselves to another eyeful of the kicking, struggling, red-faced Gherkin. Tallbob, still well in control of his adversary, nodded in acknowledgment.

'Hiyer, Sticky! How's it going, neighbour! I'll be with you both in a second – get me a beer; I'm just going to thrash this idiot to within an inch of his avoirdupois, then Bob's your uncle! Now then, you little twerp – are you going to shut up about rasslin', or do I have to wring your scruffy little neck again – eh?'

For some reason, Tallbob appeared to hold no patience whatsoever for Fig that day. Meanwhile Les, aka Les Miserables, the long-suffering owner of the bar, had been greatly preoccupied with marching Curly and the Skipper away from a profoundly grateful dining section, after pledging a massive compensation package to cover the tomfoolery. Marching them on across the room, he sat the pair down on a couple of stools much closer to the bar than harm's way – in what the Gherkin might have described as a neutral corner. Although the pair had been two of the Malt Cross's thirstiest over the years, Les still had to be seen to be in government of the sitcom – for his career's sake.

'Look, lads, I don't want to have to bar you both, but if there's any more swearing and falling about from you, I'll have to think about it – okay?' The Skipper replied with, 'Bollocks!' as Curly fell off his stool and Les himself was struck hard on the ear by yet another flying beer mat. Thrice trumped ace. Understandably, he gave up.

Back in the blue corner, Tallbob had won by a submission. He dumped the Gherkin face down on the plush, midnight blue carpet and strolled over to collect his beer and confirm his support for the evening ahead. He'd scarcely put glass to lips, when a fresh tirade of provocation exuded from the blue corner.

'Hey! Hey! Yes – *you*! Gay testicles! Get back here and fight like a man! Oooff! I'm Adrian Street – No! Steve Logan – forearm smash!' The Gherkin slapped his forearms challengingly.

'Jackie Pallo? Mick McManus? Pah! Who are they? It's the Iron Gherkin you're dealing with now – oooff!'

Tallbob calmly took a long sip of beer without giving any reaction to all of this; then, gently setting the glass back down, he politely absented himself.

'Excuse me for a second – I won't be long.'

He turned about face and marched determinedly back to an all of a sudden not so confident looking Gherkin, cuffing him crisply across the ear. Then, before he had a second to react, Tallbob set about constricting his windpipe with anaconda-like fingers. The Gherkin bravely tried to prise him off and was shaken about like a fledgling pear tree for his trouble. Another prompt submission seemed prudent.

'Ahk-k-k-khak!'

'You gonna shut up?'

'Aggurggikk-ikk-aright, k-k-aright!'

Tallbob allowed the Gherkin a second's breath, then squeezed again. 'You sure?'

'*Kkk-ik*!'

'You sure? Eh? Ask him, ref! Ask him!'

'Ahkahk! Peace – ikk! Aherk – peace – kkerk! No trouble, honest – blorkk!'

Tallbob looked the Gherkin directly in his rapidly reddening eyes.

'Good, it's settled then. One more bit of your rasslin' crap and I'll murder you, and there wouldn't be a jury in the land that'd convict me after spending two minutes listening to your life story.' He launched the Gherkin away and into a chair, then returned to the bar.

'That's put the ferrous phallus in good order.'

This time he was right. Fig had seemingly abandoned the blue corner and his alter ego, the illustrious Gherkin. Fig remained quietly seated. He hadn't been unaware of the arrival of two greasy-haired and dowdily attired women at the next table and so, curtailing his forearm slapping, he directed all resources into waving and smiling at his newest neighbours like a man surely on heavy medication. Having taken the first full account of his profile out of combat that day, it became apparent that no matter how vigorously or how often Fig swept aside the fringe of his hair, it was springing back up and out after a kind of unicorn fashion. Fig slightly dropped a shoulder and cocked his head as he now fancied himself as Fig the conqueror of hearts. The incessant waving, combined with the lunatic grin and the unicorn coiffage, certainly made him a conqueror of ribs. Our ribs.

'This is surreal. I'm aware of what's going on in his head – but what's going on in his hair?'

Tallbob told us the tale.

'Well, grip this. The dirty bastard kipped in my armchair last night. I got up in the morning and decided to go to the airing cupboard to check on my bean sprouts. He'd only *pissed* the chair and then thrown his piss-sodden jeans in there to dry. I nearly puked – the whole cupboard funked – I had to ditch the moong beans.'

'Fig, Fig, Fig.' Sarge shook his head disdainfully. Sticky squirmed. I felt my eyes narrowing.

'So, I stormed into the living room and there he was: spark out, with one hand stuffed in his pants.'

'Ha, ha! Anarchy in the UP!'

'So then before I woke him up, I tied his laces together.

Filled his pockets with garlic salt and varnished his hair up to a point… I'll iron his Gherkin!'

Sticky leaned sideways to catch a glimpse of Fig's shoes.

'Yep! No shoelaces. I wonder what the ladies think of being chatted up by a Valium-crazed Woody Woodpecker with flippers?'

Tallbob beckoned further attention. 'The best thing of all about this is that he's been spending plenty of money from his pockets, which is now circulating hand over fist via Les's till through practically everyone's fingers, pockets and purses in here. Just look around. Fig's got everyone in the place sniffing themselves.'

Sarge sniffed cautiously at his fingers. 'Shit, well I wish you'd told me ten minutes ago!'

'Ha ha ha! Make sure you've got the correct change for your beers, neighbour! That till's a bit too spicy for Sarge – ha, ha!'

Fortunately, the eight pence change from my shout was still lying around on the bar and there it could stay for me. I was eyeing some of the newly available seats next to the Gherkin's table. I could have done with bending me knees a bit.

'I reckon we owe it to ourselves to join Fig and find out exactly where we've been going wrong with the kife for all these years.'

'We all got a beer? Let's go, before the troops bag the seats.'

We dragged chairs and stools over to form a crescent-shaped auditorium around the Gherkin, before sitting down to a master tutorial in the highly specialised field of converting women into putty. Whatever ground the Gherkin had or hadn't already made, he saw the intercession of his crew as a springboard to a higher confidence. The two women – mother and daughter, at a reasonable guess – sat in a non-committal silence, studying hard at the Gherkin's barnet as the Gherkin himself cranked up the babble control to full.

'I say, ladies, it's the band! I say, girls! Girls, I say – it's my musical friends – Sticky and the Shedfixman; well, I say *friends;* I hate the bastards – and musical? Useless! Not a toon in their tiny minds, now! Jethro Tull, eh? Eh? Now we're talking music, eh? What d'yer say, girls?'

One after the other, the girls reached forward, taking hefty gulps at their ciders, as perhaps part of some subconscious, if ever hopeless effort to access the Gherkin's level of communication.

'Anyway, I digress. Sticky? Shed? This woman refuses to marry me! *Refuses*, if yer please! What d'yer think of *that*?'

'Ha ha ha!'

'Fig, Fig, Fig, what troubled days are these!'

'That's the fickleness of womankind for you, Fig; I remember well the days when women would cheerfully queue fifteen abreast right down the street for the chance to walk out on the arm of a nocturnally incontinent jester – off to town to throw his garlic around in a swanky, suave, devil-may-care sort of manner. Frankly, I just don't know what's wrong with 'em these days!'

'Ha ha ha ha ha!'

'It's not *your* fault that you're just too macho to handle, Fig. The girls can easily see you're the hot, impetuous, shoelace-hacking type of undresser rather than the limp-wristed, picking undone, "it'll be all over by then" excuse for a man "I don't think I can"!'

'He's just *too* damn swashbuckling for any blockbuster movie!'

Fig was gazing up at the ceiling, sniggering perfectly out of sequence with the joking. He was laughing, but laughing at nothing of this world. His attention fell back in the women's direction, then around to us. He seemed to be about to make a very important statement. Then the forearm slapping returned.

'Oofff! It's a sleeper! My hand never left the rope, ref! Har!

Har! Har! I say, lads! What do you think to this? Eh? Listen to this! That old trench over there refuses to marry me – what do you think to that, eh? Eh?' This removed any shadow of a doubt. Fig's head was extremely gone.

'He's gone, Stick.'

'He's gone, Shed.'

'Gherkin, Gherkin, Gherkin!'

'No need to be so rude, Fig. No one's been rude to you.'

Fig launched to his feet to beg to differ. He pointed out the guilty.

'Oh, yes they have – there! That grotesque old gorgon seated not five yards away from us! She's besmirched my good name – she's scoffed at my honourable intentions!'

'Steady on, Fig! What exactly has she done to offend you?'

'This old halibut refuses to wear my ring – *Oi! Yes! You* know who you are...'

'Fig, sit down and shut it!'

'...insulting my integrity! Well? Speak up, Trenchy! Summat up with me, or summat?' He was speaking to backs.

'Oi! Just sit down and behave, pisspatch! You're upsetting those women!'

The women in question were now adamantly preferring to remain deaf, thus negating the impact of any further derogation, but Fig was equally adamant on being heard. He sidled over to the pair, now focussing his propositions upon the younger of the two.

'Okay! I know when I've been rebuffed – *ooff*! Half nelson! Okay, okay, forget the old skate. What about *you* then, my little hen? Uh? Oh – yeah! I dig it, baby – just playing it cool, uh? Yeah? Well just relax, baby – yeah – 'cos Fig digs cool. *Ohhh*, yeah! Let Fig describe it to you, babe-uh? This is all Fig's dig! Whatyersay? Cool cat? Maybe we can – say – looose this crowd of... squares... and, like, *take off*? And then maybe... spend some time... like... tonight... just you and me... like... setting up a miniature meringue display in the Dales...'

'*Pfff-hahahhh*!' She broke silence for the first time. 'No thanks, mate – I'm busy every night for the next fifty years!'

'Ha ha ha! There you are then, Fig! Now come and sit down, there's a good woodpecker!'

'Oh! Oh! Instant rebuttal! Very boudoir! How very – *ouch*!'

'Ha ha ha!' Sarge had wandered over to collect the nuisance du jour and had set about transporting him back to his seat by the more effective option of applying thumb and forefinger to the ear, which actually prised a laugh from Henny and Halibut.

'Now, siddown!' Once again, Fig's rump was forcibly parked. He immediately went to stand again and was seized by half a dozen hands, to a choral 'siddown'.

'Chair comfy enough for you, Fig? I've got a much comfier one if you want it...'

'Don't mind if I do, sport – ooff! Ricky Star!'

'There it is, through that door with the little bloke on – you can sit there all day and drink for nothing – ha, ha!'

'Oh! Oh! Tallbob the super witty comedian! Anyway, it's obvious what I'm dealing with here... *pair of lesbians*!'

'Shh – oi! Keep it down!'

'Shut it, Fig! I'm serious now!'

Fig half stood again, purporting to a sincere placation of his peers.

'Whoa! Okay! Peace! Peace! Submit – ooooff! Oooff! Take it easy. No problem – *That's right! I said lesbians*!'

'Jeeez!'

'Get him in his chair!'

With this last bawling clearly audible to the entire bar, including the act and one or two evil-eyeing marines, action had to be seen to be taken. I took a large ceramic ashtray from the side shelving, emptied it and returned to sit and rap it against Fig's tabletop. Fig eyed it hypnotically.

'One more chance, Fig. None of us particularly wants to stop one off a pongo, so let me make this absolutely crystal. If you don't park your gob and behave, then I'll be forced to smack some polite into you with this appliance here. Okay, sport?'

'Whoa – hohoho! Easy there, sport! Peace!' He held both hands up, and relaxed back in his chair. The crooner was being applauded from the stage, having now decided to throw in the towel. He marched off to a tumultuous cheer and volley upon volley of beer mats. At the end of the bar, the house tapes were reinstated, and folk recharged glasses and sniffed fingers and – being now able to hear themselves speak – were able to discuss the predicament of the strangely attired drunkard lying belly up and spread-eagled next to the half of a broken ashtray over there.

Having issued a further brief apology to the two victims of Fig's psychological torture, I adjourned to the door with the little bloke on, to entertain perfunctories. Sarge arrived some seconds later to take similar issue at the most proximate pissoir.

'Sorry about that, Sergeant – God told me to do it.'

'Shed, Shed, Shed – in the broader interests of peace, I'm afraid we all have to cosh it into some people sometimes; it's all part of life's great jihad!'

'How are you, anyway?'

'I'm very well and very much looking forward to this evening. So! Same bill as the Mclads, eh? Big night. Will I still have to pay to get in when you're playing Earls Court?'

'I wonder if we'll still be getting skanked when we're playing Earls Court?'

'Who's skanking you?'

'Sarge, we're starting to fill venues, but the deal's always the same. We made Cueball's gaff a fair wad last week – what was our end? One beer apiece and a Chinese on Cueball's wastage account. I presume we were paid a fiver in expenses too, but only the trick cyclist who lifted it can tell you that for sure, and here we sit like grandma's last fucking biscuit and let 'em all do it to us over and over again!'

'So what would make you a happy rabbit?'

'Sarge – this is live rock 'n' roll. Up front effrontery! A change to yer advertised programme. You get five live animals before your very eyes. *There*! Not giving an Olympic toss, like you've never known toss ungiven in your life, and it only costs fifty pence! What's wrong with a quid gate, like everyone else gets? We're worth two! You can't see anyone decent for less than four fifty these days!'

'Maybe you're still no one decent, Shed?'

'Come on, Sarge! You know we put our backs into it!'

Sarge sprinkled his last and zipped, turning to the basins. 'Shed, Shed, Shed, which is better, m'man? Would you prefer two hundred people to come and pay you a penny, or one hundred people to come and pay you twopence?'

I'd been humbled by his finer humility once again. I couldn't answer that question without revealing a foolish or greedy man, as the Sergeant well knew. We exchanged mirrored grins, whilst in the process of scrubbing hands and souls. I sensed a greater profit in listening than in talking, and so indulged him his thoughts, which he voiced against the whirring backdrop of the electric hand dryer.

'Harmony is a rare bird which visits us all too infrequently, Shed. Learn to recognise it. Because it never announces itself.'

Much more than his revelations, you felt compulsion to be in awe of a man able to deliver them so readily across an inexhaustible cornucopia of circumstances and contingencies. Replete with dried digits and a spiritual sprucing up, it behoved us to return to the vale of material sorrows, just the other side of the little bloke.

'You're on board, Sarge, m'man – let's go and check on the Gherkin.'

'Don't worry too much, Shed, just remember the three Rs: Ruffians Require Remedy!'

'Ha ha ha!'

The first vista to greet us on return was that of the Skipper being thrown against the fruit machine by a stockily-built, suntanned and more than capable-looking member of the Queen's Shilling Crew, who then began to brandish a comet-sized fist.

'Gimme one reason not to bust yo in the nose, yer leery bastard!'

Unperturbed, the Skipper returned his saucer-eyed and nerve-rattlingly maniacal ear-to-ear smile.

'*Nernit! Nernit! Nernit* – I've got a Hillman Hunter!'

For a second, the marine's fist sank as he lapsed into the distance-gazing dumbfoundment inevitably induced by attempting to fathom any sense from that statement. One second was all the Skipper required to slide furtherly unchallenged down the fruity piste and crawl off unscathed – still nernitting healthily. The marine swilled from his bottle and muttered something restorative to himself, as he watched on in abject horror and hung back in fear of infection.

Over at the bar, Joe Planet had just arrived, and he and Sticky were mustering the band for a soundcheck down at the venue. Sticky beckoned me over.

'Calling all Chimneys! All Chimneys for a soundcheck – can someone get the Skipper vertical?'

By then I'd developed an ongoing romance with the Pils. It hurt to have to call it off so cruelly. 'Are you absolutely sure about this m'man? Only...'

'Come on, shithead – Joe's got the taxis waiting, so let's get it over with, then we can get back amongst it!'

The Skipper had managed to cross the room without getting his fingers stomped and was clutching at Sticky's jeans in a concerted attempt to escape the carpet.

'Hey Skipper, m'man! Hope we're not inconveniencing your good self! Are you nearly ready? Shed? Swill and go, m'man! We've got a date with fate!'

'And headlines to make!'

'That's the one! Hey, Curly! Three Mclads need a drinking lesson! How are you fixed for a practical?'

Curly's elbow plummeted from his knee, causing his chin to plummet from his fist and crash onto the table. This gauntlet to the chops was more than enough to shake the man from his deep aestivation. He glared in the loose direction of his challenger.

'Whoever said that, just send me. You send me – I'll piss more than you can drink!'

'Okay, rolling?'

'As from go?'

'Go!'

He was the least likeliest to leave, but the Ashmore kid was the first rump to pick a seat in the lead taxi, and the first belly out onto the deck of the concrete concourse which ran from the taxi bay to the Mardi Gras approach. The man Tinker had been awaiting us there for some time in involuntary sobriety, leaning lightly on a lamp post on the corner of the street until a certain fleet of sinners fell by... meerschaum tooting on as ever, for England. He'd already popped inside for a sniff-around. Now we could sign over to him and rely on his deliverance to wherever. Tink immediately delivered our entirety up to the main doors of the Mardi Gras and bade us attend while he rapped at the doors with the bowl of his meerschaum.

'Ooz there?'

Tink waved us back, then cleared his throat. 'Yeah – we're The Chimneys – sort yourselves out!'

'Oh, okay! It's open!'

We all yanked at the bulbously obnoxious Georgian handle. Trouble with the Georgians – they refused to manufacture door handles compatible for nine hands at once. Inside, we flexed biceps and blew out chests and skulked downstairs to the arena; Spartan livers – yawning for new capacities to conquer. With a provable back-up of one gallon plus, we were ready to go. No prisoners. No one ever likely to demean the creed.

'Right! Where are these contenders, then?'

But even before the echo of Curly's bellygrowl could return, the sight to be beheld from the foot of the stairs rapidly transformed the prospect of contention into a bone of contention, and eight boisterous Chu boozers into tailors' dummies. There they sat. The Mclads. The Boddingtons Bitter gurus. The pride and joy of *Viz* magazine. Ottley the bassist, sitting scratching his head, with a bottle of alcohol-free parked alongside. Zebra, sipping a Diet Coke, and the drummer sipping absolutely nothing whatsoever, in fear of a pro-parental despatch from his sister, who'd just unexpectedly turned up. So this was the competition. All I could think of was demanding a rebate for twelve bottles of Pils. The Skipper could only belch. The Croc could but fart. Curly's sole option was to lose his footing and negotiate the remaining five stairs arse first, and then belch and fart. The most conservative of tups permeated from the back of the stunned onlookers' club. Sticky, mindful of his role in setting up the gig, was first to break the ice.

'Zebra! I'm Sticky – we're The Chimneys – hey! Did we jam together once with Holly and the Italians?'

'Everybody asks me if I played for that shit!'

'Well, don't sound so surprised, then! Where do we set up?'

'Where you like – use our kit and backline if it'll save you pratting about unpacking yours.'

'Suits us – cheers! You bringing many down from Cheshire?'

'Not a clue, man! What about yourselves?'

'There'll be the *as per* bunch – we'll get busy.'

If I was about to borrow gear, I preferred the say-so directly from its owner. Having set my bass down behind the stage plan, I strolled over to the yawnful, head-cradling Ottley.

'Ottley! Shedfixman. You sure you don't mind us plugging in?'

'Sound, man – no problem – we've finished our check. Go 'ead wi' yours, if yer like.' He yawned harder as his head sank further towards his lap.

Overlooking for the moment their overtly guile-infested propaganda and current plummet on the FTSE 100 image index, it had to be remarked that the Mclads weren't a bad set of Mclads, who'd endeared themselves instantly with their cordiality and unselfishness. The sole remaining enigma was the relevance of the mystery man, sitting quietly away at the back of the auditorium. So far he'd made nil contribution to the social intercourse; he hadn't even once removed his beak from his copy of the *Observer* financial section, except to flip over pages, each flip briefly revealing a study of resolved concentration behind gold rimless specs, a Breton beret and the seemingly ubiquitous white rainmac. This was beginning to get monotonous. Another potential poofter, plying the A&R sketch? Journalist? Ghost? Maybe the Mclads get faced on onions, and he's an international shallot broker? We milled around onstage, juggling various bits of kit this way and that, exchanging rock 'n' roll anecdotes with the Mclads, and taking odd moments out to burp, stagger or drop something or deliberately incur the insignificant disdain of drumsister. No one had failed to raise at least once an inquiring eyebrow at M Brokeur du Shallotage. When we'd eventually tuned and mustered for the check, Joe – who'd been laying down the woes of now needlessly trawling along his seven-stone Peavey amplifier (not to mention the Skipper's Moog and Hammond) upon Zebra's flapping ear – sidled over to the conference. He gave a sideways tup to M Brokeur.

'Apparently he's with *them*. That's all I can get.'

'Well, that's okay, then. You know you've finally made it in the music game when you get a regular attendance of myopic Frank Spencers.'

Joe had more news. He always chose the moment. 'Oh by the way, tup, that last guy – the A&R man at Cueball's. He was genuine. I checked around.'

The drumborne Sticky shrugged. 'So? We're *allowed* to send record companies packing! We're The Chimneys! If you want to spend a glittering career planting passionate kisses upon some old slag's lily of the valley scented testicles – go and play for the Westwoods or the Red Hot Dolphins or summat!'

The Croc was approaching from the stairs, arms replete in a port and starboard biffer escort. Sticky, having observed Curly's torpor, called the tune to extricate the Croc from this palpable torture.

'Okayreadygood! Just for the charming young man over there, who can't resist staring at the inside of his own eyelids – a little incantation entitled "Let's get ugly"!'

Tap, tap, tap. Joe powered into the three-chord intro of the anthem composed in commemoration of a running battle between seven Chu and the internation of hair-shy flying jackets, pitched in the car park of the Chestnut Tree, Radcliffe-on-Trent. The Croc slipped his guard, commandeered the microphone, dilated pupils, pursed mandible. We punched through 'Let's get ugly' under God's own specifications. We were sharp. Impressive. Self-surprising. All-surprising. Boom. Chop. Sticky.

'Howzat?'

Not unpredictably, Curly's was the first snarl to rise. 'Absolute shite!'

So it was spot on then. I turned towards Sticky.

'Great!'

'Cheers, m'man – that's it then. *Pub*!'

Ottley had taken five for a fag and a listen. He now seemed more than chuffed at the co-billing. 'Yeah, man – that was the dog's knob!'

I was flattered. 'Cheers, Mclad! Now then – about this

piss-up?' The glove was firmly in their court for the sniffing. All the Cheshire eyes turned to Ottley.

'Yeah, great, we've just got a couple o' bits to sort out first, then owzabout we meet you somewhere?'

'Sparklin', Martin! Owzabout the Queen's Hotel – you can't miss it – it's right opposite here?'

'Yeah, if yer like! Sound! Say one hour?'

'One hour! We'll show you around and wine 'n' wine you!'

Curly had been bottling up a more vehement challenge of a less impersonal nature. Sticky fortunately recognised that 'bulges are bursting' look in his eye and spun him away to the staircase with the rest of the tribe of two halves – those who could, departing at a march – those who mistakenly thought they could, departing at a reeling lope, as if concentrating intently on shouldering a shitty rhinoceros.

In the Queen's, the duty barman seemed a little less than delighted at this latest marshalling of the troupe – particularly Curly and the Skipper – but this was heavy trading and seldom seen at early doors. As we all infested his bar space, clamouring feverishly for priority, Sticky banked his head Shedways to impart a succinct whisper.

'What time d'yer say the Dragon'll arrive?'

I'd completely forgotten *that* impending little conflagration, but I hadn't forgotten that this was a Chimney gig, ergo many ears milling around which would relish to happen upon my fascinating little dilemma. I returned whisper. 'Ssh, man! Later.'

The time was 5.45, which gave us around forty-five minutes to get uglier, then at least ninety minutes to entreat the Mclads to a blazing exhibition of synchronised beer removal; the likes of which neither man nor beast could ever have witnessed since time began. Then it would be eight and Dragon time, but I wouldn't give an oyster's hiccup, on account of being in a solar system far, far away. Then an occurrence occurred. A Hammer Horror began to play in my mind; a further whisper was expedient.

'Eh! Ssst! Sticky! Please be good enough to me to say that those two are going directly to the Mardi. Not here. Please.'

'Mardi Gras.'

'Deffo?'

'Absa.'

'Thank God for small ones!' Now a long shot was beginning to unfold in my diseased little mind. The Queen's was surely beneath Helen and Dawn's station – I could rely on that much, if I could rely on m'man. The mission – should I decide to accept it – would be to snatch Selina away from the Queen's and into the club just at the moment before we're about to climb on stage. Then make a large and public fuss of her at the last call – which *she'll* put down to the state I'm in – and Helen'll put down to either professional necessity or Mr Rev-up Pig and 'try to squirm yer way out of this one later, because I refuse to lower myself in order to preserve these social graces of mine'. In short, the famous 'nail yer colours to the mast' approach. Yep. That's the one.

6.50: still no Mclad in sight. Had I misread the modus, or were they pretty late? Sticky usually kept time and the better recall under extreme insensibility, even though he was at that time embroiled in a pitiful battle with Mark Anthony to land a dart as high as the dartboard. He'd just managed to arc one into Curly's full pint, however.

'Oi, Stick! You did say "Queen's Hotel" to the Mclads?'

'Yup. Six thirty!' Curly was typically profound as he displaced three quarters of a pint of bitter to fish out the dart.

'Hah! They've shit out already! Good evening, ladies and gentlemen! We're the McShitouts!'

'Ooowah!'

'They've, tup, probably been held up, tup.'

'They've obviously been fucking held up, tup!'

'I've tol' yer – they've shitted out – hur!'

'Surely not, Curl, they're men with a reputation to uphold.'

'Well, then I suggest they might make a little more effort in upholding it, dear boy!'

Tinker sloppily decoked the meerschaum and rose to his feet. He crossed the room to take a peek outdoors. Outdoors he peeked left. He peeked on. He peeked right. He tapped the meerschaum lightly against the side wall and returned indoors to his beer, and a fresh charge of tobacco.

'Any sign, Tink?'

'Can't see anyone.'

'I'm telling you – their arses have gone!'

'What do you reckon, Skip?'

'Ahaahah! I reckon I've suddenly been taken vay, vay drunk, dear boy!'

Sticky was still prepared to give them the benefit. 'Okay. We give them till seven, yeah? Then just in case they got lost, we try the Crown, the Bentinck, the Fellows, the Narrowboat, then back here. If they're not out there or back here...'

'Shit-out, *big* style!'

Seven o'clock. We trooped into the Crown, discovering not one sausage – save the usual indigenous few cheerfuls who would have marked the Mclads' accents and beaten them to death with shovels, anyway. The decision was made to sup hastily then hoppit before we met with similar or worse. Looking in on the Bentinck, the hoppit card was played by the Parson before the drinks could be ordered. No Mclads. The Fellows showed us their own hoppit card, virtually at the door. Still, no opposition. At the Narrowboat, sensing the continuity of the no-show, the hounds of hoppit began to turn on each other and the stakes were mutually raised to green deaths with a double vodka sidearm. Inevitably after this, those who could still hop, to wit the Skipper, Curly, Tallbob, the Parson and Fig, were invited to enjoy the street in their own time, courtesy of its manager. In fact we all enjoyed that fresh air, veering a path back to the more open hospitality that had been the

Queen's Hotel. Curly was first to wedge his head between the double doors and convey his unmagnanimous tidings to the attendant Sergeant and Mark Anthony, who were themselves now concerned at the lacking of McShitouts.

'Vickry to *us*, I think! Or whaa?' The final flicker of credibility for the opposition had died. Mark stood up.

'So much for the "kings" of beer, snatch 'n' curry!'

'Thassa point! We'll check the curry houses after!'

'They probably – hah! Lemme guess the order! One omelette – powdered eggs, please – and one half of a cold omelette and nothing for me and me sister twice!'

'Ha ha ha. Anything to drink, sir?'

'Nah, chuck. We've aahll had a heavy night, taaah!'

'Ha ha ha ha!'

'Told yer they shat it.'

'Dear boys! We are the bessiss.'

'They're probably detained at this very moment in some fur-lined hotel room quaffing G and Ts with no G, and putting grapefruits up each other's rumps!'

Even Joe was tupless. But the Skipper maintained stroke.

'Time for more beer – we've got twenniminniss!'

Time had been irrelevant for ever. Then the tribal jubilations were sheared in half by an 'Oi!'

'Oi!'

I knew that 'Oi' so well. I slowly cranked the millstone which was my head up onto its bar-propped-elbow-propped shoulders. Selina. Sitting alone by the window, intolerant of anything below immediate regard, impatiently drumming the tabletop, her sharp brown eyes fleeting around from character to character, searching for clues. I shoved off from this erstwhile comfortable mooring space and lumbered clumsily over to her table, armed solely with half a gormless smirk. I delivered an unwelcome ale-fumed peck down to one of the broad blushtone cheeks.

'Hiyer, babe! Drink?'

'You pissed-up bunch of bastards!' Sticky and Mark both caught the remark and simultaneously fixed on its source, only to find their gaze abruptly dispelled by the glare of Medusa.

'Whoops!' Mark chanced his life even further.

'Dragon at eight o'clock... range seven metres!' But fortunately, she was too disgusted with me to hear Mark. I was still hoping for some precious droplet of response meanwhile.

'So's that a drink or not a drink, then?'

'Lager and black!'

'Ever my pleasure.'

I flew to fulfil her fancy, leaving her to shovel copious heapings of hatred around upon various of the tribe who were now drawing in or about her to convey numerous sexual propositions of a largely unconventional nature. Here and there, the staple minimal of 'giz a snog or a date' – Sticky's adamant request being for the idiosyncratic tit wank, whereas the Gherkin plumped for the 'full nelson' followed by a 'crutch hold and slam'. Then 8.20. Showtime at last.

Still mindful of the mast and ready with the colours, I hung back at the table – purposely stalling, allowing the other 'tramps' that crucial head start. Not easy with Tallbob Weedley afoot.

'Come on, lover boy – it's teddy bears' playtime!' Which inevitably called in the Parson.

'Just look at the two of them – billing and cooing like two little lovebirds!'

Mark's head turned back. 'Oi! Bill! Come on, you can bring Coo along too, you know!'

'Ha ha ha!'

'Yeah, yeah, just gimme a sec, you bunch of runners-up!'

Lover boy needed a little time to apply some soft soap – possibly the whole bar. Not too long, though, in case she sniffed the fish from the beginning.

We shortly drained the glasses and stepped outdoors, carefully maintaining the 90-yard deficit on the crew; I wanted them on or about stage first. I took hold of her hand. She scrutinised me for a suspicious moment, then again as we crossed the road. Keep talking...

'You should enjoy tonight – everybody's coming down.'

'Yes. I can see the Biffers are here.'

Oh, not *that* old chestnut. I'd never bunked up with a Biffer myself. Security risk. But I often seriously wondered whether I'd quit messing around altogether, if she'd just resign her bloody post as Minister of Jealousy.

'Did you like The Beatles, Selina?'

'Yeah, why?'

'Because if they'd barred everyone who wanted to shag 'em from their gigs, you would never've heard of the bastards!'

She narrowed her eyes at me as I stood aside to let her go in first. We checked with the door crew and, remaining thoroughly circumspect, I made sure we descended into the dimly lit haze side by side. No sign of danger yet, but it was dark and I couldn't be sure. Maybe I was already clocked. I'd never been more sober from a whole day of razz in my life. The forum was packed solid and buzzing along with the house tapes. Aside of ourselves, the Cheshire temperance trio had obviously pulled well. I made out the greater circle of Chu, and a seemingly more healthy showing of familiar faces – some which had been missing from the flow for years. The Biffers were growing in numbers, it appeared, and there was even a bunch of my old teenage boozing pals who I'd often invited but never expected, which was nice. No shortage of sightseers for my public execution. I exchanged a yell or two – hey! Even a couple of 'Some Chicken' members – Mark Anthony's old punk band – had fallen out of the woodwork. But still, I hadn't clocked Helen or Dawn.

Wacckk!

'Oooyerbastard!' I hadn't seen the Sarge either, biding his moment to ambush me.

'Shed, Shed, Shed.' But the back pain was completely

upstaged by the terror. The band was now onstage and ready to roll; Joe was beckoning me to get up there with them. Okay – if Helen *was* there, she'd be watching me at this very moment, so I grabbed Selina and launched my tongue down her neck for a few seconds. As a bellowing 'Ooowah!' boomed through the speakers, I jumped up there for glory. While Tinker was throwing my bass around me, Joe was already powering into the first chords of 'St Ann's Well Road', and the Croc was strutting about like a peacock. The Skipper pursed his mouth, raised a fist and launched that saucer-eyed stare at the crowd. Sticky cracked twice on the snare like a shotgun and we were off.

The main spot burst onto the stage, and everything out there in front of us just went fucking bonkers. All I could clock at the front were racks of bouncing tits. The middle ground was awash with a legion of jabbing forearms and fists, and away at the back, white T-shirts leapt up and about like exploding popcorn. The Mardi was a neat little venue, designed specifically with live music in mind, and capable of enjoying three hundred guests before the bars caved in. At first it seemed that the 'Aye-aye-aye' of the chorus was the bounce-back from the opposite wall, but as you cocked an ear, it became apparent that we'd got some considerable crowd participation; the Skipper's synth wheel cutting through it like an Inter-City 125. After the usual burnout finish to that number, the roar nearly blasted us back into the amps. The Skipper let off a howl fit for Blade Runner, Joe stuck his chin out at the Croc, I turned to Sticky. We both knew it was that orgasm-topping feeling again. As some footlights went on, we stalked forwards to pick out some victims. Croc surveyed the mob.

Of course, Curly was performing the short-awaited. 'Fucking rubbish – get 'em off! Bring back disco!'

Deafening whistling. I spotted Tallbob's brother, Georgy Pyjamas with Deenbag and Leadbelly. Naturally Tallbob himself had to contribute generously.

'Hey, neighbour! Tell Joe to strum the next one without his boxing gloves on!'

'Ha ha ha!'

I scanned around the girls. Shit. Couldn't spot Selina, but couldn't spot Helen or Dawn either. Maybe the away team had postponed. Or more than maybe Sticky had been wanking my crank all along. Oh no! Crazy Jane and Nellie Hatchscratcher! Who let *that* pair of nutty mares in? They were always in danger of haunting your gig, doing Egyptian gyrations at the front whilst faithfully banging the feminist gong and orchestrating ready refrains of, 'Cocks out for the girls!' That should delight the Dragon highly. Croc got to the mike to hum 'Cwm Rhondda' to accompany their wails. Selina still maintaining silent running. Intense.

'Blimey, crikeydick!' The Skipper had just dispatched another beer to the sub-basement and caught himself in time before toppling backwards offstage.

'Good grracioussh! This place is even licensed for sky-diving! Gosh!'

'Ha ha ha!'

He reacted to the howls by flopping down to the keys and peeling into 'Smoking like a Chimney' with one hand as the other crammed a fag into his mouth, lit it and then found the next bottle. On at least two more occasions during the set, he toppled backwards, taking his Hammond keyboard with him – until the club management, possibly mindful of a hostile claim for idiotic misadventure, decided to cater for his disposition and arrange for the main house gorilla to stand behind him to catch him and throw him back on – Hammond and all – as and when...

To say we stormed the gig would have been to say the bare minimum four words. It was more important to us that we'd finally arrived with a lot of local people, and equally fulfilling was the way Mclad T-shirts were getting behind us down there. Lightweight boozers or not, it was the least we could do to hang around after the set and make a row for them in return. That's the sort of chap a Chimney was, *and* it saved bothering to shift from the bar.

The Cheshire lads came on tight as expected, then a fraction into the first number we all were to discover the importance of being Monsieur Brokeur. The rainmac, beret and specs were all discarded to reveal a Pistols T-shirt, bondage trousers and cropped bleach blond hair. He charged through to climb onstage, turned to face the crowd and then skydived right off, reliant on a human safety net. Repeatedly. So that was it. Brokeur was in fact provocateur! What a religiously dedicated career tosser. We all prayed hard for a sudden large gap in his recipients. This entire bunch could easily be mistaken for a monumental fucking joke if the personalities and their toons hadn't been decent.

I had finally spotted Selina chatting with some of the Chu and so took some drinks over. I frequently punctuated the conversations with tactically tactile body contact or ear whispers; she'd loosened up a couple of iotas by then anyhow. Maybe some of the old days and all that. Main thing was that we were overtly the item. Anyhow, the night was all but done and we'd stomped the Mclads back for an encore which they'd been poised to do anyway. Selina had been chuckling along with some yarn, which one of us had been spinning, when suddenly, one side of her smile levelled off as she focussed over my left shoulder. Somewhat curiously, I glanced round to see what the annoyance might be. Turbo. Sapphires. Helen. Just standing there. Calm. Alone. Staring. I could've thrown her the turd. Even under the 99-decibel backdrop, you could hear a strawberry fart. Fuck, now what? I stared directly back into the angry sapphires; I didn't flinch, didn't blink, didn't breathe, didn't speak, didn't crack face. Helen didn't do identically for a full ten seconds, perhaps more. Then the sapphires locked onto Selina for a second, then back to me. Her lips parted. What? What? What? What? What?

'I thought you were very good.'

'Thanks.'

She turned and disappeared. I never saw her again for six years. I turned back to the circle of Chu and a more than quizzical look from Selina.

'What did she say?'

'She said she thought *we* were very good. What did *you* think?'

She compressed her lips and nodded in consent. 'Yeah, you were quite good, I suppose.'

From nowhere, Sticky was grinning at me. He raised his eyebrows and stuck his tongue in his cheek. I took a diversional sip of beer and crossed my eyes slightly at him. Joe loped over to us all.

'I don't suppose anyone knows anything about the cash we made tonight?' Everyone shrugged shoulders, at which point some clumsy drunken bastard fell headlong into us, then fell over – flat on his face. I turned him over to get a better look.

'Well! If it isn't the world's one, only and best all-smokin', all-drunken, sky-divin', rugtime pe-anna player!'

'Ha ha hah!' The lips pursed, the eyes reeled.

'As... assay, dear boys! Anyone for tiffin up at the Noor Jehan?'

We pulled him up onto his feet, and then again. And then again. How was he to know that this visit to the Indian restaurant that night would mark the dawning of one of the most outrageously swashbuckling eras of his enviably flamboyant lifetime?

ELEVEN

The takers for a ruby – as the Mardi spilled out – included Tinker, the Skipper, Selina, myself and some smug, devious bastard entitled Leggo. Leggo was a lanky, malodorous, sullen-faced reptile, who floated to the surface every harvest moon to examine any harvestables. He was so named in keeping with his omnigratifying penchant for frequently managing somehow to break a leg. Most recently, he'd managed to achieve this by crossing Woodborough Road at a particularly nasty blind bend, during a thought-free episode and getting launched to the tune of fifty yards off the bonnet of a Ford Cortina. Moreover, Leggo was a kind of Robin Hood between the genders. Basically, he'd cheerfully rip off even his closest mates in more ways than a compass could afford; then he'd turn around and lavish fortunes on the rightest old slags – the likes of whom were usually so transparent you could see the jading back-glut of fingerprints on their tits. I'd hated the slug ever since I'd bubbled him once, substituting water for vodka in rounds of vodka and orange with Mark Anthony, just because he knew Mark was faced.

I knew he didn't give a fuck about getting a curry, unless he could skank the bill of course. I also knew he knew that the Skipper's car was parked not half a mile away, and whether the Skipper was ten times over the limit or fifty, he was more than happy to let the Skipper ferry him home to Bridgford if it meant saving three quid on one of the twenty-five taxis available across the road.

So then, even worse, as we set off, we had to constantly wait for the newark to hobble on his crutches at *his* pace all the way to People's College car park to pick up Bert. Bert was the Skipper's navy blue Hillman Hunter – just like any other Hunter, except that it had a plank of five by one instead of a dash, and 'Bert' sprayed hastily in aerosol across the bonnet – which wasn't held on by anything at all.

Having eventually made it there, and having eventually jogged the Skipper's recall as to where he'd left the car, we all jumped in, and Bert nobly, if noisily, jiggered away, up to the Noor Jehan restaurant on Mansfield Road. It was a middle-range, clean, relaxing kind of place – and more importantly, Fig was banned. Inside, we installed at a central table.

When he could eventually get a word in, and having survived the minefield of coats, kitbags, leg casts and walking aids, the waiter scribbled down our order, after some two dozen amendments. I was somewhat relieved to see Selina back on the korma, and rather surprised that no one had picked up on that one. Prior to departing, the waiter read the manifest back to us, if only to establish that we hadn't arrived solely to drive him clean beebar. He paused at Tinker's insertion. Tinker eyed him sideways without overtly appearing to.

'Excuse me, sir; you've only ordered chips. What would you like with your chips?'

'Chips.'

'Yes, what would you like with your chips, sir?'

'Chips. Mind if I smoke?' He freed the trusty meerschaum.

'No, sir. Have a look at the menu.' He held it out to Tinker.

'It's alright, I'll just use this pipe.'

'Ha ha ha!'

'No – yes – no – to choose a meal, sir.'

'I've chosen a meal. Chips.'

'No, sir, you must choose a main dish; chips is a side dish.'

'I only want chips.'

'But chips is only a side...'

'Listen, mate – we can sit here all week arguing over the most suitable shape for sheep shit. If money's been giving you such bad insomnia, I'll tell you what I'll do. Give me a main dish of chips accompanied by a side dish of chips and chips dessert and I'll pay the extra, if that'll cheer you up no end!'

'Ha ha ha ha!'

With this, the duty unfortunate crammed his biro swiftly into the notepad and stormed off to the kitchen, incurring a severe clout to the shin from one of Leggo's poorly stowed crutches en route. In fact, thus far the crutches had been twice as entertaining as their owner, and with Tinker on level par with the Skipper for comedic content on the night, we were obviously set for a rare performance.

I gave Tinker a nudge. 'You daft get, I hope that's exactly what he brings you!'

Tinker relit his pipe and grinned an intoxicated grin.

'I know! Let's liven things up a smidge!' He reached into a pocket of his cross-zip and produced a small bottle of amyl nitrate which he unscrewed, sniffed hard at and offered across to Selina, whose consternation was not unpredictable in the slightest. He withdrew, but then turned to the rest of us and politely asked, 'Poppers, anyone?'

The Skipper wasn't known for turning away any available means of getting daft. He piled in.

'And God bless you, dear boy!' He took a protracted belt then offered it over to me. I sniffed hard with both barrels then passed it deliberately back to Tink, missing Leggo out, just to watch the whinge well up on his face. He'd moan over missing out on complimentary cyanide.

'Oi! Don't I get a go, then?' I didn't mind answering that one at all.

'No – fuck off!' There was a silent pause. Then the buzz hit us.

'Chips and chips – haaahahaha!'
'Hooohahaha!'
'Aahoohoohoo – oh, no! Hoohooo!'
'If he – no – if he – just imagine – chips and *haahaaa-haha*!'
Selina shook her head in corporate disownership as she glanced around to observe the synthesised hysterics. Leggo managed to seize the bottle after all and soon became part of the hooing, haaing and rolling around. After two or three minutes of rib-ache, we managed to get a grip on composure and then sit in silence, refusing to catch one another's eye for fear of a severe relapse.
'Ahum – um!'
'Ahem!'
'Wuh! Woo! That's better.'
'Anyone for anymore?'
'What? Beer?'
'No, poppers.'
'Haaha – whoa! Steady!'
'Oh, I don't know...'
The neighbouring diners were by this time busily erecting imaginary breezeblocks around themselves. Selina took a rare cigarette from her handbag to help her through all this until the food arrived. By then the little bottle had completed its second circuit. The manager had posted a second waiter to evaluate the precise nature of whatever Tinker was taking on board the meerschaum. He perched at the end of the bar and leered on, completely overlooking the significance of the little bottle.
'Ahem!'
'Hoom!'
'Um-ahum!' No one now dared to face anyone else whatsoever.
'Sheesh!'
'Fyooo!'

'I'm going to ask that waiter there to fetch some baahehehh – hiheeehee! Jus, jus, jus look at his, jis, jis lookariz face – *aaaahahaaaa*!'

The perched one raised his head slightly, as if ready to facilitate a request I was about to make, but I waved him away.

'No, no, no, s'alright, mate. I wasn't gonna ask for any chips – *aaahooo*!'

'*Hooohahaha*!'

'No, no stop – stobbit – AAHAHAH!'

'Hic! Hic! I'm, I'm, hic dying – hic!'

'Tassalright, I'll use this pipe – *aahoohooo*!'

'Woh! Woh! *Wohooweeheehee*!'

'Hic! *Hic*! Hurp!'

'Hoo! Woo! Enough! Sensible. Sensible, now!'

'I'm calm. I'm calm. I'm calm, no I'm not – *aahahaaa*!'

''Ere, mate! Can we cancel the chips? *Hoooohahahaa*!'

'Heehee! *Hic*-hee!'

'No! Whoa! No more! No more!'

'*Oooh – hoohahaah*!'

At this point, Tinker had begun to wander around to offer a sniff to the neighbours, and in doing so encountered a barricade of revulsion. On his way back, he paused briefly to squat alongside one of his more vociferous female repellents.

'Well then! Do you mind if I do?' He crammed the bottle hard against his left nostril and sniffed furiously. The young woman blinkered a palm against her temple.

'*Hooohooo*!'

'*Weeeeeeehahahaa*!'

'Hic – help – *hic* – help!'

The table waiter was soon back with the undoubtedly expedited meals and was hastily wiping round the dinner plates and attempting to set them down in front of the reeling bodies with little help from the bodies. As the culinary odours supplanted that of the chemical aperitif, we gradually settled down to allow the poor bugger to hand some curry out, which he did with commendable tolerance. Each plate was apportioned its mound of aromatic rice by way of his dexterous double-spooning, except Tinker's, which was already a tuberous Mount Fuji. All that remained was for us to uncover the small silver side dishes and appraise the state of the steamy concoctions within. Four clouds went up simultaneously, as we commenced peeking and poking. True to the Noor's average-plus expectancy, the main dishes all passed the hooligan test. Then Leggo, perhaps not untypically, was first to spot and draw our attention to an unclaimed delivery – a yet to be uncovered silver boat.

'Hic! Whose is that one?' Curious heads panned around the table.

'Which? What?'

'There – hic – between Tink and Shed.' Both Tinker and I peered over table-berthed elbows at the mystery dish.

'Not mine.'

'Not mine – I've got all my kit.'

'What is it? Anyone short of owt?' Whatever it was and whether it was unclaimed, unwanted or unnecessary, Leggo was going to be the last bastard getting hold of it. For some reason, I instantly conjured up an image of a great white shark – just perusing – just happening by: ''Scuse me, anyone using this old lady on the rubber raft?'

'Selina? Anything to do with you?'

'No.'

I nudged my nose at Tink and half-opened my mouth to speak over a rice-loaded tongue. 'Have a chike, Tink – see what it is.'

Tinker delicately prised open the silver mantle of the boat, then rolling his eyes to the heavens, he flipped it over onto the tablecloth and coolly pressed on into Fuji as the rest of us were again laid to waste.

'No! I don't 'kin believe it, ha ha hahaaa!'

'Ahee – hehee!'

'Wooohahahahaha! It is! It's fucking chips 'n' chips – *hahahaa!'*

It was a fact. Tinker had been taken perfectly seriously, and there to the letter, sat a side order of chips to complement the chips. More chips had never been witnessed in one room on one day in your life. It was becoming surreal. To amply appreciate the sheer stupidity, the little bottle performed a mid-course circuit. As it returned to its owner's pocket, the front door opened and in swished an immaculately groomed middle-aged couple, palpably dressed to the operatics. He in black double-breasted, bow tie, razor-sharply pressed charcoal trousers. She in flowing crinoline ball gown – tucks and tresses, matching long cream gauntlets and court shoes. We all paused as their majesties swept across to be allotted their sedentures. We watched them. Tinker watched them. We watched Tinker watching them. Surely not. Would he? We partially veiled our faces with either hands or serviettes as Tinker left his seat, bottle at the ready and made his discreet approach upon the two terpsichorean patrons.

'Excuse me? Poppers, mate?'

The beau turned. He evidently required a few seconds to rationally process the sit rep. He glared intently at the bottle. He glared intently at Tinker – up, down, all over. Then his glare returned to the bottle.

'Oh! Thank you very much!' he said, snatching the little bottle from Tinker's presenting hand. Then he regally crammed it into his Rembrandtine nose – little finger cocked – and snorted for Merrie England.

'*Nffff!* Look, darling! Poppers!'

His belle had been handing her wrap to the reception waiter. As she turned and clocked the little bottle, her reaction could scarcely have been more fluently or imaginatively choreographed.

'Oh! Cheers!' She seized and loaded the bottle and

hooted away on it with a gusto which far exceeded that of her spouse, before the waiter returned to chaperone them, spluttering, giggling and whistling to their berth for the evening.

Back over at hooligan's island, the remnant crockery was jittering back and forth as we pummelled away at the table, fighting for breath.

'Hoooooowaahoooo!'

'Wha–wha–whass–whass 'appenin'?'

'Noo, noo – pull this planet over – I need a piss!'

'Oh shit! What a fuckin' sitcom! Terry and June nip out for a score! *Ha ha haaa!'*

Against the odds, and despite crippling rib injuries from the excruciating jollity, we managed to polish off the food, and after four abandoned attempts, managed to secure eye contact with the waiter for long enough to ask to settle the bill. Then, for the Dragon and me, his serene holiness the mattress was a mere fifteen-minute walk and talk away. For Tink, a short taxi haul to his folk's place in Gedling. For the Skipper and Leggo, it was to be eight hours through the fire, the pit, the pendulum and the shitscape, and first left at the morning.

After the cursory scan for evidence of the enemy, Bert and his dubious pair of occupants edged out of the back street behind the Noor, then vroomed off onto the main lanes of city night traffic. They skimmed on past the sparse scatterings of club leavers; snoggers, shirt-pullers and the ubiquitous fellowship of the mystery kebab stain society – still enjoying the recall end of the process. Now leaving town for London Road and the Bridge, Bert shared the next mile peacefully with no other traffic whatsoever. No pedestrians. Gentle shissh of warm air through the vents. Confidently competent shoosh from the radials outside. Even Trent Bridge looked bare.

Leggo called to mind certain previous exploits of a mutual acquaintance – the demon drummer, Jamso.

'Wonder if Jamso's done another jump lately?'

The Skipper eyed the passing parapets of the bridge.

'He must be due for another Trenting; it's been over a year. Must be a bit of a to-do though, when you change your mind halfway down.'

'Ha, ha! Even worse when some kid has to fish you out with a tiddler rod!'

'Ha, ha – fuck! What's that?' For one horror-drenched moment, the Skipper's roll-up clung to the lower lip of his widely agape mouth. His stare frosted over.

'What? Where?'

The Skipper nodded toward the end of the bridge. 'There! Down on the ramp! Filth!'

Leggo weighed up the police car. 'It's only patrol filth! Ignore them – your driving's cock-on, your lights are all tickety-boo, aren't they?'

The Skipper sturdily pursed his lips and Leggo felt Bert hit the burner.

'Whaa–what you doin'? Do you wanna get home in one piece tonight, or what? This is *not* the time for paranoia! Skip? Skip?'

'Bastaaads! I'll make you run, yer bastiz!'

'*Skip*!'

'Don't you worry, dear boy – they're filth! They won't catch Bert! We're on our way home. On ar wayyomah! On ar wayyomah!'

Leggo's snug, homely visions were threatening to melt all around him. His fists tightened around the metal shafts of his crutches.

'But you haven't done anything out of...'

Wooo.

'...too fucking late! Get your foot down sharpish – wha – I don't – why? They weren't gonna pull us! You were home clear, you fucking lunatic!'

'Filth – aaah! Hate 'm, hate 'm, hate 'm!'

'Well that's it, then. You hate the filth and now they hate you – come on! Give the loud pedal a bit more attention!'

'On arr wayyyyomah! On arr wayyyomah!'

Woooo.

'Okay, lemme think. Do Musters – left into Millicent – right into William, hand-brake right at the top!'

'Yeah, it's bound to be tightly parked around Epperstone – let's see if we can get 'em trashed – haa!'

The game was on, the mouse running and the cat without a doubt. Leggo, legs, crutches and all were bounced all around Bert's insides as he deftly abandoned Musters Road for the shallows with equally determined woo-woo clinging keenly to his tail. The initial gambit was banking largely on the premise that the cost of a police patrol vehicle – or extensive damage to same – could run into thousands if the driver slipped up at pursuit speed; whereas Bert was flatteringly overvalued at around twenty-seven pounds fifty pence, including batteries and a full tank. In or out of trouble; considering insurance, scrap value and road tax refund, Bert was handsomely attractive to a visit of matches and paraffin in any commonsense manual, anyway. Another fact in favour was that the Skipper had previously resided on William Road – until the petition gathered momentum – and as a consequence, wasn't unused to returning home after lavish and regular soirées, piloting Bert along it at sixty plus with one inch grace either side. The burning question was now how good the patrol driver was – and how much, if any, damage was he prepared to stand on the rug for?

As Bert handbrake-turned right, slightly clipping a Citroen at the end of Epperstone to Patrick Road, the answer to the first part of the question precluded the second part of the question entirely.

'Where is he now, Leggo?'

'Can't you feel it? He's choc bang up your arsehole! He's even had the manners to switch his siren off through a residential. He's your worst nightmare. A gentleman pig.'

'Bastahd! Right we are, then! Some more rare snippets of cunning, dear boy – that's what we need just now... let me see. We need to buy some road space between us – outrun him a bit.'

'Boot it. Right through George – straight over Musters – don't stop; he might bottle it or hit something – ha, ha! If we don't hit it first. End of George, turn left – we'll double back and lie low. I know a good road through onto Loughborough, then we clog it again and get home from the far side of Bridgford.'

'Rink tinky tinky!'

Bert boomed across the Musters Road intersection without incurring the more than foreseeable side-smack and ploughed on into the second half of George Road. The police patrol, tainted by the confines of safety protocol, tapped at the brakes. It was enough to allow Bert to pinch a precious seventy yards. At the end of George Road they swung left, killed the lights and weaved off the road behind a maisonette block, waiting for the blue flickers and the rage of the patrol car engine. If they were spotted now, they were trapped – only one way out of the yard. The patrol seemed to be slow in showing.

'Where is the bastard?' Leggo wound down his sidescreen.

'Switch the engine off, so's I can get a listen – he might be doing similar.'

The Skipper tweaked at the cluster of dash keys and Bert juddered into a resigned silence. Now the only noise in the pitch black yard came from the softly diminishing click-clacks of Bert's contracting engine metal. The Skipper lowered his sidescreen.

'Where is the b—'

'Shushh! Here he comes now!'

There was no surging motor, just a slow, casual, methodical humming. The blue light floated slowly across from the right, licking into successive gaps between buildings and out buildings, until it inevitably found and painted the walled entrance to the yard. There was a frozen moment of nerve-jangling expectancy. An invisible clash of wills. Then a gentler hum of acceleration, and the blue peril slipped steadily down the wall and petered away into nothingness, reconsigning the yard to its blackness. For a full ten minutes they sat. Listening. Straining eyes. Now deliberating the likelihood of a foot patrol.

'Do you suppose?'

'Sssh! No – it's okay! Just give it another minute!'

'You don't suppose he's sitting out there?'

'Not a chance, dear boy! He's off chasing shadows in some other neighbourhood. We'll boot it up Loughborough and crash over at my folks' place for tonight. It's safer than getting back onto Musters and I don't fancy crossing the bridge again. I'll just take a quick coastal, before we poke it back onto the road.'

The Skipper creaked open his door, slithered to his feet and skulked off into the blackness, trying his best not to scuff the pebbled driveway too loudly as he stooped and tiptoed for a clearer view of the street without consigning any movements to his predator's eye. With his shoulder blades dusting against the side wall, he edged stealthily along the driveway under its cloak of shadows to within inches of the street, before hazarding an all or nothing committal glance around the gatepost. Apart from the two opposing files of regimentally aligned saloon cars, nothing but a sleepless blackbird whistling for some company. They were in the clear. He turned back into the driveway and scrunched his way back towards Bert, pausing to relight his fag and then illuminate his passage with the lighter. A troubled Leggo bent a fat neck out of the window.

'Hsst! What's goin' on?'

'We've cracked it, dear boy! They're elsewhere – let's bugger off!'

A gentle turn of the key, a measured couple of pumps on the juice, and Bert was rumbling slowly and rockily back to the edge of the drive and poking his purple-lacquered snout once more out into the badlands of Bridgford. Off at a steady roll, they employed Leggo's extensive local knowledge to carefully wend and weave an elaborate course through to the vital extrication route of Loughborough Road. From there they could be three miles away in as many minutes, condemning the hunt to bitter frustration. It was broad enough for speed; at that time of the morning, it was quiet. It was theirs to exploit.

'Okay. Nothing out here. Stick the sidelights on and keep it to thirty-one for the time being, eh?'

'We're okay. I'd better garage it when we get back, just in case they're ambitious.'

The partly illuminated Bert swung out onto Loughborough Road, making off into its sweeping meanders at a modest vitesse and quietly aglow with a sapient cocksuredness. A well-earned stabling beckoned only a couple of minutes away now. His occupants could sink into their seats and relax. The trouble was a mile gone. Then two miles gone.

'Chuck some sounds on, dear boy – feel free – there should be some tapes in the glove... *Bastard*!'

'What?'

'Over your shoulder!'

Again, Leggo flexed his fat neck and managed to park both chins halfway along his right shoulder. The tape he'd fished out to play was slammed hastily back into the glove compartment, which was itself then slammed angrily shut, in favour of the verbal response: 'Bollocks!'

Unseen behind the sweep of the bend, two patrol cars had suddenly made ground and loomed quietly up on them out of nowhere.

'Absolutely first-class bloke! So! You know a good fucking road, do you?'

'You're the newark who got us in this shit!'

'Pointless arguing. Brace yourself – we're going on the woo!'

The leading patrol began to flicker handlamps and urge Bert to heave to. The Skipper gave the loud pedal a gentle squeeze.

'Bollocks, filth!'

Wooo.

'Right – we're off!'

With the loud pedal down to the floor, a growling Bert broke off to the shallows once again, this time with two woo-woos glued to the boot. The Skipper cast a brief, downward glance at the plank and its instrumentation.

'Bastard! I forgot!'

'Forgot what?'

'Forgot juice – Bert's been sniffing fumes for the last couple of miles!'

'Oh, fucking marvo! You certainly pick the finest times to say all the right things... Are you sure? Are you sure that these gauges work?'

'Of course they work!'

'Well, we can try and run for the top of Musters. Then, if it packs up, at least we can try and outroll them down to Trent Bridge, then do a Jamso off the side.'

'Ha ha ha! *Now* you're thinking, dear boy! They'd fish us out as sober as the judge we're about to be grinning at!'

Again, Bert lurched onto Musters Road, booming southwards and upwards of its long, steady gradient. The two flailing patrols were now joined by the originally aggrieved woo-woo and the whole wooing trinity wailed along in Bert's wake, up to the pinnacle of Musters Hill. Leggo, if nothing else, remained inspired when faced with the dank likelihood of having to exchange Axminster for concrete.

'Handbrake spin behind the summit then boot it hard back downhill – that'll buy some yards – Go!'

Bert transgressed the apex of the hill and whilst momentarily out of his pursuers' sights, crossed lanes to safely exact the rubber-squealing, chassis-juddering handbrake spin. The Skipper dropped into first and booted hard and Bert bounded off again, back over the crest and into the downward plummet. The Skipper leaned out of the window to screech abuse at the enemy, who were still erroneously engaged in the uphill leg of the competition and consequently now passing in the opposite direction – all the way to piling into each other over the crest.

'Hahaa! Feeelth! Where are you going?'

'Oi! Look – if we can leave them down here and do a right-left at the bottom, we can sneak through Fox Road behind the cricket ground and onto Radcliffe to the all night-garage.'

'That's *another* good road is it? How many more of them have you got waiting for us down *there*?'

'It's up to you, fartbreath – it's the only petrol you'll get in Bridgford tonight, or we can get captured and face the... Now what are you fucking doing?'

The Skipper was suddenly braking hard. He rammed the wheel over to the left, pulling Bert into a standstill at the kerbside. Now they were sitting ducks, helpless. The Skipper sat back with folded arms, leaving the engine to idle over. Leggo was now convinced that he was only having a terrible nightmare and would wake up when the cuffs clicked.

'Are you actually fucking *real*? What in God's... we were just beginning to... that's it – that's it – he's bonkers! He's stark, staring, bastard crackers – we're in jail, we're going to jail...'

'Shush, dear boy – bear with me a sec! Let me just have a little chat with them – see if we can smooth things over a bit!'

'Chi-chat? Chat? Oh, good! And what do you suppose they'll be wanting to chat about eh? The European Cup? The Bee Gees' new album? This is a high-speed chase – you don't get a fucking lunch hour!'

'Tsshushh! Here he comes!'

Bert's new-found propriety had taken the law somewhat aback; they'd now suddenly been forced to slam to a halt again in a processional zig-zag to the rear of the stationary Hillman. The first man out of the lead car was a police inspector. Behind, his troops were jumping out and running about all over the postcode, before he signalled things down a touch, having decided that the entire circus was safe in his capable hands. He waved everyone back a couple of yards, donned cap and gloves, picked out his silver-tipped cane and calmly and austerely approached Bert's driver side. Leggo swallowed audibly. The Skipper bared his teeth in a gorgonzola smile which ended at his ears.

'Good evening, Constrictor! Whaaseems to be the prollem?'

'We're locked up, we're ff—'

'Tssst-shh! I think he likes us!'

The constrictor bowed his head to examine Bert's cargo. 'Is this your car, son?'

'Carson? I've got a carpet! That's mine... well, half of it is! I called the wedding off, you know!'

The inspector raised an eyebrow momentarily, then reassumed his more officious disposition.

'Have we had a drink tonight, then?'

'Wassat? A drink? Oh! Cheers! That's bloody well decent of you, dear boy – I'll have a Pils – get one for yourself while you're there!'

'Okay, son. I think in that case, I'd better have these car keys, don't you?' He reached in towards the side of the steering column to switch off Bert. This uninvited invasion was an automatic prompting for the Skipper's detonation. The lips pursed again. The eyeballs popped, he fidgeted, frenetically.

'Not fucking likely, Filth!'

He slammed Bert back into first, stamping on the revs, jiggling at the wheel. *Boom*! Bert was away again – this time with an inspector of the Nottinghamshire Constabulary trailing alongside the driver door, having snagged a glove on the inside handle in the sudden excitement. His other hand was still gripping onto the cane, which scraped after him for a few seconds throwing a ray of sparks along the road before shooting from his grasp and snapping instantly under the rear wheel. Leggo was now becoming anally unreliable in the horror.

'Oh my God! Oh my God! He's killing a copper! He's doing murder!'

'Aaah! Stop this car – you're under arrest! *Aaah*! Stop! Immediately – *aaah*! Come on, son, let's be sensible, now!'

Flickering only as he slammed in the gears, the Skipper's saucer eyes fixed him full in the face through draught-pounded blond hair.

'Sussussensible? Did you say sussensible?'

'Come on, son – you're in enough trouble...'

'I think *you're* the one in trouble, Filth! Serves you jolly well right, too!'

The inspector's composure went completely and his aplomb regressed into a raucous bawl.

'Fer Gaad's sake *staaap* this *caaar*!'

'That – was – not – polite, Filth! Very well! If *that's* how you speak down to taxpayers who provide your wages, I don't wish to have anything more to *do* with you!'

The Skipper nudged the brakes, dropped Bert down to third and booted the loud pedal hard. The inspector's hand was instantly wrenched from the glove, affording him one last brief mortified glare at the Skipper's maniacal countenance before he himself parted company with Bert at some forty miles per hour to roll spectacularly off the road and into the elevated flower beds of a senior citizens' rest home. Meanwhile, his dispatcher casually picked the remnant glove from the door with forefinger and thumb, extending it over to his ghastly white navigator.

'Wanna glove? We can go back for the other one if you like? I know roughly where it'll be!'

Leggo's paralysis only permitted him to mutter, through his clenched teeth, 'Jusk keek griving – crazy gastard-uckin-anker!'

'That's a "no" then, is it?' He lobbed the glove out into the night, before casting the briefest of glances up at the mirror.

'Relax, dear boy, they're stopping to help him up – you really are making an awful fuss over this!'

Leggo's eyebrows twitched as he moaned pitifully, 'Jusk-uckin-grive!'

The Skipper floored it down to the end of Musters, upholding a commanding advantage on the nearest of the two patrol cars now pressing on to continue pursuit. At the junction, Bert hammered hard round to the right, then slipped unseen into the next left turn of Fox Road. Halfway along Fox Road, and Bert was in trouble. He began to falter and fizzle and flicker and fade. The Skipper thrashed the wheel left and right in a last ditch attempt to shake the last dregs through the lines.

'Shit! Shit! Come on, Bertie! You can do it! Only a few yards to go, now! Come on, ol' Matey!' But within a few yards of Radcliffe Road, Bert coughed up his last and stalled altogether. To conserve momentum, the Skipper jumped out to provide some running auxiliary horsepower. From the junction, he steered a direct diagonal course for the all-night garage, ignoring protestations from a couple of taxis which were compelled to either swerve suddenly or halt for the show. With a final, resounding *oomph*, accompanied by the rasping scrape of the driver door across the low brickwork enclosure, Bert was hoisted up onto the forecourt and dragged to a halt, abreast of the first available nozzle. The Skipper ducked inside the cockpit to crank on the handbrake. He feigned a frown at his mentally spent and physically inert navigator.

'Come on, Leggo! Make yourself useful for once – take the

pump and stick a fiver's worth in while I go and pay. I'll get us some milk and biscuits!'

Employing a partially successful combination grip on roof and door rim to support his elbows, Leggo prised his trunk steadily out of Bert – almost to his feet, until his right elbow slid off the roof, causing him to swing outwards on the door with shirt and jacket pulled up to his shoulders and his jeans dragged halfway down his arse.

'Bastard! Ooyerbastard! Me leg, me leg, me bastard leg!'

Gradually, inch by inch, he managed to bellyflop his way round Bert's hot bonnet and swipe hold of the fuel gun. Another flop onto his side enabled him to shuffle the length of the car and propel himself with a painful flurry of hops to the fuel cap. Without ever properly attaining full upright status, he flipped the cap open and clumsily clattered in the gun. The gun, now being firmly in place, doubled as an aid for his efforts toward buoyancy. Meanwhile, the Skipper slid a fiver under the glass, then noticing that there was an offer on for the 'Old Horrible', he checked his tobacco pouch and decided upon a refill.

'Skip?' The Skipper was busy uncrinkling what he loosely suspected to be another fiver from his trouser pocket.

'Yeah – just getting some baccy, dear boy! Any particular biccies you fancy?'

'I think you'd better look at this first.'

'Yes! Two milk, please and some choccy biccies... what's up?'

He broke off from his sales hatch conference to turn and address Leggo's perplexity and was instantly frozen in his tracks by the eyeful which had awaited him. From left to right of the picture: patrol filth; traffic filth, beat filth, German shepherd filth, troopships – and, from the very midst of the largest mass of flashing blue lights ever assembled in Bridgford, stepped a ruffled, unsteady and slightly shell-shocked-looking individual, wearing one glove and holding no cane.

'First, I'll have them keys, you little bastards – SHARPISH!'

The Skipper looked him squarely in the eye over the twenty yards of forecourt between them. He unzipped a pocket to first stow his tobacco whilst considering the position.

'Keys *now*! And we'll make it easier!'

'Yeah, and my other car's a fucking Bentley!' Still fixing on the trembling constrictor, he murmured from the side of his stiff upper lip to the pasty, white-faced navigator at the pumps.

'Leggo, dear boy?'

'Yuh? Any particularly good ideas left, at all?'

'I got you into this. When I give the word, run for it, would you? And good luck, dear boy!' Leggo's face cracked into a museful smile.

'Lovely night's work! Reckless driving, dangerous driving, drunk driving. Criminal damage, failing to stop, assault and battery of a police officer. Attempted murder of a police officer, breach of the peace, being reckless as to whether life was endangered, two dozen moving offences and now resisting arrest, eh? Well, why not? Let's try for a full house, and I say to myself, what a wonderful fucking world!'

He staggered briefly against Bert's nearside as the pump gun suddenly kicked back. He glanced down at the overbrimming froth of spilt fuel. He peered up at the meter, which now read thirty-two pounds eighty-five pence. He turned back to the Skipper.

'And now theft. Ha ha ha ha haaa! We nearly forgot theft!'

'Now! Run! *Aaaaaagh*!'

Screaming like a dyspeptic banshee, the Skipper catapulted himself across the forecourt, over its enclosure and headlong into the largest concentration of the law – flailing, milling, kicking, thrashing, yelling, knocking off helmets until he was finally engulfed in a flood tide of navy blue and Day-Glo yellow. Leggo hopped furiously, if falteringly across the forecourt, disappearing into a dormant car wash, only to emerge from the other end to a hearty round of applause from three hysterical lawmen – one of whom was doubled over, mopping tears from his cheeks. Another scream of laughter went up as Leggo's footing failed altogether, plunging him backwards into the giant brushes; yet another as the low, ghoulish murmur of 'Bastards' echoed around inside the chamber. The Chimney gig was now officially over for the night.

TWELVE

The realisation of morning shovelled us all onto Sunday like debris off the dump truck. Having collectively steamed up the windows of his bedroom, last night's Biffers hopped out of the Croc's pit awash with giggles and mischief and tiptoed across to press their collective mammary arsenal against the condensation thereon; a sudden shiver infusing them both as they stooped to peek out into the street through the circular, water-blurred patches provided by their live art. Croc hoisted a pained expression from out of the pillow and partially arose to ponder awhile. He pondered his wristwatch; pondered the two fidgety rumps presenting themselves by the window; pondered the mists of yestereve, then with an agonised sigh, slammed his head back into the pillow in order to ponder more fully how it came to ache so badly.

Up in Forest Fields, the bells of morning worship exuded their shrill salutation from the church of St Mary all the way to the wax-logged ears of Joe and Sticky as they busily administered Holy Communion to their respective dragons on either side of the partition wall, upstairs at 45, Russell Road. Sticky was happily supplying two strokes between dings; whereas Joe being content with just the one per dong for the moment. Back in Woodborough Road, meanwhile, Selina was sleepily reeling off the umpteenth amendment to the list of drinks which she'd been forced to accept from my pissed-up bunch of tramps as a preamble to her excuse for being spiritually absent from the coitus. I never did understand why people took on the morning grump – I always woke up feeling great: the shittier my head, the more cheerful I felt.

I left her lying there making scant sense and strolled into

the kitchen to knock up one of my specials – bacon and blue cheese omelette with a touch of basil and a sprinkle of sage and onion stuffing mix. One cup of coffee with three heaped spoonfuls of instant. Having taken eight or nine minutes to prepare, it all hit the sub-basement in seventy-five seconds flat. I left a coffee to get cold beside her and trooped off to the car to get a couple of hours' work in. I always enjoyed that half-day of work on Sunday, because whatever I took was mine. Not for bills, not for banks, not for the Treasury, not for the domestic upkeep: just for me, for to go out with on Sunday night and blow on getting stupid with the Chu.

Drawing open the garage door, I pranged it as loudly as possible, just in case Tallbob or the Sergeant were still asleep. I rolled it out of the garage to check all systems and click on to listen to the state of play at the Sunday morning cab club, whilst picking half the solar system out of my painfully encrusted hooter, and in so determining that poppers were a bloody waste of space – talking of which, I was in such a dazzler of a mood, I was even going to try to get on with Poley.

'Thirty-nine, coming on!' I gave the mike a couple of impatient clicks. Being far from Poley's favourite individual as I was, there would be the normal lengthy ignorance to endure in order that he piss me off a little before the grudging acknowledgement was moaned back at me; yet today Poley seemed uncharacteristically tail-up.

'Thirty-nine! Just the man!' In fact, he sounded a little too jovial for my liking. I whiffed a fish here.

'Thirty-nine! On Thursday evening, you carried a gentleman from Clifton to Sherwood – right?'

'Absa!' The arseholes were always easy to remember.

'He said you charged him nine pounds! How d'yer make that out, Dad?'

'I make that out because he kept me waiting for twenty-five minutes, Dad!'

'Well, there was no mention of that, Dad!'

'That's alright – I've just mentioned it, Dad! Plus, he told me to add a pound on for keeping me.'

'But that's part of your waiting time.'

'I did *exactly* what he told me.' Nope. I wasn't going to try anymore.

'I still don't see how you arrive at nine pounds!'

'You don't see a lot of things, Poley. You want to get on the other side of that door behind you more often. There's a world out here.'

'Before we get into straying from the issue here, Thirty-nine, this is a regular account customer you've mithered here. Tell me – what's the first rule of cabbing?'

Condescension, I decided, would not be welcome this weekend. It would have to be met at the door.

'Never pick your nose whilst driving over a speed hump!' I could hear the office staff howling in the background as he piped back.

'Now you're annoying *me*, Thirty-nine. That's not a very sensible thing to do, *is* it, Dad?'

'Poley, Dad, I've done a lot of not very sensible things in my time, but I've yet to go out for a shag and come home with half a mortgage, four step-kids and a sackful, Dad.'

Another faint howl. 'Right, if you're going to be personal...'

'Poley... tell me, Dad, have you actually got some *work* there to give out to this fleet?'

'I've got plenty of jobs here, Thirty-nine – not that any of 'em'll be of much interest to you, because I'm throwing you out of the line-up until you've reported to the gaffer tomorrow!'

'I'm struggling to suppress my indifference!'

'You what?' Dense bastard. I should have known better than to use words wider than his earholes. Being a staunch protagonist of the old adage pertaining to a job worth doing, I decided at this point to *really* get into some shit.

'Okay, how does "I don't give a *fuck*" sound?'

'You *what?*' Swearing was bad taboo in taxiland.

'You what? You what? You deaf? I said I don't give a fuck! Or a nuts or a jot or a fucking septic centipede's chuff cloud, because it's Sunday; I've just had sex; last night was brilliant – tonight could be better – *and* in order to fund it, I can make all the money I need by flying off with your hotel jobs.'

'I'll tell the gaffer *all* of this, Thirty-nine; you're in big…'

'Your fleet's waiting for some work, Poley. So if you've got some, why don't you stick to the first rule of radio-operating and just give the bastard out, you whinnying slaphead! You sound just like my missus on day twenty-two!'

That was the borderline between storming the office to shove the microphone up his nose, or putting him out of mind to get on with the day. I flicked the radio off and booted it down to the Royal Hotel to make some lager money at his spleen's expense – smile intact and none the glummer, chum.

Due to both his pursuant fortuity and the adeptness of his brief, or perhaps more largely due to it being Sunday morning and the simple fact that no one could enjoy a second's peace knowing he was around, the Skipper managed to claw himself some bail shortly after 9.30 a.m., having spent the entire night bickering over every single detail of the charges and gradually whittling his captors down to pasty, baggy-eyed nerve cases who were now clamouring bee-fashion around the drinks machine for caffeine and self-reassurance.

Twenty-five minutes later and still seething, he was leaping out of a taxi, leaving its driver to close the door. With zero ado, he marched grimly up to the front door of the Maples Street dwelling and booted it wide open. Thus it could cheerfully remain, for the rest of the world to walk in and out as they might please. He stamped into the living room and ensconced into an armchair to roll a fat fag and brood with a freshly acquired four-pack of ridiculously strong lager. From their perched positions at either side of the hearth, his two eighteen-inch sandstone eagles frowned back at him as he contemplated. Leggo had struck a bargain at aiding and abetting, and would've been long tucked up. Nope. They were only interested in the one trophy.

'Bastard filth!' He perused and pursed at the blue bail sheet – at the innumerable transgressions – at the impending date with fate. He turned it over, licked the reverse and slapped it onto the chimney breast.

'Huh! In a vehicle deemed to be unroadworthy! Bollocks! Ignore them, Bertie – they're only the filth. We'll just have a smoke, then a drinkypoo, then get some shut-eye. Then it'll soon be playtime again – *Hah*!'

He blasted away two of the four, then before long was catching himself burning his fingers in a hapless slumber, with number three teetering over the chair arm.

'Whur? Shi? Owuch! Bedtime, methinks!' He murdered number three, relit some Old Horrible and hauled his tripleweight bones upstairs to acquire some pressingly overdue kip in conjunction with number four. Then, having eased his lavishly booted rump down into the lush sympathy of Mistress Mattress, he popped the final ring pull and set the morning cap down on his bedside table whilst straining to thrash at his shoelaces one-handedly, as part of the new urgency to be economical with physical assertion. He'd scarcely passed through the portals of Nod, when in a moment, his grandest of all needs was realised in the form of the bedroom door being flung open to reveal the ever dutiful considerations of All Night Billy with teacup presenting.

'Ay! Owzit gaiwn', Skip? Thought I 'eard yer gerrin' up. Bit of a night, was it? Had a bit of a lie-in, did yer? 'Ere! Get this down yer, mace! Nice cuppa sea! 'Ello? On de ol' booze already, eh? Stahssin as we mean to go on, eh?'

'Billy?'

''Ere, Skip! Our cousin's wantin' to move into one of the

spuur rooms – what d'yer reckon, mace?'

The Skipper could only stare directly ahead, exploring the possibility of refuge within the kingdom of catatonia.

'Yeah, well! If yer see Terliff, juss ask'm forruz, will yer?'

'His name is Tarif, Billy...'

'Yeah, look! I've written 'm this letter – you can give it 'm – it's just to say thanks for givnuz a room and would me cousin be able to 'ave one udda spuur ones, Mr Terliff?'

'His name is not Terliff... it's Tarif.'

'Yeah – so, anyway...'

'Billeee!'

'What, mace? 'Ere – go on! Drink yer sea!'

'Thank you awfully much for the tea, Billy. I will convey your request onwards. Now could I trouble you to remove the utter fuck out of my face? *If you wouldn't mind terribly, that is, of course!*'

'Oh! Ay! Cool! I get it, Skip, cool! Yeah, well! See yer later den, praps – eh? Don't forget to ask forruzz, then!'

The Skipper followed Billy as he reversed to the doorway, then closed and locked the door to screen himself from any subsequent waffle. He needed fresh air. Billy had yapstarved his room of oxygen. He took a swallow on number four as he crossed to fiddle open the window; then having poked his head out for a quick gasp of natural, he noticed one of Billy's shirts hanging out on the clothes line, drying for work that night. Instinctively he grabbed the cup of tea from the cabinet and emptied it outside all over the shirt, leaving the cup on the window ledge before sitting back down on the bed to attempt to decipher Billy's letter whilst giving another thrash at the shoelaces. The note troubled him deeply.

'Whaaat? What a... I don't... I can't grip this! Another Wordsworthless slips the net!'

Discarding the note over his shoulder, he gave his beleaguered head a shake before taking a more generous neckful of number four and keeling over sideways.

It hadn't seemed more than a few minutes since the keeling. In fact it was less. He was jolted from his second bliss by a second pummelling upon the door.

'Come on, Jailbait! Start dismantling yer tent and look sharp! Leggo's come to visit us. We're off down the swiller, then on to Pez's bash this afto!'

Curly had always preferred death as the more palatable option to contaminating drinking hours with the insufferable rudeness of sleep. The Skipper had always adamantly adored sleeping hours as the economical option to waking hours, which only ever led to working hours prior to drinking hours, which often led to custody hours. Preferences aside, the Skipper hated – desperately hated – being woken. So much so, that he decided that any third prospect of this was clinically unsustainable, and so jumped up and stormed over to rip clean socks from the radiator. He then restepped into semi-recuperate trainers before reeling, bumping and scuffing back downstairs with a wealth of Old Horrible clutched in one pallid fist, the remnants of number four in the other and the phantom tea-bringer's note stuffed behind an ear.

Down in the living room, Curly and Leggo – who had settled into the Skipper's favourite ensconce – had both been trading sniggers at the latest blue certificate of crimeworthiness to co-occupy chimney breast space.

'Whoa-ho! It's the ruffian himself! Hey, Skip! They want to know if you fancy the villain's part in the next Clouseau remake? Herbert Lom's called it a night!'

'Uh?'

'Well – being as how you hate inspectors so badly – ha ha ha!'

'Ha, ha – nah! I fancy him in *Vanishing Point*, meself!'

Leggo snatched the dregs of number four from the Skipper's hand and began to glug. The Skipper accordingly planted an acute toe poke on Leggo's plaster cast, causing Leggo to both choke and pray for an anaesthetist to suddenly call. Curly perused the particulars upon the chimney breast to sustain the ribbing.

'"Did refuse to stop when required to do so. Did drive recklessly and without due care and attention in a vehicle subsequently deemed to be unroadworthy..." blah, blah... "GBH to a Prefect of the Sûreté in the execution of ..."'

'Hah, ha ha ha!'

'"Being reckless as to..."'

'Yeah, yeah, fair dos, dear boy! Actually, hard work gripping it all this morning! So! Leggo, you smarmarse! I suppose *you* grew wings and jaundice? What's the run-in for your end?'

'A caution, mate – too little to stick! They struggled in vain for ade n' abe – plus, no previous – what can I say?'

The Skipper took number four and tipped it towards Leggo's smirk.

'You could say, "Skipper? I'm afraid I'm rather a breastfed, wetbed, flat and flatulent-arsed, partially-witted sausage jockey – and above all – a rather senseless waste of the earth's good oxygen." Or something simpler and similar.'

'Hey! Don't worry, mate – I'll be in court to back you up.'

'Don't say that, please! I'm hoping to beat the rope.'

Curly had spotted Billy's note behind the Skipper's lug. 'I see you've knocked a will together! Shrewd stuff!'

'Eh? Oh that... Oddfish. Is he still around?'

'Billy? He popped out a minute ago – why?'

'Well then, feast your eyes on this cack! It's his note to Tarif. He's trying to get a fellow specimen moved into one of the spare traps. If you don't read this, you'll never believe it if I do.'

Curly rattled open the note. As he scanned along its lines, murmuring its general theme under his breath, his eyebrows ascended progressively.

'What?' He began again – this time aloud.

'"Dear Mr Terliff..." Who's Mr Terliff?'

'That's Tarif.'

'Ha, ha! Here we go then: "Dear Mr Terliff. I hope you are right and my room is thanks nice. My cousin is after plaice I said you have got a spare one. It make you twenty. Please think. It's nothing to sneeze at Mr Terliff you would make that easy be there two room empty now. Regards, Billy."'

'What the fff?'

'Is there a Liverpool on Pluto?'

'Dunno, but if he makes me one more cup of sea, I'll have to think about his express manslaughter on the grounds of persistent kip deprivation.'

'So, do we give the note to Tarif?'

'Get real! He'll go and double the rent to cover the registration of a lunatic asylum. There's a limit to the amount of PG Tips a body can take before we're all in the ruddy chimp advert.'

'Okay, bin the note – but try and get on with Billy? The poor bastard's only trying to make his way back to a life.'

One of Curly's more endearing qualities was a predisposed faith in man's better nature; whereas the Skipper expected quals and checkable references in triplicate on his desk by Monday morning at the very latest.

'Okay – that's that, then. Just keep an eye on the dodgy little paraffin. Any more pressing business, or can we go and climb into a pub for a few hours?'

'I'll get my jacket – let's scoot before he gets back and decides he's with us.'

Curly and the Skipper hoisted Leggo up onto his leg and handed him his crutches.

'Off you get trotting, then, dear boy! Up the road with you! Ring us a cab from the offy – we'll join you in a sec!'

Leggo hobbled off from the front gate, ooching, aaahing and mebastardleggining, whilst his hoisters fumbled for wallets and tobacco and sniffed around in the hall for the least offensive-smelling jackets available. Then before departure, one last forage around the fridge for whatever assailables were on offer; two glugs apiece on the milk, a bite each from the cheese, one raw egg each – shell on – and a spoonful of cold baked beans to prevent the blue fluff from closing ranks across their surface.

'Righty! Let's get Leggo, then get the cab, then get ugly!'

'Did Billy take his key?'

'I've no idea.'

'We know that, but did Billy take his key?'

'Who cares? Come on everybody – offy!'

The taxi drew up at the offy and its driver, observant of Leggo's affliction, began to crank the passenger seat back to cater for the imminent sprawl. Curly and the Skipper loaded numerous white carrier bags into the back seat to see them through the afternoon vibe in prospect, and then fought each other for the single remaining rump space all the way to town. One and a half tins later, they drew alongside the Yorker and fell beer-first out onto the pavement. Leggo, still bereft of the subtle techniques of self-elevation, hit the pavement arse-first, to the slimmest of sympathies.

'Oh! You *don't* need a hand, then! That's the spirit, dear boy! Just hop up and pay the man – we'll be at the bar.'

Having consigned the bemoaning Leggo to his dolefully over-dramatised dig for pocket change and to his hoppy, coin-droppy, head-knocky sort of antics, the Happy Shoppers shunted shoulders and beer bags into the bar to an explosive cheer from their peers therein assembled. Naturally, all were hitherto fully comp to the Skipper's nocturnal caperings, and he regally acknowledged the throng.

'And a very good day to you, one and all!'

A grinning Tallbob opened for the Clergy.

'Well? It's approaching a quarter past midday, Sterling! Where's your sick note?'

The Parson adjourned his pool table obligations to stick a halfpenny in. 'And don't we mean the sick note you left the slammer with this morning!'

'Ha ha ha!'

The Sergeant slapped him heartily on the shoulder. 'You know what? You're a menace to us decent, level-headed, law-abiding folk, and, quite frankly, society frowns upon you today and rightly so. You and your... no, I can't bring myself to say "pop group"...'

'Who can?'

'He's just *said* it!' Tallbob whacked his other shoulder, waving the rest of the Clergy aback.

'Just ignore my... no, I can't bring myself to say, "friends". As we *well* know, neighbours: society fits society – and nothing else.'

The Parson chirped sneerily in again, whilst eyeing up a shot on the table. 'Yep! It's a fact! We tried society on, once! It was too *small*.'

The Skipper squirmed free to seek an available barkeep. 'Alright, alright, you desperate shower! Now kindly let a chap see the barrels, there's good bastards!'

Curly offered them a unique diversion. ''Ere! If it's good clean character assassination you're all craving after, go for gold and just take a pike out of that window! Leggo's out there – *paying* for something!'

Half a dozen wide-eyed faces stormed the window and a spontaneous roar boomed out as the seen paying Leggo was then forced to hop the gauntlet of whistling, clapping and frantic waving of banknotes, all the way from kerbside to inside to footrail. Eric, already flush-faced from attempting to accommodate the day's first trade single-handedly, had been poised to tend to the Happy Shoppers before the pandemonium set in.

'Oi! *Oi*! Down af me seats! *Af*! An' don't be banging at me windows again... Yes, lads! Bitter, is it?'

'D'you know what, Eric?'

'Joono?'

'D'you know? I was just saying to my good friend and

faithful companion here, that it was high time we popped out for a damn clever little pint of bitter to be enjoyed, for a change, in convivial and morally inspirational surroundings – was I *not* just saying that, Mr Ashmore?'

'No, you wasn't.'

'Well then, lads, yer've cum to the roight place…'

'Yes, we know – but we thought it best not to risk the beer, so we've brought our own, if it's all the same to you?' The Skipper hoisted one of the carriers, breaking out a belly laugh at the zombified stare on Eric's face.

'Aah, had off an' shoite, yer cheeky bastards – cum! Will yez be drinkin' me beer or movin' elsewhere?' He reached over to beckon for the carriers.

'Cum on, hand 'em over. I'll put 'em in the cellar for yerz – it'll be cooler.'

So, divested of the luggage, they were again persuaded to acquire the official article before making their way towards the pool alcove to rub shoulders with some of the other party goers.

The Croc had pitched up with his biffing bedfellows; Mark Anthony was overseeing foul play at the table. Pez, the prospective host – a textbook example of why not to mix punk rock, alcohol and aspirations within the Civil Service – was seated nearby, chatting retentively with his dragon, who herself had been possibly commanding a little too much of the crew's attention as a direct result of owning breasts somewhat akin to a photo-finish in a Zeppelin derby.

Next to them perched Houdi. Houdi was Rudolf Hess's parachuting double in black leather. He never really spoke much; he just loomed. Houdi possessed a particular penchant for proudly poking pins through his penis at parties, thereby assuring himself commemoration for future invites on the novelty ticket. Houdi was little short of a fucking weirdo. In positive contrast, most of the afternoon's conversational traffic had been orbital of the ever vibrant, ever resplendent Chu man, Johnny B. Johnny B was always the Chu's dapperest dresser. At the table, and with cue ablaze, his preferred vesture of the day was matching black button-up shirt and trousers, both patterned with a random scatter of skeletal remains. Black bootlace tie with a silver skull clasp. Undertaker's top hat with trailing silk band. Silver skull rings shimmering from every finger into his opponent's eyes, and circular bands of silver skulls adorning his black suede Chelsea boots. Facial make-up as you'd expect, care of sheet white foundation, contrasting with blackened lips and eye sockets. The man was a fashion assassin. A far, far cry indeed from his dowdy, subdued contemporary, who was skulking in the corner, crouched on a solitary stool, nursing a hangover and flicking peanuts to a brown Cocker Spaniel with a trailing leash. Fig had apparently enjoyed an unconditional restitution to the establishment, mainly due to the fact that Eric was now infinitely more unnerved by Johnny B – having been offered a live burial as mandatory penalty for his derogatory allusions to JB's paranormal dress sense.

As a consequence of the previous night's outing to the Mardi Gras, the crew as a whole were encountering top-up syndrome, ergo the inevitable plunge of all decorum could doubtless soon be expected to accelerate to a positive plummet. The Clergy were progressively encroaching upon the Zeppelin zone. A claustrophobic Johnny B and the Croc had partnered up with a Biffer apiece in a concerted attempt to clear the backlog of challengers at the table. Johnny B was being made increasingly irritable and intolerant by his partner's hesitance in executing what he perceived as the simplest of play until, biting his knuckles and spinning about-face to stare at the ceiling, he could stand no more of the indecisive fidgeting.

'Tell me, woman – are you actually ever intending to *play* that shot or are you just going to stand there making aniseed twist with your bomb doors, all afternoon?'

She giggled along with her buddy at this, but Pez's dragon

was visibly offended. Tallbob – as per – was first to notice this. He loomed just that little bit closer into her life.

'Hey, missiz! Have you ever thought of getting those things weighed?'

She cast Tallbob a sardonic, head-hung sideways look.

'No!' She owned a vicious bark too.

'Did I say weighed? I meant insured, of course! Anyway! If you're thinking of getting them insured...'

The Parson leant to, in ever-keen pursuit of his lifelong happiness to redeem all and sundry of sticky situations. 'Tallbob, did I hear you say *insured*?'

'Yes, why?'

'You mean *weighed*. If she's thinking of getting them *weighed*.'

'Of course I do – you're absolutely right! So anyway, if you're thinking of getting them weighed...'

'I'm not!'

'...stop interrupting! People will think you're a bit rude...'

'I beg your...?'

'As I was saying, the *best* way to weigh them is to grab them with both hands and shout, "Weigheee!" – in your own time, missiz!'

'Ha ha ha ha ha!' She tried desperately to suppress a grin, but let it go. As the laughter subsided, the Parson cut in again, issuing first that impish bow of the head to denote his impending comment.

'Okay, is everybody behaving, then? Look – if we all sit quietly and listen, Uncle Sarge might tell us a nice bedtime story – a nice story about bedtimes, that is!'

The Sergeant snapped abruptly from his trance. 'Uh? Story? What story?'

'A little *bedtime* story, Uncle Sarge!'

'Be more specific, newark!'

'Specific? Okay, *specifically* how you ended up ending up Crazy Jane after the Mardi Gras last night!'

'Whaaat?'

'He *what?*'

'Sheeeesh!'

'Sargey, Sargey, Sargeeee!'

Sargey looked the Parson squarely in the bloodshots. 'And how the fuck did you know this, Little Lord Rumpsunk?'

'Just a little bird, nerd!'

'What little bird?'

'A little bird on her way to work this fine morn. Work? Work on a borrowed bike? Bar work? News House?'

'I think he means Nelly, Sarge.'

Sarge stuck fiercely to his guns. 'Oh, so this little bird was a fucking nuthatch, then!'

'Ha ha ha!' His levity could only relieve the siege temporarily. Tallbob pretended to be appalled.

'Sarge – you realise that if insanity was contagious, you'd be the only person left in here right now?'

'Sarge, Sarge, Sarge! Her gusset's a battlefield!'

'Ha ha ha!'

'That would not be an unreasonable supposition, given the degree of upward tilt on that bike saddle.'

'Okay, alright, so I shagged her... satisfied?'

'Yeahhh!'

'Whaaay – ooops! Sorry, missiz!'

Tallbob persisted with the derision, which usually meant that he'd either been there too, or had fancied going.

'So Sarge, I suppose next you'll be telling us that she's fully oiled and hinged and in complete possession of a full set of spokes?'

'She's not so bad, she's fairly culturally aware – anyway, last night was just a flash in the pan.'

'Oh no! He's flashed her pan, too!'

'Culturally *what?*'

'The only fucking culture in *her* life's in the yoghurt at the Sherwood Co-op!'

'Turbo romance – hey! It's yer man!'

All attention was then abruptly re-channelled, as Sarge's salvation arrived in the form of the seafood basket man. The seafood basket man was a jolly, convivial sort of oldster. He *had* to be, on a pub circuit in the city centre of Nottingham, I suppose.

'Afternoon, ladies and gents... *Bloody Nora*!' He took an overdose of Johnny B, as the alcove revealed him.

'It's the bloody ghost of Christmas future!'

'Ha ha ha!'

'Right – whew! Never mind. Right then, folks! Who's for any cockles? Mussels? Prawns? Whelks?'

Johnny B was never one to allow such a quip to go unavenged. 'Hey! You got any crabs on you, cock?'

'Ha, ha – hey! Shall we get Shed a new prawn?'

'Ha ha! Where is the slack bastard, anyway?'

'Probably back at the love nest, trying out his new-found talents on the beef and Yorkshires! We must remember to organise a cutlery benefit gig for the poor old fork-free mite!'

'Hey, look Fig's scored again, big time!'

'I've seen him pull worse.'

The spaniel was slowly succumbing to snack-food intoxication at the hands of Mr Low Profile.

Tallbob addressed the crew in a tactically lowered voice. 'Don't ask questions. Just play along.'

'Whose dog is it, then?'

'Ssst! Keep it down; Bob's yer neighbour – *Hey*! Gherkin! How's me dog doing there?'

The Gherkin looked up from the crispy mess.

'Uh? Wha? Oh, yeah! Yes, Sport! Yeah! Whose dog did you say it was? Your uncle's?'

''At's right! 'At's correck! Hey! You're not to give him any nuts whatsoever! They give him earache!'

'Ha ha ha ha ha!'

'Him? But it's a bitch, sport!'

'Ooop! Er – yeah! So's life! Are you a bit deaf, as well as drunk and stupid? That's what I said – *her*! I said don't give hff! Too many nuts!'

'Ha ha – *oi*! Stop the presses! Gay drummer in seven-inch death plunge!'

The crew cheered anew as a showered, shaven and fresh-faced larkster, largely resembling Sticky, marched into the bar, nudging the Parson as he passed. The Parson initiated cordialities.

'Yey, Stickman! What can I say? You were nothing short of breathtaking last night! Well, actually, I was busy talking at the time – but I could still hear you! What on earth inspired you to put a garden shed up on stage?'

'Ha ha ha ha!'

Mark Anthony had long been an arch-antagonist of Sticky's. 'Hey, Sticky! What's been going on with you and Mary till this fine hour? Have you finally decided to take some rhythm lessons?'

'I bet she's going crackers – he's been dropping beats all over the bed.'

Tallbob gripped Sticky in a tight embrace. 'And how was it for you, my luscious little love lozenge?'

'Gerrof, you big pole of piss!' Sticky was grinning from ear to ear, but broke free to centralise himself among the Chu. This desire to reap further attention indicated the forthcomingness of an announcement.

'Oi! Shut up a minute; Des – listen! We're playing again, a week on Thursday!'

Mark slammed down the black ball and rounded on him again. 'The Chimneys might be, but *you're* not, you crap bastard!'

'What d'yer mean? Why not?'

'Why not? Because you've been sacked for being such a crap bastard, you crap bastard – that's why not! Hey! What's the difference between Sticky and foot powder?'

'Go on?'

'Foot powder bucks up yer feet.'

'Ha ha ha!'

The Skipper was marginally more curious than drunk for the moment. He loudly requested a little hush in order to more clearly debrief his drummer. Request denied, he scooted his stool closer within earshot of Sticky.

'What's this then, dear boy? What occurs?'

'Gaffer of the Mardi Gras called me this morning – he said we were the worst racket he's ever laid witness to.'

'Super! That's jolly decent of the chap, but we already know that... and?'

'But he'd just finished totting his till, and he says it's the biggest amount of money he'd ever taken and could we play there again a week on Thursday – top of the shop!'

'Yaaay!'

'Sush! Just a sec! So what did you tell him, Stick?'

'I told him we'd think about it.'

'Good man! Wha'd he say to that?'

'He said, "You what?"'

'So whajja say to that?'

'I said, "I said we'd think about it." He said, "Who do you think you are?" I said we were too busy being The Chimneys to waste good beer minutes thinking about who we were...'

'Devil of a riposte, dear boy!'

'So then *I* said I'd talk to everyone and call him back tonight – just to sweat him over the price for a few hours, yeah? Anyway, Joe's cool and I've rung Shed and he's happy.'

Croc was sending a double thumbs-up across the room.

'Excellent! Good man! So it's Thirsty Thursday, is it? I'll get the flyers printed up at work tomorrow – that'll give me something to do.'

'Okay, and I'll book the bowling green for this time next week.'

'Righty! That's *that* little lot sealed, stamped and sent, then – well! Round about this time, I generally prefer to order yet another beer – mmm!'

Eric was preparing to close for the afternoon to repair to four hours of The Lord's sweet peace. After the last towel was thrown on, he popped into the cellar to retrieve the carrier bags, which he passed over to Curly. As the party goers began to muster, Fig sidled over to Tallbob, leash in hand, spaniel aside. Tallbob threw a bewildered stare at the pair. Fig smacked his chops and tugged the dog to heel. Tallbob looked nervously around, as if fearful of something abroad. Fig tugged again.

'I say – I say, sport! I say! Alright if I take the dog along?'

Tallbob somehow remained deadpan, though he felt his eyes popping out of his head. The others, though still a little perplexed by all of this, had long known that playing along with Tallbob was always in the best interests of high entertainment.

'Er – yuh – ha – haumph! Ahum! 'Scuse me, yeah! That's perfectly fine by me, Fig – but don't let him get away for God's sake, will you.'

'Pff-fff! Fffufff!'

'Ooh no, sport! No danger – hey! It's a bitch – what do you mean *him*?'

'Are you getting deafer? I *said* her!'

'Oh. Did you?'

'Fff-uffff – I'll be outside – I can't grip any more of this!'

'I can assure you this dog's in the best of hands, sport! She's safe with me.'

'As long as you're sure, then – can't wait to see this!'

'What? See what?'

'Nothing, cloth ears! I said I can't wait for a piss!'

'Oh! Come on, girl – here! Come on – hey! Tallbob! What's her name, anyway?'

Tallbob paused for a second's thought. There was the

chance for a minor howl, but he had to be quick to avoid Fig's suspicion.

'It's... er... what did Uncle Jack tell me? Oh yeah, Eileen! The dog's called Eileen! Are we ready?'

'Ready when you are, sport!' He yanked on the leash again.

'Come on! Come on, Eileen!' There ensued the most frantic of rushes to get outside upon hearing this.

'Pfff – ha ha hah! Toolooriyey! Come on, Eileen – toolooriyey – ha hah ha!' The Parson, typically, had already weighed up the jape. He sighed at Tallbob, 'Do you suppose he'll twig?'

'Nnno. Doubt it.'

The Victoria Centre flats complex – which amongst other known shacks embraced Pez's nineteenth-floor, luxuriously soft-furnished des res – lay a mere seventy-five yards townwards from the Yorker. This was probably the sole morsel of ergonomic order in the entire weekend. The revellers loped loosely off towards it in a variegated spillage, with a randomly meandering irresolute towing a stubbornly reluctant spaniel in vague pursuit of them.

Upon entering the complex, some twenty of them in all then began the tedious procedure of waiting turns to be ferried upstairs at the mercy of a rather sluggish lift system. The final embarkation eventually comprised of Mark Anthony, Fig and the now vehemently resisting spaniel. Once inside the car, and for the moment having succeeded in becalming the canine, they selected button nineteen and commenced on the upwards. Some halfway aloft, Mark turned with a gross indifference towards the proud dog-handler. Mark, too, had weighed up the jape. He generally knew best when the chortle was getting to far enough.

'Fig?'

'Yes, sport?'

'Take the dog back.'

'Uh? How d'you mean, take the dog back? It's Tallbob's uncle's dog!'

'Tallbob hasn't got any uncles, Fig.'

'Eh?'

'Fig. Listen to me – let the coin drop – he hasn't got any uncles – it was a joke, Fig. Just take it back, eh? Before someone down there goes spacko?'

Fig appeared suddenly and thoroughly shell-shocked.

'Gaw, no! The bastard! What a bastard! Fancy pulling a dirty, low-down stunt like this! Bastard – just wait till I see the bastard...'

'Alright, don't spit your dummy out – all you've got to do is sneak it back into the pub.'

'Ooooh, the sneaky, low-down basss...'

Now at floor nineteen, Mark strode out into the strip-lit corridors as the steel doors swept methodically together behind him, relegating the chunter-locked Fig back to earth to face whatever symphony awaited him back at the Yorker. Mark had wasted enough breath on Tallbob's latest victim. He pressed directly on to the first sequence of door numbers, looking left, looking right, until the venue gradually announced itself via the pounding bassbeat of 'Red-haired queer' by Gina X, leaving small doubt as to which door he should barge into.

Having barged inside, he immediately popped a lively one from his four-pack, which upon chishing, managed to shower the legs and feet of a couple of hall-haunters with beer foam. He mumbled a 'Scuse,' then shouldered past to add to the Chu's forward line, who were effecting an entrenchment in the living room. Pez and Houdi's section of the populace, being fully comp à vis the Chu's awesome capacity for alcohol clearance, stood fast in the kitchen, shepherding the outflow of it to the more tentative thirsts and telling themselves to keep telling themselves that everything would be fine. In fact, given the polarity of earthly purpose between the two crews, a negative development was a much safer 'when' bet than an 'if' bet.

The 'when' bet was to fructify in roughly one hour, twenty

scratched LPs and two tons of spoken horseshit later, when Pez's painted scouts returned to the kitchen with the news which he hoped would never come. The Clergy's flagons were all presenting at forty-five degree angles – bottom upwards. Curly and the Skipper were sharing. The rest of the Chu were shaking stray cans and looking around. The stark prospect of a cruel, cruel thirst was stirring up unrest amongst the troops. 7 p.m. was still over two hours away. Could they hold the kitchen in the face of such predation? Pez and Zepzone hurriedly stashed a nominal supply of tinned lager in the washing machine, and then having conferred with a couple of also-rans, decided upon a cosy mingle in the living room. Pez – evidently icebreaker elect – headed the delegation. But the obsequious ring to this gambit was picked up on by the Chu, almost before he'd breathed a word.

'Everyone cool? Yeah? Aha?'

The Skipper removed his tongue from the bottle for a second. 'Absolutely tickety-boo and seven-fifths, dear boy!'

'Bollocks!' Curly didn't have a drink.

Pez then turned to his flanking also-rans. 'Yeah well, guys – this is the Skipper; Skipper – Matt and Jim! These boys haven't seen The Chimneys yet; you'll just have to have a chat and find out for yourselves what a really crazy bunch of loonies these guys are – yeah?'

The acrid funk of sycophancy was uncared for by the three Clergy who glanced silently around the room, exchanging knowing smiles. It was more visibly intolerable to the main body of Chu, who glared icily up and down and through Mattikins and Jimmipoos, causing their superficial smirks to twitch at the edges. But worst of all, to describe the Skipper as pathologically immune to pliancy would be to plumb an ocean of understatement. The Skipper despised arse-kissers and fawners with his very life. His eyes narrowed as he gazed at the space between them both. He drew hard on a roll-up, without blinking. Then as his lips parted, his eyes widened again, bulbously. The smirks withered altogether.

'My dear boys! We are... the best!'

An immediate chorus of *'The best!'* supplanted the music to fill the air. Jim jumped. The sudden block attestation was neurologically unbudgeted for – and while Matt, Jim and the compère were still wondering what to do or say next without tripping any wires, Houdi burst into the room as if on cue, with penis flailing affront and safety pin completely through it from side to side. The host gasped, then cackled nervously at the entertainment – perhaps through surprise or horror or sheer cringing empathy; but for the Clergy, Tallbob was champion of the unimpressed.

'Put it away, child.' But universal attention was Houdi's meat and ale.

'Eh? What about this, then! Eh?'

'It was a laugh the *first* time, Houdi. That was three years and three dozen parties ago. Now you're a yawn, so just put it away, you poor, confused fucking freak!'

An indignant Mattikins chinned up at Tallbob. 'Oi! He's just having a laugh, mate! Leave him alone – it's *his* prick, all said and done!'

'And whose prick are you?'

'What was that?'

'I said, when I want your opinion I'll look it up on the letters' page in *Bunty*!'

Jimmipoos peered out around his colleague's shoulder. 'I wouldn't, mate! Matt's been in the Forces.'

'Oh, the *Forces*! Well, that changes everything! What regiment? Royal Mounted Handbags?'

'He'll clump you one!'

'Whaatz? I'll manhandle his spotty little rump *any* day of his menstrual cycle!'

Matt spoke up for himself at last but least. 'Do you *want* trouble?'

Tallbob clenched his bucket fillers and bared his teeth.

'And do *you* want to shit my shoelaces tomorrow?'

At this point Pez was nudged into action by an overriding urge to preserve the household and its contents from the impending tornado. Bidding a hasty farewell to the harmony promotion, he bounded in between the two clusters to issue a plenitude of *whoah-whoahs* and to evacuate the two missionaries before the cauldron was lit.

Houdi cast a nervous nodlet in the Chu's generality, before carefully tiptoeing off after the others, cupping over his redundant trademark with both hands. Tallbob reached into his trouser pocket, took out a twopence coin and flicked it after them.

'Here! Treat yourselves to some fucking personality!'

Mattikins wheeled around for further remonstration, only to be bear-hugged away by Pez and Jim.

'Whoah! Whoah! Man – hey! Cool, eh? We don't need bad vibes – eh?'

'Big bastard think he is?'

'Whoah, Matty! Come on, man – have a beer in the kitchen with us, eh? Cool!'

Upon their departure, Johnny B stood to restore order and jovialities. He had calmly appraised the sitcom and now delivered his findings.

'Okay, gentlemen! Well! The ale's running dry in here and the party's about to run right off the rails and down the embankment – once again! So! Before I bugger off home to frisk the missiz, might I recommend the usual?'

Mark clarified the 'usual'. 'You mean liberate all the beer and portables, wreck what we don't need, then bugger off jeldi-jeldi?'

'That's the one.'

'Only trouble *is*, dear boy, we've already cleared the pop – apart from whatever the Odd Squad have got cribbed away in the kitchen, that is; and as for the portables, just look around you! What do you honestly see in this dearth of pseudo-culture that you could confidently offer houseroom to? Look at it! I'd rather fill the space with oxygen!'

Curly contorted the weathered leather visage and growled out a poignant reflection upon the third objective. 'So! It's just the wreckage, then!'

'Let's see!' With scant ado, the Skipper unplugged a ghetto blaster from its wall socket anchorage.

'They like loony? They shall have loony!'

He launched the item clean out of the window. Tallbob, meanwhile, slid the window frame further aside to better facilitate all subsequent departures at the hands of the mobilising Chu. The dining table. A large reading lamp. Then a general dispensation of books and records, two carpets, a radio, three dozen eggs – previously stolen from the kitchen for later on with some toast – loaf of bread for same; two armchairs, a television, Leggo's crutches, the pictures, the toaster, the cutlery, the cornflakes – sprinkled – a kettle and a crash helmet.

The Sergeant, being far too faced to participate, was content to lean back against the adjacent wall and passively follow the parade of condemned articles with his eyes. The Biffers sat happily on the bare lino, clicking fingers and humming the theme to *The Generation Game*, before going on to correctively recall and describe the flown goodies and repeatedly congratulate each other on how well they did. The Croc 'Oowwahed' as he perused every cupboard and shelf to adjudicate between the ejectable and the adoptable. The Skipper was poised to eject a posher, all-chrome sandwich toaster, but was halted in mid run-up by Johnny B.

'Hey, Skip! Hold up – I can do with one of them for my flat!'

'Okay, I'll place it in the goods wanted section.'

The hallway mirror was set aside for evacuation in a corner beside a food mixer, some tapes, some acceptable records, stereo amp and speakers, two handsomely mature spider plants and a tumble-dryer from the hall cupboard. Mark, having quantified the extent of the piracy, saw fit to intercede with a titbit of practicality.

'Okay, you shambolic shower! Bag your booty and let's become a rarity before they start wondering what happened to the noise and the comeback comes back!'

Two dozen sweaty mits descended upon the corner stockpile and converted the job lot into hand luggage, then one by one, they sidled out into the blackened corridor to await the clarion for departure – having first made certain that the 'Odd Squad' were still interengaged around the washing machine in the kitchen. At the last moment, Mark had detected an absence.

'Sssst! Curly! Where's the Skipper?'

'Woll – I jissappened to mention to 'im that, by rights, we oughta rifle all but the kisshen sink – urrrp!'

'You're joking! Whyd'yer tell him that for?'

'Ssorright, s'right, obviously there's no shansa gettin' near the kisshen sink – so he's in the bathroom gettin' the kisshink's brother.'

'Uuh?' In a trice the bathroom door was yanked aside to reveal the dusky, doubled-over figure of the Skipper, attempting to trundle fifty pounds of brother towards the brethren. Mark rolled his eyes.

'Put it back.'

'Why? We can sell it – or grow mushrooms!'

'We can't carry what we've *got*, you radish! Come on – let's piss off before some muppet pokes his head out and bubbles us for the lot!'

The sink was laid down in the bathroom door area as the procession shuffled on towards the main outside door. Mark had barely laid hand upon its handle when a firm, resounding clout was laid to the other side. Someone had called at the flat.

'Bastard!'

'Shit!'

'Isshh!'

'Mark, have a look! See who it is!' Mark peeped out through the fisheye peephole.

'Sheeeet!'

'What?'

'As you were, and drop the shopping – it's the filth!'

'Fuck!'

'Quick!'

There followed a processional double-reverse back through to the living room, and as the last bodies jostled for concealment, Pez's quizzical countenance was suddenly illuminated at the opposite end of the corridor – discernibly more quizzical as the second *bumph* resounded from the front door. Meanwhile in the livestock quarters, the shopping was being hurriedly restacked in slop soddit fashion. The Skipper was cocking an anxious ear towards the hall. Murmurings were being transacted – murmurings which grew uncomfortably louder, menacingly clearer, raspingly closer. The Skipper turned back to the Chu.

'Er... demure and blasé, dear boys – demure and blasé!'

'Luxalordee!'

'Ffff!'

'Oooowahh!' An enormous gloved mit had swiped the door wide open.

'Ooo! It's the *Carry On* cops!'

'Ha ha ha!' The Chu flinched into a rough demure and blasé as the three starry, starry knights flooded the doorway. A constable fixed the Parson.

'You'll get carry-on, you little bastards!'

His sergeant loomed large alongside. 'Right! What's been goin' on up 'ere?'

'Sargernoon, aftergent! And how might we assist your steward's enquiry, old horse?'

'Look – ignore him! Just you carry on, sergeant – sorry – not *you*, Sarge; I'm addressing the *real* sarge!'

'Ha ha ha!'

The real sarge scowled directly back at the Parson. 'I'll wipe the grins off *all* of your silly fucking faces in a bit! Now! We're pursuing complaints made by local residents. Who's first wi' the story?'

The Parson once again felt personal projects outweighing all possible punities.

'Nineteenth.'

'Nineteenth?'

'That's correct – but I'll check for you. Sarge? Tallbob? This is the nineteenth storey, isn't it?' Tallbob held a five-inch middle digit to his lips.

'Sshh! Keep quiet, everyone! Stay calm – you know what walls have, don't you?'

'Ears?'

'No – sausages!'

'Ahh ha haa!'

The real sergeant's other flanker lurched towards Tallbob. 'Let me knock his fff!'

Tallbob leered straight back into his gnarling face, unsettling him visibly. 'Let's go, Perky! We're *both* out of uniform!'

'I'm *in* uniform!'

'You think so?' The gloved mit swiped again to forestall his flanker at the chest.

''Ang on, Ralph – it's gone far enough out of 'and! I'll give 'em one more chance. *Right then*! Who's been chucking t' kit out o' t' windur?'

'What kit?'

'Fukkit!'

'Anyway – which bastard's been complaining – eh?'

'Bet them muppets in the kitchen've blown the gaff.'

The real sergeant glared down at Leggo's plaster cast.

'So you're saying nothing's been chucked outa this windur?'

'Haven't the windiest, dear sarge.'

'We see nerthing, we hear nerthing, we knerw nertheeng!'

The real sergeant glanced over his stripes and away into the corridor.

'Right! Bring 'em in!'

Having patiently awaited his cue, a further trooper promptly loomed at the doorway, bearing a pair of crutches and the grin of the harbinger. The real sergeant's more studious espial now visited Leggo's cod-like expression.

'Still a bit in the dark over this then, lads?'

'Oowah!'

'Cheats!'

'Low blow, Joe!'

''Ere! Dyew moindah!'

'Right, that's it, Ralph – we're going to be nicking all the gobshites – so that'll be Rutger there; the fuckin' Grim Reaper; that little bastard and the big drink o' water! The rest of you, pipe down! You're under the microscope for the rest o' the day. Right! You four! Let's be having you! Names?'

'Why are we going to Letsby Avenue?'

'I swear I'll crack you one in a minute, you little bastard...'

'Look – don't crack me one; let me crack *you* one! Aherm! *She was only the fishmonger's daughter – but she lay on the slab and said fillet*!'

'Ha ha ha!'

'*Names*!'

'Er... okay! A vase. A... vaaaase.'

'Skegness!'

'Mardy Mardy Mustard!'

'Joking George the Third!'

'Right! Cuff 'em!'

The seizure began. Pez and the beautiful people turned out in the hallway to bystand the marching away of the Skipper, Tallbob, Johnny B and the Parson. The Skipper entreated them with a parting salvo.

'Bye-bye, dear, sweet things! Keep dancing!'

'Uh – cheers, mate...'

'Around your handbags, that is – ha ha ha!'

The remainder of the Chu – and at a healthier distance, the Biffers – followed the pinch all the way to the lifts, before hailing the proximate car to that of the captured. The police sergeant, it seemed, was dutifully persistent as guardian of all protocol.

'Where's *your* lot think yer gooin'?'

Mark stared him directly in the eye. 'Just making sure my clients arrive safely in and out of your charge, Officer!'

Ralph bucked out his chest and tucked in his chin. 'Bugger off, before we nick the rest of you!'

'Indeed we *shall* be buggering off, sir.'

'Off-icer!'

'Ha, ha!'

'However, it would appear that these four accused men wish to retain the services of our legal department.'

'You what?'

'They wish us to represent them. Our practice is exclusive to the day-to-day legal interests of these men.'

'I kid you not, kiddoes – we'll nick you hard!'

'We advise our clients to refrain from any statements for the moment, in the absence of the formulation of any substantial charges...'

Ralph reopened his blue-bearded mouth to swap feet.

'Juss lemme – just let me!'

He lunged towards the Parson, but Mark instantly curtailed his vigour.

'Oi! Read your law, m'friend! Anyone can represent anyone; in any case – five Bills cannot arrest twelve people in one lift, or you'll be in breach of health and safety!'

'We'll be the judge o' that, me duck.'

'No! *We'll* be the judge of that, *me duck!* As legal advocate to these men – might I inquire as to whether formal charges are forthcoming?'

'Yes.'

'Then might I inquire as to the nature of these charges?'

'Yes.'

'Then would you be so good as to equip us as to the specifications thereof?'

'I'd love to be so good, me duck! Owzabout kicking off wi' breach o' the peace, being reckless as to whether, damage to public property, dumping litter on City Council property, occasioning actual bodily harm to a publican at the White Hart public house in Glasshouse Street, resisting arrest – and if I can possibly swing it, riotous assembly goin' on civil commotion – and *that's* two to ten alone! Off the top of me head, like, me duck!'

Mark turned dispassionately to the captured.

'Fair enough! Shag the legal trade – we'll go for a burger instead! See yer, lads – best of British!'

'Tootle-oo, dear boy! Look after dear old Blighty for us!'

The Navy Blue closed ranks around the captured as the lift doors closed around the Navy Blue. Downstairs, they marched across the cloister of shops, four cuffed to four, then out through the glass doors towards more awaiting enemy poised in a white long-wheelbased Ford Transit van. Meanwhile, reeling around the pavement some fifty yards away, having casually strolled out of a pub with a pedigree animal belonging to someone he'd never met in his life and taken it for a ride up and down in a lift before somehow losing it God knows where, was the indirigible prospect of Fig. Fig was stooping, staggering, supping at a third of whisky and whistling to four winds for his wayward charge. He turned, rested both shoulder blades against a shop window, clocked the pinch and hoisted his bottle aloft.

'Hah! You've been nicked – *hah*! Well, d'yer know somethim? Eh? Yer bastards? I'm glad – I'm fucking well glad! Hey! Copper! Watch that lanky bastard, sport! He hates coppers – says all coppers are gay bastards!'

Tallbob's arrester scowled.

'Does he now?'

Tallbob glared grit-teeth at the Gherkin.

'Oh yeah! Yeah! Nah – it's all very well – he comes round yer house: "Can I borrow a bowl o' sugar?" Yeah! Yeah! That's how it starts! Yeah! Next time it's, "Can I borrow a bowl of fivers?" Yep! I know it! A dog ain't just for Christmas – it's for life – phweep! Come on, Eileen! Here, gal! Tell you what, I'm glad – phweep! Yep! *Hah! Glad*! Eileen? Where are you, boy? Phweeeup! Where are you, girl?'

Any displeasure kindled against Fig for this performance would be short-lived, however. Two days later, having completely forgotten all about this, Fig popped into the Yorker for a quiet pint after work. At the bar, he rested an elbow and turned to nod and smile and bid a very good evening to a total stranger standing there next to him. The stranger returned the nod, as one might. He smiled, wished him also a good evening and promptly and cheerfully smacked him clean over the nearest table, before calmly finishing his beer and leaving the place to Fig to come around and stagger around, trying to work it out.

Procedure as usual down at Nottingham Central Police Station, as the freshest four guests checked in to be frisked, de-valuabled, de-shoelaced and shunted downstairs and along to separate cells for an unquantified spell of bang. The Skipper chewed at his jowls, mindful of the fact that he was now in serious breach of the bail secured over the river, less than one day beforehand. There wasn't much time to think. He had had half an idea – and to employ it, he firstly needed to screech it abroad to ensure the others took heed before his incarceration proper came into being.

'You can't lock me in there! Do you realise who I am? I'm Travers Manners-Liversidge! I've campaigned for the Rushcliffe seat! I demand the statutory right of a phone call to my lawyer – immediately and bar all delay, sah!' Ralphy's enigmatic wit had not forsaken him for a second.

'Hur! Your lawyer's up town, tucking into his cheeseburger – remember? Lord Liversidge, me old duck? Any road up, I won't forget to mention your name upstairs – hur!'

He nudged the Skipper into the cold, bare, piss-festered cell and clanged shut its hefty door. The Skipper grinned. Then he laughed. The other three had nodded, or winked or smiled. His apprehender was deludedly delighted that he'd let slip his real name, and the Chu's collusion in the matter had been secured at the last moment.

When the mass of keys next thrashed around in the door, the last one brought out for interview – one Travers Manners-Liversidge – was led back upstairs for processing. He gave a fleeting glance at the mountain-bellied jailer's Sekonda, only to realise in abject horror that almost two hours' drinking time had elapsed.

'So then, you're absolutely sure you don't mind granting the gaffers this little audience, Sir Travers Manners-Spanners?'

'Bollocks! Oh, sorry, dear boy, but I'm in grave danger of becoming sober at any time now!'

'Don't fret... Just behave, and the lads'll have you sorted and shipped out in two from the noo!'

He was marched back upstairs, through several double doors and along into the main processing area. Across the shitty green carpet squares, they encountered a stoaty-featured, but clear-eyed and immaculately groomed inspector carrying a buff A4-sized folder. He imparted a general air of seen it all, done it all, nicked it all.

'Cheers, Frank – we'll do him in number three, I think.' He shoved open the nearest available glass-panelled door.

'Come this way, if you'd be so good, Your Lordship? Let's get comfy and hear what you've got to tell us.'

They seated themselves on moulded plastic tube-framed chairs either side of a black ash table and the Skipper folded his arms to circumspect the monotone of the drab, magnolia-painted brickwork, whilst across the table Inspector Swayne coughed, excused himself and began turning over the limitless sheets of paper. Sheets of complaint, sheets of memoranda, sheets of statement, blank sheets. Scanning through the statements, he nodded in turn at each one. He sniffed. He gave the Skipper an upward glance.

'So, er, what was the surname again – Travers...?'

'Manners-Liversidge, T.'

'And where are you currently in residence, Mr Manners-Liversidge – T?'

'Up yer *strasse*, mate! For you, Tommy, *za vor ist ofer*! Geneva job, dear boy – I only have to give my name, rank and number and I wish no special privileges over those of my men – with whom I expect to be allowed to circulate freely!'

Swayne scarcely batted an eyelid at this.

'Well, Mr Liversidge, T, you can carry on with fucking smart Alec; but your next performance'll be on Tuesday afternoon, at the earliest. That'll be having spent the best part of two days back in your little stalag downstairs, sharing magical moments with a mental dosser who tends to enjoy a loud wank or a piss up the furniture every twenty minutes. Or you can demonstrate a little common sense – which I can tell you've got – and provide me with a sensible statement to my satisfaction. *Then* you might still get out for last orders with your bunch of buddies, waiting in reception for you. Which is preferable to *you*?' Swayne had read his man to perfection, dangling both the ripe and rotten carrots of beer and *habeas wankus*, whilst wedging in the odd modicum of buttering up. Beerwise, the Skipper possessed the breaking strain of a Kit-Kat and decided to tow the line. But first, Chu honour had to be upheld.

'Might one then enquire as to the substance of these... alleged complaints, dear boy?'

'Sure! Well – ha, substance, eh? Here we are, then. Item:

Complaint from landlord of White Hart public house, Glasshouse Street. "...after being pelted by a sudden shower of eggs which were apparently falling from a particular section of the Victoria Centre apartments, I did manage to locate a camera and take several photographs of one particular apartment and its occupants, before sustaining heavy bruising and concussion from at least one egg." Item: "I am a landscape gardener, currently contracted to Nottingham City Council to carry out shrubbery replenishments to roof garden at fourth level, Victoria Centre. As I was doing so today, I was suddenly alarmed by a loud crashing sound over my shoulder. Upon turning round, I discovered that an armchair had appeared behind me. As I ran for cover, what appeared to be a disabled person's walking aid fell down into the side of the armchair seat." That's just for openers, Trav!'

'Ooops.'

'Here's some more substance – you'll love this one! Item: "I am currently a resident on the eleventh floor of the Vic Centre. This afternoon I was in bed with the wife when a kitchen table came through the window, showering us both with glass before hitting me on the back of the head." Hmm! Tough one to fathom! Freak gust of wind, perhaps. Well, Sir Travers! Shall we start with name and address, or is it more substance you're after?'

The Skipper turned through the patchy pages in his barrel-fevered memory to forage for a suitably bogus and checkproof address. All roads led to the Croc's pad.

'Manners-Liversidge, T. 53, William Road, West Bridgford!'

'Phone?'

'Disconnected.'

'You keep *that* outside too, do you? Right. That didn't hurt too much, did it? So what can you tell us about the junk shower from floor nineteen?'

'Haven't the faintest, dear boy! Some rather dodgy teddy bears at that picnic! Wouldn't have trusted most of them with a dead elephant!'

'Are you saying you had nothing at all to do with the weird and wonderful freefall display this afternoon?'

'Innocent as the driven, dear boy! I'm afraid you've been barking in the wrong forest entirely.'

'Yes, well, if nothing else, you're consistent with the other toe rags. Well, you've all had some hours to sober up. Personally, at this stage and in light of the degree of consistency in your general corroboration, I see nothing here that I'd bother wasting a court's time with... *unless* any additional information emerges from the landlord's camera, *or* if his injury transpires to be more serious. In the meantime, make no mistake, m'laddo – this situation is ongoing. I'll tell you *exactly* what I've told the others. For the moment, I'll be issuing you with a formal caution. You'll be fingerprinted and photoed while we check you for form; then you'll be issued with your caution sheet and your property and released for the time being. In other words, Trav, we're playing this one by ear, and none of you are off the hook yet. So expect a visit just in case, eh? Okay, sign your caution sheet at the Duty's desk and get lost.'

He was practically home and dry. A name that didn't exist couldn't show form.

'I think you'll discover that my friends and I are of impeccable character, dear boy. Let me apologise without reserve for any misunderstanding over the matter...'

'Yeah, yeah, sure. On your feet, then, Trav! Let's get you done, so's we can boot your entire shower out.'

Elated with the unexpected upturn in fortunes, the Skipper remained grinstruck throughout the mugshots and dabs, and all the way back to the foyer; back into which he strolled, still wiping the ink from his fingers onto a standard issue tissue. The latest blue shitsheet had been sharply folded and stowed, half-protruding from his cross-zip top pocket. The others, hitherto joined by Curly and Leggo, had been in attendance for over an hour, strewn lazily around on the benches in thirsty resignation. They jumped to their feet at his arrival – apart from Johnny B, who continued to sit, picking and blowing specks of dust from his topper. The Skipper glanced around for a receptacle in which to cast the inky tissues. Flummoxed, he sauntered over to the reception desk and its starchy-bloused WPC sentinel, and casually tossed the whole grubby mess onto the daybook in front of her.

'Erm... could you sort this lot out, dear girl? No bins this side, you see – ta!'

Her jawbone almost hit the daybook. 'Don't make a mess of my desk!'

'Well, I find that rather rich! Look at the mess *you've* made of my fingers!'

Johnny B and Curly stepped forwards to claim an arm apiece and ferry him off discreetly to the revolving exit doors.

'Come on, Jailbait, let's blow before they start sucking again.'

'Yep! Let's not push it now, Travers!'

They dallied at the revolving doors for the mandatory clown around, taking two revolutions each – except Leggo, who was held prisoner inside and forced into a series of backward and forward hops by several hands at the handle. Suddenly, the Skipper grabbed at Johnny B's wrist.

'Luxabastardlordy – it's gone niney! Can that be the timey? Well, folks! Rind abite this time, I usually pop to the nearest pop shop for a large glass of coping fluid!'

Curly seemed equally parched after the excruciating hiatus in suppage.

'I'm with you on that one, Sir Travers!'

The Skipper began to smack his chops and search all horizons. 'In fact, I'm ruddy well *starving* into the barging, old horse! Fancy a deep pan pizza or something?'

'If we must – who's with us?'

Johnny B was the first decliner. 'Sorry, troopers – she's still at home, waiting for that frisk!'

Tallbob seemed ill at ease with the distinct possibility of more horseplay leading on to yet another incarcerable conclusion. He loathed the prospect of bang-up, let alone *more* bang-up.

'A pizza? With *you* two on full? What d'you take *me* for – a walk?'

Leggo, mindful of a bisection of the taxi fare, decided on a hobbleabout to look for the others, until Tallbob announced that he was heading home to rifle his barrel of home-brewed stout; whereupon Leggo announced an amended proposal to wit shag looking for the others and tag along for some stout. With minimal ado, they dispersed in their various directions off into a balmy Nottingham summer evening.

THIRTEEN

Having declined to omit any of the five pubs en route, thereby clawing back all lost time and quantity, as Trojans would, they eventually reeled into the entrance of the Market Square Pizzaworld, innocuously whistling away at several bars of 'Mr Slater's Parrot' by the Bonzo Dog Doo-Dah Band.

A sceptically-inclined young waitress therein had dreamed of toasting her plump hooves against a home-fire by a foot spa – when the muse was rudely pierced by this latest of intrusions. She rolled her eyes furtively and sighed audibly and led them off to a central location where they could be better covered by beadier eyes. Once successfully seated, she flapped menus greased by a thousand eventide paws in front of their faces. Curly meticulously realigned the gingham pattern of the tablecloth with the edges of the table and then realigned every tabled object thereon. The Skipper ignited a jowl-rippling belch and turned to glare and hiss at the indignant response from several of the nearest tableful of butterchins. The waitress flicked an insubordinate tress of brown hair over her ear and cast the Skipper a well-repertoired look of distinct mistrust.

'Anything to drink at all, *sir*?'

'Damn hellish good idea, *sir*!'

'Two beers each, my dear, if you wouldn't mind so awfully much – I thank you!'

She wheeled instantly about and pounded a sturdy retreat to the duty barman, who finicked and fiddled at his bowtie, whilst muttering mouthside to her that he was confident of the sufficiency of just the one in their particular neck of the woods. The Skipper had detected his antipathy. He smiled at the barman and clanked together the pair of freshly filched earthenware cruets in his jacket pocket.

The waitress patiently awaited her colleague's pristinely poured preparations and then, plonking them down onto a small plywoodn't tray and deliberately slopping them both all over it, she briskly ferried the whole headless mess back to the suspect bandidos' table, where she remained, swaying her weight from one hip to the other in sardonic attendance of their next pleasure.

'Ashley, dear girl, I'll leave it to my man here to deci… you know, you realise, we've been together allese years and not one cross word?'

'Really? Well, we'll be happy to…'

'No – nah, we're crap at crosswords!'

'An' cross-country.'

'An' cross-dressing.'

'An' cross-sniffin.'

'An' crossin' over from the pub…'

'I'm sorry, but it's getting late! Can I take your orders *now?*'

'Cuzzucan, dear girl! Wine yer say so? Standin' there…'

'Wurzup wi yer? I'd like a twelve-inch Messicano, pleece – hurp! *Boop*! Wupsah!'

She switched a frown between the insensible grins.

'Ah – ah – ah'va twelinch anythin'! Susprise me, won'tchah?'

'Surprise him – yeah – hey! Where're the beers?'

'Beers? They're in front of you! I've just brought them!'

They both grabbed the beers and drained them in three seconds flat.

'Nah – *orppfah*! He means the beers *after* these beers!'

'I'm sorry, but the manager has closed the bar!'

'Man can only be described as a blithering idiot!'

'Blithering eeyut! How yer think my work record's gonna look if I keep showing up on a Mondee, juss 'cos blitheeyuts have been shutting bars all over this town – uh? *Uh*?'

'I'm sorry, but...'

'Geesh – look, it's only eleven fiffeen! You're lice till midni – oop! Brip! *Alloah*!'

'*Oi*! That bloke's getting a fresh drink over there! Woss goin' on in the world? Uh? Oo?'

'But...'

'An' he's got salt 'n' pepper! Would it intress you at all to learn that me good friend here, and meself are feelin' vittimised an' issulted by the ope-*erp*-ernly hossile reception at this istallishmen?'

'Well, with respect, the manager thinks you've already had enough to drink – we'll...'

'Ho! *Ho*! Does he, hindeed? Howzeh know this, then? Has he been through me pockets or somethin'?'

'Surely he can't see me pants from there?'

'As I was saying – we'll be happy to serve you your pizzas – then that's all! Let me know when you've made your minds up.' She stormed off again on a tidal wave of scowls from the unquiet ones.

'Hur! Witch!'

'Bitch!'

'Witchbitch!'

'Ditchwitchbitch!'

She returned from a windowside table, fully laden with plates, a wine carafe and a glass with tomato-stained napkins stuffed inside. As she passed them, the Skipper pulled out his Zippo lighter, flicked it on and held it out in her direction.

'Burn, Witch! Burn!' But it was all taken in her stride as she then paused to scoop up another empty carafe in her remaining free fingers.

'And two big Messicanos while you're at it. *Urp*!'

'And unless you put those cruets back, you won't even get your food – it's your choice!'

The Skipper eyed her with raising brow and pursing lips. As

she barged on into the kitchen, he slowly, grudgingly, retrieved his trophies from the dark hole and methodically resettled them onto the gingham. Once assured of their restitution, the kitchen rushed out the pizzas in priority order, to expedite the farewells to this particular pair. Curly picked and analysed; he harboured a dogmatic mistrust for food un-British. The Skipper's face was partially obscured by piping hot steam as he incised and devoured, free of all international constraints. Through the steam, that look of impending skullduggery had begun to muster in his eye. Curly knew the look well. He'd seen that look a thousand times.

'What?' the Skipper responded through clenched Tarantellatone teeth.

'Right!'

'What?'

'So this is what we do!'

'What?'

'When I say run – *run*!'

He slipped the cruets arrogantly back into his pocket, and continued to wolf at the last intact fraction of Mexicano. At the bar, an enlarging combo of staff conferred as to whether they'd actually heard him say 'Run'. Leastways, Curly now had to frantically raise his game to try to catch the Skipper up. Within a couple of minutes it was looking all over for both pizze.

'Isst! I'll just go and get a piss while you finish, Curl. Don't forget! Issa runner on *run*!'

The block attention of the serving staff fascinated upon the Skipper from table to washroom door, like that of a troop of neurotic meercats. Curly tucked on in, throwing them the odd beaming toothy smile, tastefully embellished by the odd lingering strand of mozzarella, which was untautly connecting his chin to the plate. Then, after one of the uneasiest and seemingly most endless of suspenses in downmarket catering history, the washroom door wrenched open to a backdrop of hissing waterworks. The Skipper paused for a second, then marched out, arms at his side, staring nowhere but ahead. He marched on. He marched up to the furiously masticating Mr Ashmore and then beyond. The march was hastening. Then, all at once came the kick of heels as he altered tack and bolted for the outside.

'*Run*!' He was away.

Curly sprang to his feet, nearly keeling over the table in his own surge for the off. The staff had nurtured confidence in having one bird still on the ground. Now feeling confidently mugged, they were hurling themselves into the main aisle like a parachute display team in dire want of rehearsal. Curly had already thrown his chair behind him to hinder all pursuit. He threw another.

'*Oi*! Come back! You haven't paid!'

'*Fuck off*! We never *do*!'

At the spearhead of the chase, the pursuant manager's inexpedience in hurdling the first chair led to his overhauling and overturning by the more zealously pursuant waitress. The entire hunt clattered to a standstill around him... and with that, Curly was gone. They were too late. They could but stare from the jarred back main door as the Deep Pan Duo traversed the square like tandem greyhounds, weaving indiscernibly among the milling multitudes. Revellers. Reelers. Skateboarders. Gone. The manager turned back inside, patting his breathless waitress on the shoulder as he passed her.

'Okay, forget it, Donna. I'll just call the police – we've got some good descriptions.'

Meanwhile across the square, concealed behind two marbled pillars in front of the Woolwich, the deep pan caper caught some breath, belched, peeped and gathered themselves; their fraught faces becoming occasionally reflected in the facing sheet glass window pane by passing bus and taxi headlamps.

'You–you–sil–silly–bastard!'

'Whur?'

'Well – thanks! Thanks–for... the–more–than–adequate–notice... you tosser!'

'I said "run"... didn't I?'

'Fffeee-fffooo! Oh yeah! You said run when *you* were... halfway to Moscow, you... fffeee... fffooff... bastard! I'm surprised you... fffoo... bothered warning *me* at... all! Why didn't you... just... bugger off home and ring me at the... fffoooff... restaurant? You could've got the staff to page me. "Mr Ashmore? A mister Curly Ashmore of eleven Maples Stre... eet? Yes sir! We've received a telephone message for you, sir! No, sir! The caller didn't give his... name, but he says *run*! Ffffooofah!'

'What's the matter? You made it, didn't you? You've dined for gratis, dear boy!'

'Yeah, what an ungrateful swine I am... I'm about to throw up a disgusting slab of cack which I had to barrel down in five minutes flat... before taking on all comers at the John Wayne school of furniture swinging... ffoooo... then smash the world hundred metres record with a three-gallon handicap on board! I wouldn't mind if I'd been hungry in the first... bloody place!'

'Soz, dear boy!'

'Forget it. Now what?'

'We split up. Stick with the crowds in town, heads down and then separate. Back roads home – see you at the house!'

'Right! Go!'

They casually emerged from the shadows, Curly taking west, crossing over to Beastmarket Hill; the Skipper east into Exchange Walk. There were adequate bodies to mingle alongside.

Away from the square, Curly dug deep, fishing out a half pocketful of bits; there looked to be an easy sufficiency for a taxi to halfway home, perhaps further. There was a strong case for immediate evacuation, given the normally nominal police vigil around the Square – ergo, halfway looked fine to him. He slumped into one of the cabs which was flying the end of Angel Row, slammed the door and he was away. Safe.

Back in Exchange Walk, the Skipper had ducked into a doorway to construct a fattish roll-up and to plot a course home. It would be a right turn into Wheeler Gate, left, away from the Square along Friar Lane, Maid Marion Way up to Canning and slip home through the Radford backstreets. That was it. Simple. Anything looks dodgy – taxis on offer all the way. Then home. Get in, check fridge for nightcap, seven hours' kip before work or ring in sick, dependent on head. Okay. Quick toke, quick lookabout, head down, collar up – go. He slinked out of the shadows behind a party of revellers who were sauntering down to the bottom of Exchange Walk, then peeled away, banking right into Wheeler Gate.

'Oooyerbastard!' Looking up, ten yards ahead of him, he saw the pavement was awash with starry, starry knights. They hadn't seen him yet. He performed an instant one-eighty and began to creep away. Yep. Yep. Yep. Yep.

'Ah! Good evening, Sir Travers!'

Nope. Was he clocked? For a second, he froze in momentary indecision between runner and bluffer.

'Oh, please don't ignore us, Sir Travers! After all, we *are* your humble electred here assembled!'

The Skipper slowly turned, head first.

'Can I help you in any way, Officer?' He faced the half dozen one-sided grins escaping from the helmet shadows.

'*Now* you're talking, Sir Trav, me owd! Well! We were rather hoping you'd indulge us with one of your increasingly popular interviews! Just an informal little chit-chat back at our place, *if* you've got nothing else on tonight, that is, of course?'

'Ssstard!'

It was a case of two wrongs making a sensationally fortuitous right. The police, armed with a description loosely befitting one Travers Manners-Liversausage, had taken it and taken off like proverbial gatebulls and scrambled to the *wrong* outlet of Pizzaworld, to their own gross embarrassment. Then what? The Skipper had only dropped a *fine* chop in designing his escape formula, being pissfully forgetful that Pizzaworld also had a Wheeler Gate outlet. He'd done no other than carefully hatch a cunning plan to walk straight to them, and in so doing, had kindly cancelled out their bungles and blushes. Good ol' reliable police inefficiency was the dog finally having its day.

After the brief sojourn to the *correct* outlet for physical confirmation by the manager, staff and sundry disgruntled butterchins, Sir Travers found himself once again negotiating the famous revolving doors in the wrong direction. He was booked in at reception to the popular acclaim of his electoral winovers.

'Ah, Sir Travers! Good evening, sir! Will you be staying long?'

'You can rely on our vote, Sir Trav!'

'Dreadfully sorry, Sir Travers – looks like we might be messing up your manicure again!'

'You again, toe rag?' Looming large in the custody wing doorway, Swayne was somewhat less platonic than his legion.

'Get in!' He stood aside as the Skipper was uncuffed and prodded towards him.

'I'll take it from here, George – thanks! Well done!'

Well bloody done? Well bloody done who? They marched abreast once again down the corridor with no end.

'Room number three again, Trav? It's your favourite!'

Thing was, what did they know? Were the sarcastic platitudes an indication that his identity was bubbled? No, no – that's just drink paranoia. He'd stick by the Liversidge wicket. They sat in number three. Swayne stared hard into his face.

'Well, Trav – I have to say, I thought you smelt a bit

soonish earlier, but not *this* strong!'

'I refuse to make any comments, pending proper legal representation.'

'Really? You know, Trav? When your description was flashed through, I said to the chief, "Chief? I must have a thousand more important things to do than waste my time buggering about with Sir Travers again" – and then something funny happened. I couldn't think of *one*. Isn't that funny, Trav? Not a single one.'

'Hysterical.'

'Indeed, hysterical.' He sat back to open the desk drawer to rummage for something which turned out to be a copy of the Yellow Pages, which he launched against the Skipper's chest.

'It's "pick a brief" time then, Trav – and make sure he's half decent, because I'm a less than happy man.' He grabbed the telephone, twisted it to face the Skipper and clanged it down in front of him.

'One call. Bilking a restaurant. Theft of restaurant property, for which you are about to be searched...'

The Skipper felt into his cross-zip pocket, took out the cruets and clicked them down on front of Swayne, twisting the 'S' and 'P' sides toward his face.

'Highly desirable. And using threatening behaviour to a member of the restaurant staff. Two minutes; empty out the rest of your pockets.'

With all the declared booty aboard the desk, Swayne performed the statutory body search as the Skipper attempted to focus on the list of firms of solicitors in the open book on the desk over Swayne's shoulder. The knocking about was less than conducive to his concentration, but he'd taken Swayne's two minutes to be literal, and so, unable to engage his usual brief due to his deed poll complications, his eyeballs fell all the way to the 'B' listings – to be precise; to the firm of Bernard, Cursham and Wright in Friar Lane.

Some thirty-five minutes subsequent to the distressingly garbled Mayday, the firm of Bernard, Cursham and Wright dispatched representation in the mountainous form of Mr Lee Siddons; a six feet three, twenty-two stone, moustachioed, curly-haired giant of a jolly and highly optimistic disposition. Siddons wasted no time in securing his client's transfer from piss pen back to number three, to firstly offer him reassurance of his own success record in the defence trade and then to get down to brass tacks and legal aid. Munerations aweigh; it was then back to piss pen.

Within fifteen minutes of his reincarceration, the Skipper was overly tickety-boo to discover that the thrashing of keys in his cell door was not a further temptation to salivated tea, but news that Lee Siddons had bargained, bartered and badgered for England and secured the bail. This was evidently reached on the basis of his client's drink-induced claustrophobic dual incontinence and notwithstanding his standing in the looming Rushcliffe by-election, let alone the fund-raising Rotary Tea Dance for the Bridgford elderly and infirm. The headiness of all this rhinoceros shit even astonished the Skipper into a two-minute silence of ingurgitation.

By three o'clock in the morning, Travers Manners-Liversidge had provided his curve-throwing masterpiece of a statement; was charged, bailed unconditionally for twenty days, re-propertised and readied for the world with a brand new blue bail sheet, nuzzling beside the earlier one in the cross-zip front pocket. He wiped his palms down the sides of his jeans to exchange a hearty handshake with Lee Siddons in the foyer, then thanked him sincerely for his efforts, moaned about his pay structure, and bade all a very good morning as he hopped towards the revolving doors, taking his baccy and Rizlas in hand. At the doors, he abstained momentarily from passage to allow a young woman police officer priority of thoroughfare. Upon her entering, she smiled and thanked him. Then as he paused to roll another fatty relish before the rush of good air, a chilly cataract of cautiousness cascaded down his spine. He thought to think and not to move. He'd seen her face somewhere before. Old flame? School friend? Barmaid-turned-filth?

Behind him, something had been niggling *her* equally as much. But in a mind better conditioned for recall, she'd got there first. His infamy was to be his undoing.

'Morning, Mr Snowis! Not been frying any bricks lately, then?'

Shit. *That's* who it was. Farmer, from Bridgford nick. What the wankery twank was *she* doing in this postcode? Swayne was still busy babbling with Lee Siddons at the opposite end of reception. He didn't hear that. Too far away. Time to slip out, in case.

'Snowis? Are you familiar at all with this individual, Farmer?' He *did* hear. It wasn't far enough away from the bastard's Gibraltar.

'Course, sir! It's Paul Snowis – aka the "Skipper". He's legend over the river!'

Oopa bastard doopah! The Skipper froze in mid-creep. The balloon was up. Swayne maintained his mechanical dignity to wag a beckoning index finger.

'Er, Sir Travis?'

'Ha ha ha! Yes, dear boy?'

'Would it be convenient if we extended this little... *chat* of ours, in the light of this, er... *unexpected* development?'

'Development, dear boy?'

Swayne turned aside to the briefcase-clicking Lee Siddons – who, due to his natural mastery of mood-gauging, had already suspended the final click.

'Mr Siddons? Would you at all mind giving your further attendance, please? Because personally, I'd say you were in for some good overtime, mate.'

FOURTEEN

The front door of 11 Maples Street was dealt its freshest kicking in at around five forty-five of that morning. The stone eagles almost tutted in disownment at the latest three blue sheets to be posted above them on the chimney breast. Available space thereupon was indeed fast becoming a scarcity. The named miscreant then wearily reconsigned his fastly diminishing gob of Blu-tack to a sideboard drawer. He was tired as never, and the armchair was demanding a generous grope of his arse. The Skipper crashed seat first into this cushy heavensend, and as his head fell lower and the first rasp of a pressing schedule of snores exuded, that sweet voice came to him, yet again.

'Skip... Skip! Come on, mace! 'Ere! Get dis down yer! A lovely cuppa'll set you right for the day – but mind, it's piping hot, mace!'

The Skipper's ten-ton eyelids cranked slowly and painfully apart. There'd been more than enough trouble for one week without incurring another blue sheet for justifiable homicide. The Skipper capitulated, uttered a bleary 'thank you' and sat there sipping and nodding his head at the teabringer's tide of twaddle until the tea was all gone. Then in a final rallying of determination, he managed to escape to his room to slide into soft sanctuary for what would be twenty-four deep and dreamless hours.

That week dragged its heels throughout. August was generally deathly for all of our daylight professions – particularly mine. I'd spent six days doing seemingly little other than sitting on my arse, cooking away in the cab in wait of a rare spark from the radio; then one, maybe two, jobs per hour. By the time Sunday came around again, I was chomping to get amongst it. Bowls. Rehearsal. Booze for England. I left Woodborough Road at 10.30 a.m. armed with bass guitar and a bundle of blowing cash. I'd left fresh from another blazing row with the Dragon over the usual nothing. She was probably on day twenty-two, unless it was me – ground down to miff after the week of sheer shite.

The vista on offer as I arrived at the Forest Greens offered little cheer to the brood I was nurturing. The weather was glorious, the greens couldn't have been greener, the bowls were attendant at mat and from the green painted trellis gate, the body count appeared to be one hundred per cent. The initial chishes of the day could clearly be heard escaping their boozy brown cylinders. Everything was perfect, except for the fact that – even in the face of universal discouragement – All Night Billy had shown up again. I'd suspected being in receipt of an airborne perfusion of his claptrap long before actually seeing him, but had refused to believe the evidence of my ears.

'Ay! Ay! Ay up, Shezzy mace!' Worse than that, he was on a top-up from the night before, which meant he'd either worked pissed or pissed work; neither being conducive to a fistful of currency. Either way, he was already staggeringly shitfaced.

'Shed!'

'Oowah!'

'Ah! The Shedfixman! And how the blue blazes are you, dear boy?'

'Well...' I set the bass down with the other kit already stacked around one of the benches, removed my cross-zip and rolled up my shirtsleeves. '...to be savagely candid, I'm fucking uncheerful. What's the newark doing here again?'

The Skipper placated hastily. 'Steady on, dear boy! Nice day – nice drinky! Free country and all that bollocks?'

'Not happy!'

He drew closer, lowering his voice out of range of the others. 'Just giving him enough rope. Trust me – I'm a Chimney.'

'I trust you, m'man – you're a Chimney, but I'm still double plus undelighted about this. A bit.'

Billy was swaying in the breeze, hands in pockets, with a deeply concerned look in his dilated pupils. He was palpably still trying to process the previous remark.

'Ay, ay! Woss-woss-wossa newark? You'll after teach me some o' these Nottingham sayins – ay?'

I was delighted to oblige. I was still bloody livid. I looked him in the best eye.

'A newark, Billy? A newark's a mixed-up wanker!'

The Chimneys ranged between grin and snigger. I kept the look fixed on him in case he fancied a go, but far from being offended, he broke into peals of laughter. He roared. We looked around in beguilement at each other. He was certainly a one-off, if little else.

'Aaa – aa-aaaha! Aa-aa! Shez! Newark! Wanker! Aa-aa, like ud! Like ud, mace! 'Ere! Cum 'ed! 'Ave a zrink, 'ave a zrink o' this, mace!' He waved a half-full flagon at me. I accepted for the others and for the hopeful peace of the day. To be honest, I had to chuckle; I couldn't help warming to the way he coped with the rubbishing.

'Shed, m'man! How's the Dragon today?' Sticky offered, switching subjects.

'Don't ask.'

'Hey! I take it you've heard about the great Pizzaworld caper?'

'Yeah, can you grip it?'

Joe sucked hard on a cigarette as he polished away at his first wood of the day.

'Tup, I had a bit of trouble with one of them pizza delivery companies once, tup.' His seriousness seemed a tinge phoney to me. Joe always told a good tale though, so he could usually grab your attention and amply reward it.

'Yeah... ordered fifteen quid's worth of kit from the Sherwood Pizzeria. After I'd put the phone down, I noticed at the bottom of the menu leaflet it said, "For security reasons, the management regrets that our delivery staff are not permitted to carry more than ten pounds in cash." So twenty minutes later, yer delivery man knocks at me door, hands me the nosh and says, "That'll be fifteen quid, please."'

'Yeah?'

'So what d'you say?'

'I said, "Hang on a mo – how much cash have you got in your pocket, mate?" He has a quick count and sez, "Six fifty, mate – why do you ask?" I sez, "Right then! Here's three fifty. I won't tell 'em if you won't! Now fuck off, before you get the sack for breaking the rules!" Ha ha ha!'

'Ha, ha! Get out of it, you daft bastard!'

'Stick around, dear boy – I might need you in court soon.'

With all the unease dispelled, we got on with the game in the customary spirit of verve, decorum and drink – and in spite of Billy's frequent raving interruptions. Sticky, it transpired, had booked some kind of funk band to support us on the next outing, and by way of a departure from that, a decision was subsequently formed to rehearse 'Hunting Tigers' by the Bonzos later that afternoon and include it in the set for a trial offer. For the rest of the allotted hour we preserved some semblance of sporting a sporting interest, as Billy's slurring and swaying accelerated to burn-out point. By ten minutes to pubs open, he was virtually unconscio – sitting with his feet in the storm gully and slumped forwards, head in hands with a rope of saliva trailing from one side of his overtaxed mouth. The Skipper was tapping at his watch face.

'Okay, nearly time! Woods into the buckets?'

'Nearest pub?'

'Sherwood Hotel?'

'Tup, what – all of twenty yards, eh? Bit out of the way for us, isn't it?'

'Can we afford to invest such time?'

'Sticky's got his motor.'

Sticky's attention turned to Billy's demeanour. It was clear from his facial response that he'd neither bargained for, nor relished the prospect of hauling a naturally malodorous sicksack around in his pride and joy. The usual four scapegraces were more than enough.

'Sheesh, behave! Would you look at the state of that!'

A sudden downpour of japery revealed itself to me, as if by divine recommendation – a means by which to salvage the sitcom.

'Fret ye not, young Chimney. Leave this to yer own – yer very own – Uncle Shedney. For he has a plan. Anybody lend me a pen or summat?'

The Croc turned open a lapel and selected a broad marker pen from a readiness of three. He handed it over.

'Might one inquire as to what's in the offing, dear boy?'

'You may recall expressing very recently a whim to lend yon beleaguered wastrel some rope, or did you not, sir?'

'Indeed, I do recall that, sir.'

'Healthy. In which case then, I'm about to give you satisfaction, sir.'

The others begin to gather their goods and chattels in preparation for the off, as I marched over to the corner of the green to reach down and upheave the metal eye pin which anchored one end of the white nylon border rope passing just in front of Billy. Drawing out the pin, I then trailed the rope down to Billy and around behind his motionless, squatting form and carefully threaded the eye pin through the rearmost belt loop of his jeans, pulling the rope through after it – yard by steady yard. Then, trailing it all after me back along to the corner, I replaced the pin into the turf, rotating it until the rope was as taut as I could physically get it – which keeled Billy forwards a couple of inches. Then I gave the pin one last good stomp for luck, and to the backdrop of distant sniggering, I strolled back to Billy, and through four or five cautious attempts, managed to squat in front of him in order to scrawl 'MULE' across his clammy forehead with the marker pen. I sauntered back over to the sniggerers, tossed the marker to the Croc and picked up my bass.

'Sherwood Hotel, then?'

'Oowah!'

'Flawless, dear boy!'

'Ha, ha! Sparklin' Martin, the attendant will make his rounds in a minute or two. We'll have a grandstand view from the Sherwood lounge!'

We crossed the Boulevard to the Sherwood, bang on time for midday refreshments. Sticky brought his car round and onto the concourse while Joe procured the fruits of the hop pole and the rest of us organised the premier viewing configuration of seats beside the middle lounge window.

'Hurry up, Joe!'

'Gimme a chance!'

'Don't want you to miss this – the attendant's clocked him – he's walking over... ha, ha! He's trying to wake him up!'

Joe and Sticky clambered over seats to the window. We all itched for the next instalment. Out at the greenside, the bemused attendant had been patting Billy on the back for a full minute now, unable to raise a glimmer.

'Come on! Come on, son... time to go! Your mates've all left! Come on, now – let's be off, eh? Up and away! Eh? Come on!'

A bellowing roar echoed around the Sherwood lounge as Billy's head then groggily rose, fell, rose, fell, rose and wobbled through left to right, trying to make out where the hell he was in those first waking moments. The attendant, largely relieved by his patron's revival, strolled off to accumulate the discarded woods, before pressing on with his numerous horticultural assignments around the garden section.

Billy took a second, more co-ordinated appraisal of his environment, then checked his sadly forlorn flagon for dregs, sighed visibly and launched to his feet for one hundredth of a second before the rope twanged him back down like bolt lightning, dropping him arse first into the ditch and whipping his head wildly around into the deal. The returning clamour was all-deafening in the Sherwood lounge. Three more times he tried, convinced that it must have been an attribute of his drunkenness; three more times, his rump pounded the ditch bottom. Not far away, five dispossessed men fought hard for breath, whilst mopping away rivers of tears. The drinks were hardly yet touched. There hadn't been chance. Billy sat for a while, in clear pursuit of some primitive equivalent to rationalisation. This provoked yet another desperate howl from the Sherwood. But this time, Billy had it 'worked out'. There could be no doubt that the rope was attached somehow behind him. He felt around for a second or two. Right. He was on top of this. Yes – the answer lay in his belt. So then, in one calculated flowing movement, he could unbuckle his belt, pull it clear of his trousers and spring to his feet. The fledgling triumph was visibly welling up in his cheeks. Up! TWANG! BANG! OWW! Down!

This time he was almost horizontal, as it fetched him back *really* hard – in return for his far more determined effort. For a while, he disappeared from view altogether, as the entire length of his body filled the gully bottom. As we rolled over the furniture, screaming blue murder for mercy, Billy was enjoying his second brainstorm of the day. He'd now arrived at the momentous conclusion that the rope *was* probably passing through his rear belt loop, and had started to shunt-hop his battered rump along the rim of the green to the eye pin. Having completed the voyage, he was to undergo two more glamourless dumpings as he twice lost his grip in attempting to pull the pin out before unwinding the necessary slack first. Having at last worked the pin free, Billy's next move was at best unfathomable to man or beast. Taking the pin with him, he tramped back to the middle of the green, reseated himself and began pulling yard upon yard of rope through the loop from behind to his right until finally, with mere inches to go to the plight-redeeming pin, he took it on board that he'd gone the wrong way and began pulling back through to the left. I'd truly never seen men so close to dying of laughter before – but Billy hadn't finished yet. The pinnacle of his performance had been saved for last, as he now stood and unfastened and lowered his trousers to try to bend over and take a look between his legs, whilst still yanking away sideways at the rope. This was more than a measly two lungs were ever biologically constructed to cope with.

The drabness of that past week had been redressed ten times over, but none of us could healthily take anymore. We raced the beers off and strolled out to the car. As Sticky swung out into the Boulevard and began to make revs for Maples Street, there was still provision for a final howl as we glimpsed over in fine time to spot the admirably sympathetic greens attendant endeavouring to give counsel and support to the trouserless Billy, who was again dolefully encamped in the ditch and thrashing around outwardly and upwardly in his cloud of nylon spaghetti.

FIFTEEN

The very first job on the list of things to think about on Thirsty Thursday was to pop home to the flat at around 4.40-ish to make sure the Dragon had kept faith and stood by her decision to work through until ten that night.

With two or three bellowing hellos having gone unanswered in the hall, and no further evidence of life in bath, bed or living room, and given that she would normally have been home forty plus minutes beforehand, the coast appeared to be clear to implement thing to think about number two. Ring Sticky at work to make sure he hadn't accidentally booked a pair of Bangkok shilling shaggers to fly in to meet us tonight, and somehow forgotten to mention it. It took an era to finally get his secretary; I'd just stretched the cable round into the kitchen, popped a cold lager and taken a huge gobful on board when, inevitably:

'Good afternoon – Mr Dickens' office! How can I help you?'

'Ulp! Wug-worg-wlooap!'

'Hellooo?'

'Wup-waah-ahem! Ahork! Sorry, is it convenient to speak to St... er, Mr Dickens, at all?'

'I'm afraid he's still in a meeting! Can you call back?'

'Er, impossible, I'm afraid; the flight's already boarding and there *is* a brief and vitally important bulletin which he must have before the Hang Seng opens in one hour. He'll consider it of prime urgency! Can you get a line through to the meeting, please?'

'Can you convey the message through me?'

'Uh? My dear girl, are you trying to get me the sack?

There's a multinational contract involved and it's rumoured highly likely to be poached by IBM. *Woop!* I rather think I've already let on far too much, but very well – if you wish to stick your neck out and play God here...'

'I'm just taking your line through...'

'...just mention Mardi Gras Corporates to him.'

Cutey Miss Duty secretary tentatively tapped at the door and entered the file-cluttered, impromptu meeting room where Sticky was busy holding court to a smarmy array of jacket-off, brace-trousered, fish-faced corporate wonders in Disneyworld ties. She delicately curtailed his flow of parp by setting the phone down on the desk by his left forearm.

'It's urgent: MG Corporates.'

Now Sticky had never heard of an MG Corporates, let alone known of any trading with them. But he wasn't in the business of not knowing who people were, and more importantly, he *definitely* wasn't in the business of being *seen* not to know who people were. Here was a plated peach to put one across his aquatic-featured congregation. He snatched up the receiver.

'Hi! Mick Dickens! What's the news at MG?'

I held fire to put him under the microscope for a few seconds and took another large, loud gulp on the lager. At the uncomfortable end, Sticky was embarking upon a facial improvisation of many facets. He soon felt his repertoire succumbing to a reddening.

'I'm sorry – it's a terrible line – would you mind running that one past me again?'

I drained the can and oowooorbered and clarified the mystery in his mind.

'I said, do those boring fucking stiffs in there realise that all you wear in bed is a fluffy pink bra, stuffed with cornflakes, you prancing great sausageer?'

He ground the receiver into his ear, suppressing the mirth as best he could.

'Oh, ha, ha! Yes – I believe we've been introduced.'

'What time soundcheck?'

'Mmm, we could offload at seven point one five... clear at eight point two zeroish?'

'No kife invited?'

'Oh, no – that's a *beeg* no-no!'

'What time do you finish?'

'Ooh, difficult to estimate! Heavily dependent on the hassle factor.'

'Okay, get rid of them...'

'Actually, I had *you* in mind for that, ha, ha!'

'Well, get straight round here after work. I've got a hefty consignment of lager in the fridge and the best before date says half past six tonight!'

'Yep, that's on board – yep! I think we can accommodate that offer, this time around. Well, thank you for taking time out from your schedule to call me and I'll look forward to probably seeing you on the fourteenth! Bye!'

He turned back to the sea of smirks. 'Now! Let's get this to bed...'

So with peace on earth provisionally guaranteed for the night, it was then time for thing to think about number three stroke four – which was to stash the taxi for the night and give the domestic lager a sound thrashing. Sticky arrived on the sixth; eight, earlier than the fourteenth, but we wasted no time getting there between us. Soon, and with three remaining of the fifth and final four-pack, Sticky had turned clock-watcher and the pace had dipped under a gas attack. He was more than aware through bitter experience that the drummer was generally considered the pariah to be avoided whenever rock 'n' roll inflicted the ravages of gear-humping upon a band. Consequently, he preferred to be in essence and direct charge of his vested thousands, rather than be in absence, imagining wreckage at the hands of men opting for the lesser cumbersome career of guitarist or singer. Men who were, thereby, far happier to employ the second adhibition of the term 'drum roll' rather than unduly exerting themselves to properly carry his weighty share of the assets. He dispatched number seventeen to the sub-basement and grabbed the phone from the table.

''Fraid it's a cab job, Shed – it's twenty-four minutes from Tulsa. Sooner it's set up and done with, sooner we can get on with the drinking – gimme a number.'

'We'll use my lot for speed: six triple zero two seven.'

Sticky punched in the number as I cracked eighteen and exchanged him for his spent one. Under the trust of a five-minute guarantee, we left immediately to be ready and waiting outside the complex. But the taxi was already drawing up – this haste was beginning to feel rather injurious to the breadbasket.

'He's here – tins down in one, Stick!'

'Wuupoo! I've got a stitch – I'll be sick!'

'I'll pretend you said nothing to that! Come on, just one last biggy – it's for Engaland, you know! Orrp! Wowzheezh!'

We forced down the last bubbles of heartburn, lobbed the tins over the ramp wall into an illegally over-utilised builder's skip and clambered headlong into the back seat of the droning dralon dromedary to dictate preference of passage. Its well-seasoned chauffeur retained all dignity and aplomb, in spite of the sudden gust of youth, butane and alcohol, to first acknowledge kinship to a fellow tradesman, then ascertain point de deliverance.

'Pub.'

'Any pub in particular, cousin?'

'Nope – any pub in particla, driver!'

'Well? We got the Newcastle Arms up ahead?'

'Earlpp-wbb!' Sticky's attempted protestation was snubbed by belly gas each time his lips parted.

'Newcastle sounds bellissima, drive – and just wait for us a min, man.'

'No! Shh... ulbit... ulbm!'

'Easy now, young drummer – trust yer man, m'man!'

Within two more of Sticky's belly rucks, we drew onto the double yellows outside the Newcastle Arms in North Sherwood Street. For reasons which he seemed only five per cent capable of disclosing, Sticky had laboriously attempted to indicate a preference to remain seated and continue the journey.

'Shid – no! Woolb! Ib! It's...'

I grabbed him by the forearm. 'Trust yer man! It's just a quick medicament to sort your guts out, then we're awayski! Honest!'

'Lyin' bastard! Oooo! Ulburrr!'

As another torn Chimney fly-poster was being used somewhere across town to conceal a Martini bottle at the bottom of someone's dustbin, back in the Newky, y'man me drummer was slumped in headshaking disbelief at the bar, as y'man meself procured triple James Beamses – *purely* to banish the burps, and for no other reason springable to mind whatsoever. The Beams were caned back before the change of the tenner returned, then we were back out to the dromedary. Similar at Phil's. Similar at the Piano, similar at the Coach and Horses, similar at the Tavern in the Town, similar at V53, similar at the Salutation and Royal Children, similar at the Bentinck. Then as the dromedary reached its ultimatum, drawing up at the Queen's Hotel, similarity came to a very sombre halt in the wry, unforgiving form of Joe Planet – self-appointed sentinel of sensibility. Mission: to wring a soundcheck out of his band, like it or not, before half past seven.

Sticky made the chauffeur's patience worthwhile, bade him a burpy adieu and promptly tripped on the rubber floor mat and launched himself head first towards the pavement, where I was mercifully on hand to arrest his earthbound noggin between my knees, before the pair of us keeled over at Joe's feet. Joe was less than tickety over all this.

'Tup, not you two as well? Come on, chaps – we've got enough on with the Skipper, tonight.'

'Whur-sup? With the Skipah – uh?'

'You'll see.' Joe impatiently bundled the both of us across the street to the Mardi Gras, whereupon the next problem to surmount appeared to be the negotiation of the half-naked, drunken vagabond who'd decided to pass out in the doorway, clutching a drained whisky bottle in fond embrace. Inside, the stairs were very, very steep. We opted for an arse-bound descent, one stair at a time, holding hands. Sticky had looked somewhat puzzled since the doorway.

'Ahse-ahsayerwhat, Shed, ah sure ah've seen that bloke in the doorways before. Somewhere. Before. I'ave.'

'Yeah?'

Joe was still on hand to allay his mystery, whilst continuing the drove.

'Yes. You probably will have seen him before, tup, it's the Skipper.'

'Whu?'

'Chokin'?'

'What a state to land in – New Hampshah, tharriz!'

'Oh, don't worry! You two look much worse – tup; now, if you'd both be so good as to crawl up there onto the stage, I'll go and carry him down and then we'll see if we can remember any songs, tup.'

After the fourth attempt to enthrone him at his keyboard stool and halfway through a glaringly painful rendition of 'I never dream of you', the Skipper's lifeless head came crashing down onto his synthesizer, triggering a deluge of feedback through the system. Joe and the Croc exchanged signals to halt proceedings for the time being to place faith in two hours of abstemious restoration. We resigned the stage to the supporting band in order to reconvene for the time being over at the Queen's Hotel – all except for the Croc who was expressing the need to chat with a hitherto unseen petite and demure little blonde who'd arrived asking for him.

Harbouring a bilateral dread of the tup tycoon, Sticky and I arrived back over at the Queen's, marginally quicker than the National Grid could've arrived at its light bulbs, given identical notice. Inside the lounge, we cast our cross-zips sloppily over the cloak-stand beside the Gents' room to feign its usage, then immediately fled through to the back bar to evade further frownings; and as the lounge began to swell with Nottingham's summer sound scene scientists, the quieter back bar became end station for any flimsy aspirations we might have entertained for pulling ourselves together. Sticky slammed the driver's change of a twenty onto the copper-topped bar, clung to the handrail for dear life and turned to try and fine focus on my tightly clamped lips.

'Sh-sh-Shed, m'man. Righp. Thisssit! Choice! Whassit to be – throttle or handbrake?'

'Throrrul, course! Do I look like some kind of greens-eating, crust-cutting, cocoa-to-bedding, sister-pleasing, Cheshire chew-arse?'

'Hah! Ass m'man – whoop! Shurrup – it's the barmaid! Shhp!'

It's the barmaid floated along the bar to us upon a föhn of Femfresh. Under a swirling black pall of semi-permanents, there at the hand pumps she tarried, clingingly rigged in sprays of Palais des Doges pastels, which were a pleasantly contrived diversion from the Guernica-esque grin in between, which could easily have derailed a man's beer appetite for good.

'What can I get you, gents?' There it was again.

'Shem'man?'

'Y'know, Stickm'man – I've often sat awake at night wonderin'. How many Barley Wines equal one pint.'

'Oh, four – easy!'

'Not fivey?' We were singed by another blast from Guernica.

'I think you'll find it's just over three, gentlemen.'

'Wauhh-ahh! Then ther'll be just enough room for a splash o' lime! Game, Stick?'

'I'm yer man, m'man!'

'You both want triple Barley Wines with lime?'

'Me first, miss!'

'And don't drown 'em.'

'Bloody hell! You pair been at it all day, then?'

'Not yet – erbhahhp – yet – djizzun.'

She lovingly wrung the likes of six Barley Wines into two poised pint pots, then administered the lime toppings. Joe's ghoulish snigger could now be heard above the general blah from the other side. Sooner or later we were going to have to retake his exam; contingencies had to be drawn up.

'By the way, miss, we normally refer to this pertitla beverage as a "hand shandy" – so if we need an... *when* we need another, you'll know wosswot, yeah?'

She winked knowingly over her shoulder.

'Nicely, nicely, Stick, m'man – let's get back to the others! If Joe gets tupping – amembah – mum's the word, Bob's yer neighbour...'

'And life's a wingnut sandwich.'

'Uh? Now you're just bein' delivrutlee persnickative – and that's a comeetlee diffrun' kettle of surrealists, alberobero.'

We turned for the door.

'You first.'

'You first.'

'Just take a biggy and go for it, will yer just?'

As luck was to permit, our migration back to the lounge had coincided with the Skipper's *own* swashbuckling advent. Whereupon entering, he wasted no time in firstly jarring a tableful of beers with his arse before sneaking over to where the Biffers were incognisantly sitting, to yell '*Boo!*' – which caused one of them to shower a complete stranger with her cider. We swerved around him, as he then approached the bar to offer to buy his jacket a drink. Meanwhile, a sedentary Joe, who for once appeared imporous to antics, was disposed in fervent conversation with two young gentlemen of a studious application.

'Who's he waffling to, Stick? They the support mob?'

'Nesseenem me life, mate; anyway, let's bug!'

'Don't say it's anoth... I tell you what, m'man – whatever happened to the Seventies? Remember? You used to get chatted up by *women* at your gigs? I'm beginning to think Phil or Eric or one of the other four billion people that hate our guts've gone and got us registered in the bum-plumbers' directory for a laugh or summat!'

'Ha, ha! Shush! Faces serious!' But Joe's reception was one of formality and professionalism.

'Er, chaps? Sticky – our drummer – Shedfixman – our bassist. This is Robin and Gus from the TPSU. They want to do us a feature in the first term newsletter, and look at a booking for Oct/Nov.'

Thankfully, Messrs Robin and Gus weren't handshakers.

'Stick! Shed... er, man! Pleased to meet you – here! These seats are free! Now! What we thought of, was this! Brief interview – to be quoted over gig report and individual personality focus.'

'And if we can just...'

At this point, I finally lost the samples. And knew it. Gazing twitchily out through the permaglow of my mind's champion lush green hedge, I could see that Sticky was also struggling hard to contain his indoopiworg. Back on earth, we'd both had brushes with media muppets before. And come out at best misrepresented, misquoted and mispackaged – like stew in a newspaper. It was an historic foible. You could come to Nottingham and play Rachmaninov; but do it in a leather cross-zip and they'll say it's psychopunk. Do it in a Daffy Duck wristwatch and they'll stick it in the panto revue. No matter whoever began the script with whatever good intent, that was always Nottingham's fast and invariable edit. It was best to be cagey and yet, here was Joe not being cagey. But he had a smile on at least, so we sat and played along for peace.

Robin, stoat-faced mouthpiece of the duo, did little to sway my impressions. He exuded little to nil in the departments of patience and concession. From the off, he seemed insistent on injecting his own inflexions into every reply he was given. Nottingham at work, already. Gus sat knowingly nodding – occasionally fidgeting to line up the focus of a Pentax camera, which his chubby digits would then press into his far chubbier cheeks to line up the shot. He, of the pair, seemed the more sinister and irritable. Somehow, he inspired the feeling that someway down the road, you wouldn't have been surprised to discover him in some tabloid headline, aspiring to notoriety as the BUDGIE FOUND PADDLING IN THE RAVIOLI serial rape strangler, sparking an international manhunt. I didn't particularly relish the patronage of either of these little cacks and rose again to order the 'hand shandies'. Upon returning from this, it appeared that the Skipper had joined us to give them something *else* to think about. Joe was puzzlingly entranced with the 'shandies'. Robin was thinking up fast questions. Gus was thinking about the nerve-jangling grin which the Skipper was broadcasting directly at him and his Pentax. Robin had thought of a question. It could have been posed to anyone; but in order to both quantify the danger, and to deflect its attention from the TPSU's newest photographic investment, it was tentatively offered to the Skipper.

'Well... the Skipper – I believe – is it? Well, do you usually make a point of enjoying yourself at all of your gigs?'

'Ummph?' The Skipper had managed to clamp his lips together just in time to arrest an accidentally discharged beerwork.

'I mean – meant – er – you're having a good day out, then?'

The Skipper thought he may have half-detected a faint whiff of patronise. The eyeballs ballooned outwards. His head zoomed closer in on Robin. Gus was thinking of lending him the camera after all.

'Rrrinky-tinky-tinky, dear boy!'

Robin rode the gift horse.

'Er, is that *good*?'

'Good? We are the best!'

Robin's eyelids flapped shut instantly in the blast. Then the paining smirk wandered back across his teeth.

'Well, the best! Ha ha ha… nothing but, eh?'

'I've got a Hillman Hunter!'

'Really? A Hillman Hunter?'

'Bert.'

'Bert?'

'Bert.'

'Who's Bert?'

'What's Bert.'

'What's Bert?'

Gus crammed the Pentax further down in his kitbag.

'A Hillman Hunter!'

Robin changed tack and Chimney, in quest of the advent of anything rational.

'Soerrr – Sticky! How's Notts Forest going to do this season, eh?'

'Notts Forest. This was direct indication of an out-of-town, patronising prick. I disguised the shudder with speech.

'We don't know.'

'Come on! None of you into football?'

'Football's not our game.'

'So what's your game, then? Cricket?'

'Nah.' From now on, any sport would be all ours.

'Don't tell me!' He scanned our faces in eager expectation.

'Don't tell me – it's ice hockey! You're Panthers fans!'

'Nah.'

'So what *is* your game?'

'Blow chess.'

'Uh?'

I'd thought of a pacier one. 'And fruit gum dog.'

'Uh? Fruit gum dog?' Robin thought he'd misheard.

'Yeah. It's an old country pursuit. Me grandad passed it on to me dad just before he got shot.'

'Your grandad got shot? What for?'

'For wearing an English uniform in the German half of the battlefield, so – no...'

'Ha ha ha!'

'...no! The ojject is: you wanna laugh. So get a packet of fruit gums, purrem all in yer gob at once, then when they're just beginning to get soft, give 'em to your dog to chew...'

Gus parked his lager in expressed disrelish.

'No, honest! You'll piss yourself watching the poor bastard trying to get his jaws apart!'

'Ha ha ha!'

'Well, moving along for a second; one thing that strikes me is that none of you particularly owns a Nottingham accent.'

Cheeky little bastard. I could see him standing in some boozer back in Aber-fucking-soch, spouting Midland and claiming he's lived here all his smarmy little shitnosed life. Sticky kept the ball firmly in our court.

'No, actually we're from the highly trendy and "with it" County of Suitshire.'

'Suits me.'

'Gravy, booby.'

'It suits us all, dear boy – mmphrrr!'

Directly opposite, it was gradually dawning on Joe that, by virtue of this brazen exhibition of non-compliant nonsense, something was very much less than tickety-boo with the booze. This dawning was in turn detected by Sticky, who then opted for all-out attack as his first line of defence.

'Nah, but seriously, foce – we all went to Grammar school and lost it. Then we lost the accents – ha, haaah! Well, all except Joe, that is. He had to be content with one of those – "other" schools.'

'Hey, bollocks! Tup – I went to Grammar school!'

'Okay, okay, huc! Tell me the capital of Spain.'

'Madrid!'

'Nope, huc!'

'Tup, it's Madrid!'

'Nope!'

'*It's Mabastard-drid*!' Sticky fumbled to his feet, setting out for a fresh import of hand shandies.

'Actually, the capital of Spain is Pesetas, you newark, ha ha ha! More shandy m'man?'

'And I know your pair are still on the sauce *without* the benefit of any education whatsoever!'

The TPSU opted for a last ditch attempt to acquire one scrawny strand of sense which might survive the edit, and with the Croc still maintaining an uncharacteristic absence, the opportunity to supply it was looking to befall my unworthy shoulders.

'So, Shedman-fix-man...'

'Shedfixman. Tough one, eh?'

'Sorry, Shedfixman! How did you get *that* name?'

'Long story with big long words and no pictures to give you any clues.'

Joe's eyebrows tilted slightly. Robin resumed.

'Well, won't go into that, then. But I *was* about to ask what you thought about the shooting dead of Fela Kuti, just last week?'

'Livid.'

'Livid? Really?'

'Yeah – livid. It was all over the Saturday afternoon telly and I was sat waiting for three late kick-off results.'

'But, but, the man lost his *life* for his art!'

'We all do – so what? We make these choices. We do.'

'Well, for a start, I think and feel he had a statement to make, and was very skilful in using his music as a vehicle to both reach out to and preach – and passionately so – emancipation to the masses.' Oh dear.

'Really? I never saw it that way – hey! Have you got any of his records? We can play one at the Skipper's court case when he's up!'

'Some people might consider your remarks to be at best cynical, or at worst racist and empathetic to a stereotypical white Anglo-Saxon system of archaic and self-perpetuating dogma.'

Oh double dear. Time to let the dog go.

'That's just the sort of thing *some* people *would* consider – hey! It wasn't *me* that shot him, you know! I'm from Woodborough Road – he was from Africa; so's the bloke who *did* – well, so far, anyway! You never know, they might pick *you* to knock his biography up, then *you* can explain exclusively to the entire planet how and why *you* suspect he was the unwitting victim of some dogmatic Anglo-Saxon bloke sitting quietly in a pub somewhere in Nottingham, craftily pretending to mind his own *fffucking businessss*!'

His dilating eyes bounced off walls, faces and windows. His snotglazed hooter smelt scoop. On he badgered, in fearless disregard.

'So, but when it *really* comes down to it, what *is* your honest opinion on this issue?'

I had to keep myself talking to save a horrible murder.

'What's *your* honest opinion?'

'My opinion's irrelevant.'

'I haven't got an elephant!'

'Pardon?'

Oh deary, deary, dear. Mercifully unpestered by the savagery of perception. Joe buried his head under an arm to sigh for the passing of yet another attempted PR exercise. The Skipper was leaning clumsily on one elbow, chestily sniggering before suddenly snapping from his muse to peek inside his Old Horrible tin, only to remind himself of being tobaccoless.

'I say! Either of you Trent Poly Wallydoodles got a fag? I appear to have leff mine in the machine!'

Sticky was now desperately trying to land the rim of his glass anywhere against the front of his head. Tupfully exhausted, the beaten Joe's eyes cast one final prospect of abdication to each of the toperous triumvirate in turn, before he resignedly produced and unwrapped a fresh pack of cigarettes, drew one out, stuffed it between the Skipper's soggy lips and methodically procured him a flame, to save everyone's trouble. At this point, the door was dealt a hefty shove open, revealing a keenly circumspect Tinker, flanked by the Sergeant and the hitherto absent Crocodile. Tinker's busy scrutiny ended at the interview table. He unhooked an equally busy meerschaum from his lower jaw.

'Oi! Chimneys! We're on!'

Sticky desisted momentarily from licking the inside of his beerglass.

'Yuh! Right wiv yer, m'man – ten minutes!'

Again the meerschaum was curtailed to standby. 'No – we're *on*!'

The intrepid Robin saw his last chance to ply another interrogative of mind-boggling insignificance.

'Shed! Just one last...'

A football-sized cloud of dyspepsia was coaxed from its deep moorings, and somewhat haughtily, I belched the word '*Tilt*' loudly and directly into his face. I then got up, drained the last of the hand shandy and made off towards the door. The Skipper stole the remnants of Sticky's refreshment and followed on, offering a brief snippet of practical advice to the questionnaire as he passed by him.

'I suggest you find a jolly big sausage, then go and wedge it aft, dear boy!'

Sticky remained ensconced, wrestling with nearsight on an empty glass, which he could have sworn on every mortal oath was not. Tinker bellowed across once more.

'Sticky?'

'Yeah, yeah, yeah, gimme two minutes.'

'They're announcing us *now*!'

'Wuh? Woooo!' He scrambled to his feet and began to negotiate a wavy line to the door, as if standing in two separate canoes on a white water course. Joe was last man out. He glanced around, performing the conclusive body count before departure.

'Okay, everyone's here. Let's go for it.'

I felt a massive surge of pep, as we strode out for the Mardi to the choral 'Go!' I felt great – I felt ready – I felt sober – I fell over. Twice, thrice, times four; I attempted the stand up to no available avail. Although commendably lucid of thought, considering, my legs – it sombrely appeared – had accepted total responsibility for the day's downpour, and in order to so do, had reacted with fresh air to form jelly.

'Er, chaps – *er, chaps*!'

The others had already crossed the road – even Sticky was halfway. Joe glanced over his shoulder, glanced again, then glanced to the heavens.

'God give me strength!'

'Yeah! Well, while he's at it, ask him to chuck a bit over here will you? Me legs 've packed in!'

'Tup, come on, Shed! It isn't funny.'

'Can you see me in hysterics here? I'm telling you they've packed in! I can't get up!'

Sticky was giggling and aping a Presleyan hipshake'n'knee-tremble from his point of progress in the middle of the road, which did little to support my appeal to the others, especially Joe.

'Packed in – bollocks! Come on, man – we're already late!

My frustration with my body was rapidly becoming temper, which perhaps luckily was the only form of sincerity Joe was ever likely to accept, given his current frame of mind. Still, I falsified a stoical contentment.

'Bollocks? Fair enough then – bollocks it is! You lot carry on in there and enjoy yourselves and I'll be lying outside, just across the road if you need me for owt. Don't forget to turn it up a bit, so's I can whistle along and not feel left out so much – *the bastards've packed up*!'

Joe, whilst outwardly unconvinced, realised that the time for argument was long departed. We were expected on stage. How we got there was of brutal indifference to all.

'Right! Shag this for a game of snakes and ladders – Croc? Get Sticky inside. I'll hold the Skipper steady. Tink, Sarge! Go and fetch *him*, will you? Bullshit or not – another *shandy*'ll probably persuade this sudden *paralysis* to wear off. *Miraculously*!'

'Yeah, you'll know when it wears off, mate. Your fucking sprouts'll be dancing on me instep!'

Upon being duly and ably hoisted aloft, I was whisked quick time across Sheriff's Way; legs trailing, toe ends of my Docs scraping along the tarmac all the way to the main doors of the Mardi. Just inside, the two neckless beauties standing guard had seen all this, and were gleefully squirming shoulders and cracking knuckles in preparation for the latest masterful delivery destined to have Wilde spinning in his box.

''E in't cummin' in!' Just goes to show how you can sell a man short. Tinker withdrew the meerschaum.

'Sorry to you too, lads! He's in the band – he's *got* to come in.'

'J'urright 'en!'

With the others already on stage and poised for the kick-off, Tinker and the Sarge decided between them on a temporal saving and beat a path straight through the cluster of bodies out front to haul me with the aid of a further surrogation of many public arms up onto the platform. Once in prime position, the final four stabilising hands were successively removed as the Croc – noticeably superzealous – ploughed headlong into the first count; evidently whether or not I was ready. Confidentish of my standing, Tinker fetched my bass and dutifully placed it in my hands. I recall looking at that bass. I'd had an identical feeling twenty-three years earlier, when at the age of four, somebody bought me my first little plastic guitar for Christmas. Sure, I'd seen the gets played hundreds of times – but was I supposed to hug it? Drink cherryade off it? Or just introduce it to grumpy old teddy bear, who was bound to feel outdone and demand to know my intentions towards it? The jelly had obviously been bounced from legs to brain in haulage. Within the first two bars of 'A Chimney is born', all options were thinned dramatically as my fingers put paid to two – *two* strings. Bloody bass strings to boot! Two at once! The activity stage-side became hectic. After a brief conferral, Tinker dashed back on to equip me with the support band's Fender Precision bass as the opener drew to an end. Surely, obviously, The Chims had been aware of my shortcomings and would hang fire to accommodate the changeover. But not a bit of it. The Croc barrelled straight back in before the last echo, and 'Let's get ugly' was looking much the uglier for no bass line.

'Arms up, Shed! C'mon – quick!'

I hastily obliged, wondering initially how the bloody thing may have been tuned. But as the guitar dropped onto me, that revealed itself as the least of my anxieties. If we'd have taken trouble to watch the support, we'd have soon remarked that its bass player was not only a very skinny lad, but also that he preferred to strap the bass topchest high. That it surpassed my head was a wonder alone. The crowd relished watching me spend the entirety of the second number wandering from pillar to post with both forearms strapped closely against my face, my fingers wriggling helplessly in the air and my nose sniffling over the curvature of the guitar each time I swallowed. During the lengthy struggle to maintain facial contact with the proceedings, I twice asked Joe for help in muted pleas; twice he lapsed into hysterics and waltzed off. In desperation, I turned to Sticky, who was by then himself so incredulously shitfaced, that whilst gawping at me, he missed a shot on the crashride by two inches and fell head first off his stool, following the drumstick. The gig was out of control – yet the reaction of the packed house indicated that we'd been presumed to have concocted all these antics; we'd just turned up the slapstick a cog, that's all. This new greater threshold for future misbehaviour was fine enough, but it was now palpable that we were beginning to lose our fear of big audiences and could no longer rely on *that* adrenalin burnout to suppress the alcohol.

Later, as the last minions milled around in the exits and Sticky sat lapping his face and neck with a bar towel, I overpaid the barman for the last time and wandered, bottle in hand, to the dressing room in search of pointless conversation or to check that my kit was safely stashed or something else unimportant. I'd expected the room to myself, as the place was now so quiet, apart from my wailing eardrums, but there was the lone Crocodile, standing, staring, hands in pockets, full bottle fizzing quietly on a desk alongside.

'Hey! It's you, Shyboy! What was all the frisk about tonight – hey? What? Not a Biffer in the postcode? Wossup m'man? Got a headache? Eh – trust yer Uncle Shed – we can cure the dreaded glum! We'll go on somewhere, yeah? The night's yet but a baby! What say you, Crocodile?'

'Shed... me mum died... this afternoon.'

I'd have been less flattened by a fully subscribed double-decker bus. I slammed the beer onto a draining board in case I fell over. My eyes welled, I suspired torrentially. My heart began to slam against the back of my teeth and I felt snugly akin to a smug, stupid, selfish, prize prick. I'm doing my best bit to fuck the gig with anything and everything ready to hand, and this guy witnesses his mother's last breath, then marches straight off to play bobbydazzle. I was small. He was tall. He'd just redefined Chimney. He'd just redefined Chu. He'd just redefined guts. Permanently. Now I realised why the Skipper always protested him to be the salt, the spirit, the flame, the aura which begirt the entire concept – yet unassumingly. Instinctively, I threw my arms around the salt; gave the man my fiercest hug.

'And you just got up there and brassed through the lot? Fuck it, man. Talk about the show must go on!'

'Oowah!'

'I love yer, Croc!'

As with ever-impeccable timing, the Skipper came staggering into the dressing room doorway, only to witness his vocalist and bass player in the intimate clinches.

'Ooops! Asorry, chapsss! Leave you both to it, then!' His eye sockets could've snatched a volley of tennis balls. We fell about the room in hysterics; the Skipper wouldn't sleep for a month over this. Now, from habit, *that* question entered my head again.

'Ay, Croc! Don't suppose you know who's shanghaied the gig money?'

With equal spontaneity, and bearing the now compulsory footnote to a gig evening, Sticky's high regions tilted around the doorframe.

'Oi! You two coming for some pizza?'

'Oi!' What?

'Ooiee!' Just hang on! I'm very, very unhappy about this. You pan me off with some archaic rhomboid pertaining to quadrant zhelvai twenty segment as of last month's omniconfiguration – plus tempus two arc and say 'please find the kids?' Wanna know where I found your fucking brats dealing illegal mononuclear replication – or rather, getting some five dozen clones to do it for them while they're washing, drinking, smoking and watching fucking television? Yeah, that's what I said – *washing*! No? Only the Milky bastard Way! Try cube at cuboid with a bi-monthly ovarian impulse – and not only Milky Way! Solar *A One-Alpha* ring any alarm bells? Yeah? Third joiner – no? Earth? Earth? Patafucking-gonia? Valais? What about Roswell, or the little shooting down business near Bloemfontein by some projectile which some of Onrad's Bacillae could've knocked together between strainburst – 'find the bastard kids'. No, I don't want to sit and have a cheeseburger – no, I don't want to share a neighbourhood with the grinning bitch – get your fucking hands off my shoulder – get off, gedoff, gerraaaff! Just leave me alone, leave me alone, leave me *alone-uh*?

'You paying for the pizza, sleepin' beauty?'

Whur? Where the...? I'm sitting next to a bass guitar in a select corner of what I would presume to be the Wheelergate Pizzaworld, surrounded by... police? Whoa, whoa, whoa – let's just wind back this tape. Uh. Uh. Uh. Uh. Uh. Uh. Someone's knife and fork left on a couple of used plates across the table from me. I know *I* haven't eaten, because all I can taste is Barley Wine. Wait. I came for a pizza with Sticky. Sticky. Sticky?

'*Stickeeeyerbastard, yer*!' I was slammed back into the seat by two starry knights.

'Oi! Simmer down! Payment, or what?'

'I've had scoot all to eat!'

'Never mind! Your pal's done two house specials, me duck! 'E's gone – you're not. Paying – or what?'

Sticky. Bastard. I suppose this is getback for the phone call earlier. Obviously I did some toe-stepping thereabouts. Okay, I'm Shed, he's Sticky; he'll lose, I'll win.

'I'm paying for shag every.'

'S'alright, Sting! Then you're nick-edd! And naturally...'

Luxalordy! Does being a Chimney automatically dictate the

bare minimum of an inspector response, these crimes? Standing there, rapping his cane against the woodwork to keep me awake and spruce.

'...you've never met the bloke before in your life?'

'Never... what? Never met the bastard? Crank your buggy up, lads! I'll take you right to the little shit-kicker's des res – *right now*!'

'Sure you will.'

'I'm *telling* you I will!'

In a slightly different world where Sticky had supplied me with some adequate warning of this cocky little plunge, I would have gone oyster on them. But here was a deliberate stunt – a snider at that – and it begat an instant retaliatory strike.

All the way up to Sticky's gaff, the trooper at the wheel kept chuntering on about how he wouldn't have had time to get to Forest Fields, but I knew Sticky. He'd not only competed admirably in a few Robin Hood marathons, but he'd quite capably complete a Rubik's cube in each trouser pocket simultaneously, whilst wearing boxing gloves and using tweezers, before letting himself get captured running a restaurant.

'It's there – forty-five, with the alcove and knobbly glass door.'

The wheel chunterer overshot the address by some twenty yards and was then forced to reverse carefully back along the tightly parked Russell Road. He chuntered afresh upon noticing the Dickens residence in complete and utter blackness. As the inspector disembarked to begin a nonchalant browse along the slab stone pathway to the house, I was allowed out of the car, cuffed to one of the two troops for just in case, in spite of confessing an inability to even roughly calculate how to sprint for it, lugging a bloody great guitar in its case.

'There's no answer.'

'Told you.'

'And I'm telling *you*! He's *in* there! I can smell the cheeky get! He's in there, all right!'

The inspector turned again to rap his cane against the heavy, oakleaf-patterned glass, blinkering a glove to his eye to strain for any sign of movement in the hallway beyond.

'Nope – still no answer.'

My bondage twin gave a sudden yank on the cuffs and marched us hastily off towards the others on the path, turning a switch at his lapel to suppress the radio traffic.

'Ssst! Chief! Someone's heading this way – down the street!' The three of them stirred clumsily into action.

'Right! Everybody into the alcove! If it's him, we'll be ready!'

Yeah, and he won't tumble in the slightest – with a bloody great patrol car stuck out there, blocking the road. Twats! Two troops, one inspector, one villain and his bass guitar, packed fish-fashion into a daft little alcove. The mortified gaze on the face of Sticky's neighbour as he walked past was more than worth preserving for future referral by the Academy of Method Acting.

'Uh? That you, Shed?'

'Hiyer, Nobby! Alright?'

'Er... yeah, yeah! Er, enjoy yourselves, lads! D'don't let me interrupt you!'

'That 'im?'

'What do *you* think, you biscuit? I've told you he's in *there*! Tell you what – I'll kick the glass in! *He* can drive me up to the phone box, *I'll* report a break-in, and *you* can be sharply on the scene to investigate the break in. Suits *me*, because I must admit to being a little bored with this, now. Suits *you*, because you get to nick the *slippery little bastard*!' I knew slippery was harkening well. 'So, what d'you say? Well?'

At first, the inspector seemed more than taken with the idea, but then common sense began to creep in. Just my luck.

'I'm tempted, son, I'll admit. No – we'll have to nick you on approval until he turns up with the dosh. I accept that you've been more than helpful, so I'll see to you getting bailed around breakfast time.'

Around breakfast time? Well fine and bastard dandy! That would sit so spectacularly with the Dragon. Here we go again; see it already. Arrested? That the best you can come up with? Biddle-abbiddle-abbiddla-bloody turbo.

'Sticky – you shifty, horrid little drummer! Your wagon's fuckin' painted for this one! You hear me? You're processed as a fuckin' pea, my son!'

'What? Drunker than *I* was at the Malt Cross, when I gave chunky Kevin's ear a sound cuffing?'

'Yep.'

'Easily.'

'Surely not as drunk as I was at the Asylum Club, when I popped into the back between numbers and fell asleep there through the rest of the entire shebang?'

'Yep, *and* Sticky was.'

'*And* more.'

'Faced as you like – legless? Look it up in your dictionary – it'll say see *Shed.*'

'Crikey! Right, well that's it, then! The ruddy gloves are well and truly off from now on, dear boys! Off, twice across the mush and lobbed squarely down at the tootsy boats or I'm a ruddy Chinaman! Blowed if *I'm* playing third fiddle to a pair of freshwater admirals!'

Of the party of cheermongers aboard Bert, as he berummed faithfully away from the night's last thrash over at the Nottingham Irish Centre, the Skipper was the least cheery. Being usurped as performing high drunkard was not to his relish. Taking the bronze was barred from nightmares. Tallbob, Tinker and the Parson were forthcoming with neither consolation nor platitude in the grave matter. Bert's loud pedal was administered a spring-wringing crunch as they banked into Maid Marion Way; Tallbob's ear was squashed against the passenger sidescreen.

'Oi! Steady onish! Let's get home in four pieces!'

'Who's dropping first?'

'Tink's farthest.'

'I'm crashing at Tallbob's.'

'So who's's closer? The Parson's or yours?'

'About the same.'

'So who's *dropping first?*'

'Doesn't matter.'

'Us.'

'Me.'

'No – go on, then – you.'

'You go, if you like.'

'Oh, for fuck's sake! Do you all think you could notify me by post before my tax disc runs out?'

As Bert raged around Theatre Square, accelerating sharply into and along South Sherwood Street, the altruism raged even louder.

'Drop these two first, then.'

'It's up to you – you're straight on – there's fewer lights.'

'So where am I going?'

'Right.'

'Left.'

'So was that *bastard* right or *fucking* left?'

'Left.'

'Right.'

'I'm losing the bloody lights! I'm going straight through, unless you tell me – *noww*!'

'Right.'

'No, left.'

'Aahh, lookout!'

With barely a spare second for the Oxbridge debating society to cross forearms over their faces, Bert slammed thunderously into the elevated kerbing which filtered three directions and soared nose-high for some twenty feet before crunching down onto the offside rear wing of a stationary Ford Escort parked to the left. The Escort's boot lid bounced clean away and sailed skywards as Bert ploughed on, careering into parked vehicles both left and right of South Sherwood.

'Woooeee!'

'*Sheerrt*!'

'I didn't see that boot *land*! D'yer see that?'

'Never mind that, Tosh – I've got no steering!'

'Hit the brakes!'

'I've got no brakes!'

'Handbrake!'

The Skipper cranked up the handbrake, then sighed pitifully as the lever flopped back down with a resigned 'clank'. He grappled on at the wheel as the car rebounded on towards the Shakespeare Street lights.

'Do something! They're changing to red!'

'I *am* doing something! Can't you smell it?'

'*Look out*!'

'*Waaaaah*!'

With the traffic lights already at red, Bert veered straight through and around into Shakespeare on just two wheels, before the nearside kerbing hooked his grounded front wheel sharply to the left, drawing him onto the concourse and burying him face first into the metal shuttering of a drive-in garage. It was over. Tallbob counted heads.

'Booh! Everyone alive?'

'Won't be, if we're still here in five seconds!'

'How d'you mean?'

'Recognise this place, at all?'

'Some garage?'

'That's correct – *some* garage. And to be precise – Traffic Division's car pound some garage.'

'Ooozitz… wotzat?'

'Shit! He's right! We're on Candid Camera! Leg it – fast!'

'Split up! Stay backstreet!'

With everyone out and beating the almightiest of hasties, the Skipper turned and paused for one last glance at the crippled Bert. Rents, crumples, sideswipes, hissing radiator misting up the buckled metal slats with his perspiration. Gnarled 'Bert' logo on the now wrinkled-up bonnet.

'Oi! Don't move! You!'

Tinker hadn't been far amiss with the five seconds. This was 999 land, and the Central Fire Station security cameras had notified the next door Central Police Station of the whole event. They were so close that it was a waste of time fetching a car round.

Instead, two hefty runners were dispatched from the desk and were heading Bert's way in swift and angry resolve.

'All the best, my dear old boy!' The Skipper began to beat the greatest hasty of them all, staying backstreet through the bleak morning's rainy overtures until he was safely home.

'Zznerr! Zznerr! Izzzanurrr! Uh? Blick? *Awaaaachoo*! Buh? *Wachoooo*!'

Billy's horrified gaze emerged from the molehill of tea. He wailed out another air-piercing sneeze, which sat him up in bed, spitting hoarsely, rubbing his eyes and furiously discharging his nose as the brown, speckly cloud rained gently back down upon and around him. A figure was standing alongside his bed.

Sssnip. Rustle. Skish… snip… sskishisskishh…

'Wuh? Who's? Skip? That you, mace?'

…sssnip. Russlywapple. Ssskishhh…

'Skip? *Waaaathoooooze*!'

'Yes, dear boy?'

'Woss… woss goin' on 'ere?'

Having restored upward movement to one eyelid, he

squinted around to finally acquire the unblurring vista of a bedraggled Skipper taking tea bags one at a time from their tin box on the dresser, clipping them in half with a pair of paper scissors, then emptying them out over *his* head, before discarding the papers into an open suitcase which appeared to contain some of his clothes.

'Skip! You goin' mad or sump'n?'

'Yes.'

'Eh?'

'Yes. I'm going mad!'

'Wha?'

'I'm going mad. Obsession *is* a type of madness, wouldn't you say, dear boy?'

Sssssnip. Wuffle.

''Ere! Pack it in! Give over, will yer?'

Ssskishh. With another teabag dispatched to the case, the Skipper placed the scissors quietly down beside the tin box and turned back to the Y-fronted waif sitting cluelessly atop his Darjeeling drift duvet. Billy goggled on nervously.

'I'm going mad, because I'm obsessed with tea! Is this making any sense yet?'

''Ere, eh? Wasting all me tea...!'

The cobalt blue eyes blazed. 'I want to kill teabags! Dirty, evil, sinister, oozy little teabags! Ungrateful, arrogant, insolent, crafty little bastards!' Then the Skipper's smouldering hellfire subsided into mournful appeal. 'Will you help me in my quest? Will you? Will you join me?'

Billy thought carefully and fearfully for a few silent moments. Then he gave a sideways nod and began to swing his pale, craggy knees off the bed.

'Ay! 'Ere! Tell you wha' – I'll make us a nice...'

The eyes blazed twofold; *four*fold; the lips pursed. The Skipper jerked forwards two inches. Billy retreated behind a scrap of duvet, evacuating from it a speckly brown cascade in the process.

'What? What – was – that?'

'Er...'

The Skipper was slowly stirring the air with his nose. 'You weren't... just about to offer me...' his voice fell to a whisper... *'a cup of tea,* were you, Billy?'

The Skipper's nose was still stirring the air. Billy's head did likewise in hypnotic fellowship.

'Er... ner... n–no–no! I wasn't, er, goin' to offer you... to do tha'.'

The Skipper's nose transferred to up and down motion.

'You *were, weren't you*, Billy? You *were* about to offer me a cup of tea, *weren't* you?'

Billy almost found himself nodding involuntarily back at the Skipper before spontaneously erupting into a jittery rationale.

'W-w-wah-w-well, ay, look. I just thought a nice 'ot cuppa might...'

'Yeraaagh!'

'Aaaaah!' Pinced between maniacal talons, Billy was launched face down onto the floor with mattress, pillow, tea and bedding on top of him.

'*Out*! You're *out*, you fucking wanker! And before you ask, a wanker's a mixed-up newark – *right*! Keys? Good – here they are!'

He grasped Billy's house keys from the dresser and jammed them into his pocket before shunting over the three-quarters packed suitcase near enough to hand to scoop, swipe or throw into it sundry items of esoteric worthlessness from dresser, bookshelves, wall, drawers and floor.

'Seems to be everything – *right*! Who's out first? *You*, or the *other* junk?'

Billy's muffled appeals squeaked out of his bedding as the Skipper wielded the case.

'Ay, come on, Skip! Not me case...'

'Not you, the case? Fair enough, then! You know best!'

The still partially-concealed Billy listened to the rumble and crash of the suitcase as it met with the terminal stair and burst open across the foyer. Poking his head out of the mattress, he gulped despairingly at the other rumble and crash of welling thunder over neighbouring rooftops and the thrashing of rain against the windowpane. He gulped again at the depressing vista of leaden skies thereout. Then came a third rumble and crash, as the Skipper lunged back into the now threadbare chamber.

'Actually, looking at some of that crap, I'd say you made the best choice – *out*!'

'Give us a shance – I need to...'

'Ah yes – bag of washing in the kitchen! I'll just fetch it while you pop downstairs to smarten yourself up a bit... no doubt you'll be wanting to knock 'em dead out there!'

'Ow! Be'ave!'

Down in the kitchen, the Skipper began briskly around, thumping numerous malodorous carbon-datables into a veteran black bin liner, before tightly knotting it at the top whilst egressing back through to the foyer. Directly behind the door he found Billy, clumsily hopping into a sock which could quite credibly have once been waved to goad a Maxim gunner at Paschendaele.

'Skip, I...'

'Ah! See you've taken your own good advice. Well, can't disagree there, dear boy! Big impression! Speaks volumes! Well, mustn't keep you hanging around any longer! Goodbye, and good luck in your new career as a male model...'

'Buh...'

The Skipper bared his teeth as he hastened man, bag and baggage on towards the front door.

'Outttt!'

The whole of the foyer shuddered as the sonic boom born of door on doorframe enforced a resounding endorsement of Billy's sudden, short and unexpected notice of quittal. Leaving his hopping shadow to the other side of the stained glass panel, the Skipper stormed back into the living room to thrust rump into the fave armchair. He caught up on breath. The eagles frowned on.

'Well? What d'you expect? The filth've captured Bert! He *had* to go! Bert didn't!' His eyes slowly raised until the chimney breast and its infestivities began to appear under the rim of his eyebrows.

'Blooo papers! Blooooo papers! All mine! All my little blue papers! Vehicle deemed unroadworthy... vehicle deemed... unroadworthy... vehicle... vehicle... vehicle... *vehicle*!' The crash of metal shuttering reverberated through him again. Yes, it was the case. They had his car; they had his details. They had all the details. It wasn't a patrol – it was running footfilth in short-sleeve shirts. A camera! A ruddy CC! A link between modus and description, then description and vehicle, then vehicle and details, then all of those and him! They had the whole jolly job lot and they were coming! They were on the way – any minute now! *Pissed*. Pissed as a monarch. Easier rap, if he was captured sauce-free.

'Bloody good point, you two!' He launched from his respite, snatching up wallet, lighter and baccy from the hearth tiles and made for off. But where, at 3.30 a.m.? He sat down again. Clubs? Shut. Friends? Coma or nicked. All night greasebath noshery? In town – hotbed of stinkers. All night snooker hall? Not a member. Friends who were members? Coma or nicked. All-night cinemas? Town. All-night dosshouses? Been drinking. Bugger it, then: it's the kiddies' tree-house on the Forest Rec until opening time. He leapt to his feet, marched into the foyer and tugged open the front door.

'Aaaaah!'

'Waaaaah!'

'Ohmygod! Fooo!'

Billy stood goggling him directly in the face, suitcase in

hand. Shit. Could've been *them*. Only Billy. Only All Night Billy. From the All Night garage. Tick. Tock. The *All Night* garage.

'It's only you – shit!'

The incompatibles hurriedly composed themselves. Billy attempted to exude his thoughts several times over, faltering in fear of further onset.

'Look... whadda mean's this – look, Skip. Why don' we pop down me garage, an' I'll buy y'a zrink – *No! No! Not tea! Coke*? Orrunge? Ay! Jules might even 'ave a bottla vodka – ay? Then we can talk about it – man to man – ay? Wotja say?'

'Damn belter of an idea! Let's go! Chop-chop!'

'Uh, pardon?'

The five-minute march down to the all-night garage nurtured little in the form of two-way conversation. With the Skipper's supersaturated trainers eeking away double sharpish and his pale, apprehensive fingers regularly plucking up his lapels, he was no ready paragon of patience to his counterpart, who was jogging to keep up whilst lopsidedly banging a forty-pound bin-liner-stuffed suitcase against the backs of his legs. The neon-skirted parapet of the Bobbersmill Allnighter was a more than welcome alleviation from the deluge. Beneath it, the Skipper fluttered his lapels and scrubbed aggressively through his waterlogged blond mane as Billy scooted his suitcase up to the sales hatch and rapped cheerfully against its perspex voice vent.

'*I! Oi! Jule*s! Ay – Jules! Me!'

Upon recognition of his well-washed comrade, Jules – a dry, bespectacled, Greco-featured lad of modest stature – set his pricing gun down on a shrink-wrapped carton of lemonade and reported to the vent, against which he held the distinction among his colleagues of not having to stoop.

'Hiyer, Billy! What's up?'

'Ay! Cum on! Lerruz in for a bit, Jules – we're zrown'n! I said I'd buy me mace a zrink. What ja say – ay?'

Jules perused the Skipper, then more briefly perused Billy.

'Soz, Billy. No can do.'

Billy tossed his head. His erstwhile cheery expression regrouped to form a pained grimace. 'Ar-ay? What's gaiwn' on? Half an hour – surely...'

'Can't do it, Bill – big gaffer's new rules! Stuff's been disappearing! Can let *you* in. Not people I don't know! It's me job, man.'

'But ay – it's me 'ousemate – it's me mucker! It's chucking it...'

From his hinterground perspective, the Skipper had now decidedly heard enough. And had enough. The Forest Rec was now double pneumonia away. He patted Billy's sodden shoulder to sever the dialogue. And the idea. And the partnership.

'Don't worry, dear boy! You have a pleasant drink – you may well need it.' He swung about face, marching grimly away.

'I'm going back for Bert.' His pace quickened.

'But, Skip!'

'This's one thing the bastards *won't* be ready for!'

'Skip! Skip! Look – we can take some drinks home...'

'Won't work, Billy – you're just not one of *us*!'

'But... talk... whaddabout...'

'Good luck, dear boy!' He rezipped his jacket, plucked up the lapels once more and strode on to whatever fate back in town. Billy was beginning to flap now.

'Eh? Know what you are, Skip? Ay? Ay? Yer a bastard! Did y'ear tha'? *Bastard! Baaastaaaard*! Loud 'nuff foryer? Ay?' He was beginning to augment the rave with a Saint Vitic soft-shoe shuffle.

'Ay? Ay? Ay? *I'll* speak ter Terliff! 'E'll sorcherout! Yer bastard! Yer bastard! Then we'll *all* get the authorissies on yer! Bastard! Ay! *Bastard! Bastaaad! Zeersee–rott'n–baastaaar*!'

Almost out of earshot now, the Skipper peered back for a moment. The faraway figure of Billy in the rain. Jumping, thrashing his arms, screaming, kicking open his suitcase, strewing his clothes wildly around, then slowly twisting down onto his knees beside the open case. Screaming louder.

'Just one shanse! Will somebody just give us just *one! Fuck'n! Shanse!'*

The Skipper turned and resumed his march. That was the last time anyone saw All Night Billy.

SIXTEEN

The tentative stillness of that next August morning did its best to belie the document of history which now recorded that pandemonium had been temporarily rehoused in fifty acres of Nottingham for the previous night.

And if Central Nottingham Police could only have convened an emergency court session at the nearest judge's bedside upon suddenly fathoming the identity of one particular guest attendant at Bert's towing-away do, they would have neither spared horse nor budget. In the event, the very least they could afford was to deny ground to his feet all the way to the 9 a.m. sitting of the Nottingham Magistrates where, in stark overtones of citizen harassment, Lee Siddons, from behind his customary sandbank of printed precedents, wasted short time in blasting two hundred hours of police overtime clear out of the water by declaring his client unfit to enter a plea, due to still being heavily fraught with the unquantifiable effects of impact shock.

With the prospect of any formal mental assessment rendered unfeasible by the temporal proximity of his *other* ongoing litigations, the Skipper was reluctantly accorded an adjournment and bail, conditional upon the surrender to the police of his driving licence within thirty-six hours, and his body to the County Courts by 9 a.m. of the date decreed in his previous summons. He was subsequently set at cheerful liberty to return home and bicker afresh with the eagles over a suitable fireside allotment for the newest of the ever-supervening muniments of blue.

Relief came to the bassist's bacon at around 10 a.m. when, only minutes after tramping home to another blazing up 'n' downer with the Dragon, a knock at the front door was answered to reveal Sticky's barefaced cheek shining in to corroborate my rubbish from the doormat. Yep, he'd been at home all the time, alright. Upstairs, neatly folded into a pine ottoman until the hammering had died down, but – hey! What on earth had there been for *me* to crow sour over? I get nine hours of good life to spend surrounded by cold, piss-stinking concrete as reward for not booing a goose; whereas Sticky bilks for England, spends the night in weapons grade luxury, rises mmm... puh? Then he tucks into two truckers' breakfasts and makes a casual phone call to the Bill. The Bill then arrange to arrive at a mutually convenient hour to chauffeur him from his doorstep cautioning – firstly to settle the trifle at Pizzaworld; then to drop him cushily off at Shed's emporium for coffee, biscuits and unbridled gloatage. The leery bastard even had the front to nudge them into doing a crime prevention check on his doors and windows before setting off – as God is yer judge. Sticky may have relished all of the legend, the impunity, the coffee, the biscuits, the one-overmanship and the whole brimming rumpus of sundry kaboodle. But it would all still remain as but a fraction of the dish due to him from Nemesis.

SEVENTEEN

The dwindling of the summer of 1987 bandied around its thunderbolts in every which direction. The Crocodile shrugged his biffing legions and – out of the blue – married his mystery petite. A few days later, Sticky marched into a liberal Saturday night attendance at the News House, firing off Havanas whilst declaring the pledging of his troth to Duty Miss Cutey – in spite of my insistence that the best thing for troths was Brasso. Joe's fiancée did a bunk with some beacon-faced bum-plumber from Basford; we never *did* work that one out, but to be perfectly honest, Joe seemed content into the bargain; even his tupping became practically extinct overnight. For nearly a week.

My personal bolt occurred shortly after we'd wowed a full Sunday house at the Test Match in Bridgford. The audience had been swelled with a drop-in visit by a West Midlands chapter of Hell's Angels. It wasn't particularly their bag, but they took good piss and tolerated it back in good humour. We'd finished the gig and were packing up the kit. I was bollocksed, hungry and looking to get my cut of the gate and shoot off home in best haste with Selina, who was busy dialling for a cab. Life was simple. Drink. Gig. Sweat. Drink. Taxi. Curry. Drink. Shag. Sleep. Simple? Little did I know that simple had buggered off for good. I heard the clack of the receiver.

'Okay, Chims, we've got a cab coming, just weigh me in with a bit of gate and we're away.'

The Skipper turned away to find something else to do. Croc left. Joe laughed.

'Weigh you in? What with?'

'Come on, m'man, don't fuck about – I'm tired. Weighbridge.'

Sticky flopped a warm palm onto my shoulder. 'Shed, m'man, there is no weight to be weighing you in with. To be precise; nought point nought per cent of buggerall of a sausage in the sense of shag every to the power of minus nil. Ish. Situation.'

'So, who's got it?'

'Nobody, nobody's weighed.'

'Yeah, yeah, so where's the money?'

'We took fifteen quid. We owe twenty-five outgoings.'

'Fifteen fucking quid? There must've been two hundred and fifty bodies in here. One quid per, less twenty-five. I make that perilously close to the region of two hundred and twenty fucking five, m'man – lest yer be wanking one's crank!'

'Well, tup, that's all the gate man said we took, tup.'

'Who did the gate?'

'Tup, Jamaica Stan.'

'Whaa? Jamaica Stan, fffsake! Who put Stan on the gate?'

'No one else we could trust, dear boy.'

'Look, look, Chims – don't misunderstand me – Stan's m'man. But. Stan's everyone's m'man – he probably let everyone in for a hug and a handshake! Are you sure the Croc hasn't darkholed it?'

'We told the Croc just what we're telling you.'

'Yeah? Well, bugger this for a fucking bus pass bonanza... Selina? Let's get outside and wait for the cab!'

Her eyes widened. 'Have you seen the weather? It's barrelling down out there!'

'I don't give a papal wank – I can't stand the funk of bullshit in here.'

'Shed, m'man...'

'Shed me no fucking Sheds, m'man – everything in this garden isn't fucking Lockwoods... Selina? We're out of here!'

Outside, sitting on a gnarled old wooden bench in the

driving rain, waiting for this bloody cab home. Selina burying her pretty face under my jacket, trying to keep her hair dry. I shut my eyes and faced the deluge. Just to calm me down. This caper was beginning to transgress the borders of put up with.

'I'm sorry, doll – I just don't see the need for this cack.'

'Do you still love me?'

'Don't talk bollocks – hey, here's the cab!'

We scrambled across the concourse and she ducked into the back door, shuffling her rump over to accommodate boy and bass. I barked out, 'Woodborough Road – city end', slammed the door shut behind me, and we were away before the chassis'd stopped rocking.

Skimming, skating, skooshing along through the rivering roads of West Bridgford. Screen wipers scarcely able to cope with the clattering salvos ahead. I felt Selina's shivers, felt her eyes on me. Then again.

'So, was that a yes or a no?'

'Whaaat?'

'To the question I've just asked you.'

'What question? Don't fuck me about, Selina. I'm not in a be-fucked-about mood. Sorry. I'm just not overly tee-hee-hee at this moment.'

'I'll talk to you tomorrow.'

'Tomorrow? It's already tomorrow! Only trouble is telling these fucking puttydicks it's tomorrow. I'm playing in a bloody good band of highly talented, highly intelligent, highly high drunkards. We drag bodies out of the woodwork for miles around. We play any old tosh and they howl for it. We get shitfaced beyond all credence of popular medical opinion and dish out abuse to make the Devil wince, and they stomp and howl for it. Alternatively, if we ever fancy upping the jazz a touch, we can play tosh, get faced, dish it out, puke up, wank over the monitors, pop over to the bass drum for a shit, then fall over with dirty arses and stay there for a kip onstage – and they'll dance and hop and whistle and cheer and stomp and howl for it… and you know there'll be more of the bastards there next time, waiting for you to do it to *them*. It's nothing less than absolute licence to print money on the strict condition that you do what the fuck you please, to whom you please, as often as you please. We're in raw, raving, ruddy paradise via the back door, on the QT. We've got the gigs, the guzzle, the girls, the good times. The only episode of this fucking sitcom which we've yet to star in is the one where the house Jack Russell comes pirhouetting on at the end in a gold lamé tutu and roller skates, then croodles down and shits a hill of Krugerrands. And this is the *band* I'm talking about! How are you supposed to expect the pubs and clubs to part with it, when the fucking newarks you're playing with don't give a toss in a tuck shop whether they get the golden gong or a tongues-in kiss off an ashtray – uh? I'm telling you…'

'I'm pregnant.'

When my balls had eventually crawled back upstairs from the impact of my jawbone, I turned to look into her eyes. She said it alright, and she meant it. Bolt. Wowzerbugger.

No one offered peep all the way to the city, then she slid an arm inside mine.

'Are you mad at me?'

I turned to look at her again, then faced front without a word. My larynx was still paralysed. Finally, as we turned into Woodborough Road and still harder rain, it cranked back into action.

'Pull over just here, mate, would you?'

'Ay? We're not there, yet!'

'Here.'

She turned to me again, I could almost feel her panic wave ripple against my skin.

'I want a takeaway.' I jumped out of the cab. Took a couple of steps, breathing in the rain, raising my head upwards, to see how long I could keep my eyes wide open before the stinging droplets slapped them shut again. In all honesty, I didn't have the Fig's iguana *what* to do next.

'Have I screwed things up?' She was behind me, leaning against the rear wing of the taxi, copping a parallel drenching. Shivering. Scared out of her wits. I closed my eyes again and hung my head to feel the rain streaming down the back of my neck. I stretched out an arm and then its hand and its fingers behind me. I heard her heels begin to click towards me and felt a hand slip into mine. Keeping the hand, I turned to face her.

'You fancy a curry?' She hung back on the answer.

'Fuck the curry – have I screwed us up?'

'Are you *sure* you're pregnant?'

'Positive. I think.'

'You *think*!' As she broke into tears, I pulled her tightly against me, clumsily massaging her back, shoulders, arse, head.

'Do you *want* to be pregnant?'

She could scarcely gather enough bits of voice together to stand words upon. She subsided into hysterics.

'All – I – ever – w-wanted was you – and – a – ba-baby!' Then she was inconsolable. I loved her so much at that moment I was beginning to crush her. Again I ran my hands over her shoulders.

'So, er, will you just settle for me and a curry for tonight, then?'

She motored into a loud, nervy laugh, still crying in between the chuckles.

'If you w-want m-me and the baby!'

I grabbed her face and kissed it hard. Then our eyes found each other. Our lips and faces slowly withdrew.

'Listen. Nobody's screwed anything up. If you're not pregnant, I want you. If you *are* pregnant, I want you and the baby – but right now, the baby's mum and dad aren't doing baby too proud, standing around here, fishing for double pneumonia, right?'

'Ha ha ha!' She took a long hard sniff at the rain. 'Come on, Shed – are you pleased or what?'

'Yes, I'm pleased; yes, I'm proud of you; and yes, I want you to get this cab home and get into some warm while I go and get us some fierce nosebag. It won't take me twenty minutes. Okay?'

'You're sure you're pleased?'

I kissed her again, full on. 'Positive! Absaturbo! I'm just a bit shocked, that's all! Now get in there and get my kid home out of this shit and warm some plates – I won't be long. Promise!'

'Don't be...'

'Just get in!'

She ducked back inside and the cab roared off, ladling a swirling eddy across the pavement in its wake. I watched it away up Woodborough Road for a while then I turned and yawned – probably through nervousness. I sighed – perhaps as torrentially as the climate. I walked to the pavement edge and back several times. What to do, what to do, what to think, what? What? What? What? Tilt! Freak! Fuck! Overload! I was on; I was off. I began to stride. Suddenly, fiercely, I knew exactly what was required. What was required, was not knowing what was fucking required anymore. I urged on, faster, more faster, then I ran. I ran into the rain, I ran hard – anywhere – over busy junctions – through lines of night traffic – anywhere. Felt sick. Saturated. Exhausted. Lungs bellowing. Chest cramping. Override it. Go. Get wet. Go. Keep going. I was back at the bottom of Mansfield Road before I knew much else; walking uphill... looking for some food, I think. Searching neons and air ducts for the optimum allure. I passed the Yorker, thinking of all the drunken Sundays after finishing rehearsals in the cellars of the volunteer centre, opposite. I passed the derelict shop doorways serving scant shelter to tonight's trapped itinerants. Down. Splayed out under rags and cardboard. Practising death due to disenfranchisement by democracy. Hopeless. Haggard. Ill, sick, worse, getting worser by the sleeping hours. Glue bag. Sherry bottle – not quite finished until it's kicked over to temper tomorrow's envy. That's how it began for them, too – as babies, passionately cradled in the arms of a young girl who swore to love them more than anything for ever. If she'd just clung on harder to them – to the years. If time and tears between then and now could all be taken back. What would've happened if she'd seen this coming? If she could've only stayed younger, longer. If time could only slow down on dangerous bends. On. Past half a dozen coin-importuning ghosts, reeling. Change? Change what? I wouldn't know where to start. Your life? Your clothes? Your breath? Or your fucking surrenderous outlook? Don't be content with the rut. Never feign sickness. Never surrender. You're not doing your level best for yourselves here, humans. Then Christ knows if any of us are. All *I* need is for time to slow down on *this* bend, but it won't. Ever. On. Past four or five grease barns – ever see yer kebab with the fire off it for four hours? Outlet, then outlet. Then I saw him. Shitfacedly self-resplendent on the other side of the rain-pothered window of the doggest Indian restaurant this side of beef. We always walked on to some place decent, but there he is – in there. God surely wants me to see this. Sole occupant at the back table. Flagging coffee cup swaying in a semi-prehensile fist. Unchecked coffee, streaming down shirtsleeve to elbow to pool of previous coffee, symmetrically matching the pool around the other elbow; featuring chutney, yoghurt and ground-in poppadom flakes. His lolling head more inert than the coffee cup. Fig. Dining after the usual fash. Alone. Eyes closed, but nattering mutedly away to an imaginary Nuremburg Rally. No point popping in or tapping at the window – he won't even recognise you by now. Walk on; you've seen this film sufficient times. He'll mess the shop, mess himself, ask for the William, pay for at least three items which they've *forgotten* to ship out, get up, say goodnight, forget where he came in, walk into the kitchen, get ejected, get refused a taxi, get ejected, get back to a flat which he moved out of nine years ago, get ejected, get a night's kip under Trent Bridge again, wake up freezing, make his way to Sneinton Market and Thelma's Allnighter for a Full English, then off out for early doors and rebound for all the same again. Now I've seen the two paths and both of them give me the galloping rumpshakes. On. Get up to the Himalaya. Reliable. Five minutes out of the storm could well make the healthy difference tomorrow, eh?

I practically fell off Mansfield Road into the crisply civilised dryness – the warm aromatic bliss of the Himalaya's open corridor. Frazzle of the rain now surmounted by frazzle of onions, cumin and garlic. Dopplerised traffic by spirited yells between waiters and chefs. Insanity by industry. Breathe. Blow the rain off my lips. Rest. Hoo.

'Please! Come inside and sit for a while, my friend! Is it a table or a takeaway, sir? You look very wet, my friend? Can we offer you some food?'

'Uh? Oh, sorry! I was miles away, mate – er, yeah, yeah! It'll be to go, please!'

'Come! Sit inside – dry a little! I'll bring you the menu. You okay, my friend?'

'I'm fine, thanks – it's a hell of a night!'

His palm swooped to pull out a stool by a table beneath an ornately perforated arched partition, through which beamed fleeting orange rays of candlelight from the subtly obscured alcove behind.

'Please. I'll fetch a menu.'

'Just my usual, ta! Thank you very much.'

Get a grip. Wipe the water from my face. Let industry drive for a while. Risk the wall's freshly refettled whitewash on my jacket back. Sit and breathe easy. Grab a piece of context here.

'Shed, Shed, Shed!' My back grew automatically rigid.

'Sarge? Sarge – is that you in there?' The main diner was on the other side of the arched partitions, but I was far too tired to hoist my rump again and far too proud to go squelching into and across relative decency, looking like Houdini's cat. All I needed for Polaris was the dry vibrato tones and the verifying scent of meat bhuna to know I was in company with the Sarge. See him or not.

'You're looking like a man looking at trouble, Shed! *Do* talk to yer Uncle Sarge about it!'

I breathed hard and long.

'Look at it this way, Uncle Sarge. Selina's on board for Jinglebells, m'man.'

No reply. Did I imagine all this? Who's there? Then Polaris.

'Wellah, wellah!'

I strained to get a clearer view. Gave up.

'So, er... I predict the impending necessity of er... a snippet of parental advice. Off yer. Like. As it were.'

'And what calibre of advice could a man like me *possibly* have to offer a man like *you*, Shed?'

'Come on, Sarge – if I want food, I'll look in the pantry. If I want drink, I'll go and look for a boozer – if I want rock 'n' roll, I'll go looking for Tallbob Weedley, and if I need sense, I'll come looking for you – you've got the all answers, m'man – you're a "Dad". What comes after the chicken omelette?'

'Shed, Shed, Shed! Don't you know? There are only *two* names for the man with all the answers: "God" and "Ignoramus". Which would you attach to *me*?'

'You've brought a child here. To this place. Aren't you scared shitless?'

'I've tried "scared" on, Shed – several times! It doesn't fit me. So what are *you* scared of? The baby? The rain? Or just yourself?'

'I'm confused, Sarge.'

'It's easy, then; do nothing and think no more – most *have* done and we've *still* survived and thrived for ninety thousand years to amount to this conversation.'

'But it's like I'm standing at a crossroads, Sarge, and the signpost's painted with a question mark for each direction. No clues, all guesses.'

'Ah! Life's great mysteries, Shed – these seemingly eternal ravages of testing and torment! Machu Picchu! The Turin Shroud! Why *was* Dan desperate? Why, regardless of whatever colour clothes you wear, is the fluff in your belly button always blue?'

'I'm serious.'

'I'm pleased that you're serious. Is it your first crossroads then, Shed? I doubt it. Does direction begin from your eyes, or from a post in the ground? You've travelled miles. Far more than me. You've seen thousands of signposts. How many have worried you? How many have chosen your direction for you? How many have chosen your view? If all points are unknown, then they're all as good. What do you see from life's window, Shed? Each component of the view holds a different pleasure or displeasure to every eye. You have green eyes; mine are brown and therefore given to inconcurrence. Or can you only stand at a window and give an account of the glass, because the window chose your view?'

'I think I see the view.'

'Then we share a common handicap equally. But then between us, you have the sharper eyesight. Perhaps it's time to use it. Select your rosiest components, m'man.'

I needed a couple of moments to take it all in, before the backed-up head traffic filtered off a little. Of course he had the answer – which was always the one staring you unacknowledged in the face. Who *ever* knows what's down any avenue? And even if you *don't* know, then what's worrying all about? You make the best of what's revealed.

Screw up? You can always get back on the bus. The aromas heightened suddenly and noisily.

'One of the usual!' I snapped to, and dug for a tenner to meet the waiter with, halfway across the room.

'Keep the change – goodnight!' I turned to take a pace back to the arch.

'Night, Sarge – cheers, m'man!' No response.

'Night, Sarge!'

Unsure whether he'd heard, I shuffled perforce through the passageway into the main restaurant. At the table where I expected to find the Sergeant motoring around his meat bhuna, a waiter was stooping to gather up the remnants of repast. Quickly, I glanced around. I covered the main room. Foyer. Main room again. The Sergeant was nowhere. He couldn't have left the room without passing me. He wouldn't have left without speaking. I checked again. The waiter was disembarking the table with his harvest of crockery. He smiled warmly as he passed by my shoulder.

'Er, excuse me?'

'Sir?'

'Sorry, but the Asian chap – the one sitting there. Where is he?'

'That gentleman at *my* table, sir? He left a long time ago.'

'He... uh? Are you sure?'

'Yes, sir – a long time ago.'

'But, I didn't see him leave... surely I would've seen...'

The fifth calling arrived one week later, as the hour of the Skipper's grand summoning was nigh. Fearing the largest of all likelihoods, we'd rallied *chez lui* the previous evening to facilitate his conscientious indifference to all, before falling en loose masse back into number eleven Maples Street at approximately 4 a.m.

His fixture with justice was designated for 9 a.m. At 8.15, we were busy shouting, slapping, pinching, punching, shaking, shaving and dressing him – nudging toast and coffee at him – anything to provoke his vital signs. We even told him that Ferrari were considering swapping their racing colours from red to shocking pink, just to keep him with us.

By the time the three taxis had arrived at 8.40, he was suited, booted and ten per cent tickety. Bloodshot and bleary, but ready. Solemnly, he ignited the day's first roll-up and then beamed hysterically.

'Okay! Just tell the mahoots to keep the chocs on, chaps! Just popping up to freshen me gob a tinge!'

'Shheesh! Well hurry up, Paul, for God's sake – before you get clattered with a bail breach as well as.'

Having shoved the bathroom door to and lowered his trousers, the Skipper enthroned himself for the condemned man's final fart and reached over the bath for the mouthwash as his Praetorians were sighing, fidgeting and tapping redundant digits against various vinyl fittings within taxis. He emerged from number eleven at precisely 8.45 to squash all anxieties, awkwardly lading his rump into the nominated front seat of the lead car and clicking tight the seatbelt. In the seats behind him, Curly, Sticky and myself afforded him a brief last scrutiny as he turned to the driver.

'Right! County Courts, dear boy and with all horsepower, if yer please!' He peered round at Curly.

'Oh, er – by the way, I owe you a bottle of mouthwash!'

Traceably perplexed at this, Curly nevertheless gave the word to go. Mindful of the perils of the rush hour, I offered the suggested route of Mount Hooton then Waverley then play it by ear, mate. Primarily unhindered, the earplay saw us all the way over Clarendon before encountering the unavoidable crawl of Maid Marion Way. It was somewhere along that first leg of Maid Marion that an itzy, bitzy discrepancy raised its undesirable head.

'*Aaahahh*!'

'Uh?'

'Eh?'

'Whaat?'

'*Ahaaahah*!' The Skipper was, for no good earthly reason, peeling into hysterical fits of laughter.

'*Aaaahahahaaa! Aheeep! Weheeehoohaaaa*!'

'Uh?' Concerned looks were exchanged in the rear.

'What's up *his* kilt?'

'Is he still going from last night?'

'I don't know. Are you?'

'No. Are you?'

'I'm fine.'

'He wasn't *this* faced last night!'

'So, what – what the fff? *Oi! Paul! What's your game*?'

To unanimous horror, the Skipper popped open his seat belt, leapt out of the car and, despite the total unavailability of malarky time, set about performing toilet against the British Telecom showroom window before then selectively stalking amongst the bounteous supply of rush-hour pedestrians for the self-beknown purpose of gurning directly into their faces.

'Shit!'

'Get him! Just hang on, driver!'

Three car loads of courtesans flooded out onto the concourse in a combined effort to secure the cannon as it weaved knavishly amid the unnerved flocks – determined not to be secured. He'd managed to set the whole excursion back another two or three unavailable minutes before he was finally swooped upon and manhandled back into the cab. His seatbelt firmly reapplied, the convoy reloaded and continued with the crawl.

'Exactly *what* is going off here, you mad bastard?'

'Paul, we've got all of five minutes left to get there – are you playing or what?'

'*Ahahaa! Arinky-tinky-tinky*!'

'He's faced!'

'He *can't* be! *Paul*! You alright, mate?'

'Hehaaa! My life is my own, dear boy! My life is my own!'

'He *is* faced! Check his pockets.' Curly loomed forwards and, gripping the headrest, snaked alternate arms around the seat to tap the Skipper's jacket pockets for signs of the secret to his high jollity. This having proved fruitless, Curly returned to his seat. He turned to shrug his shoulders to the bewildered faces in the following cab.

'Nothing. He's not carrying any booze and he hasn't had the chance to get any drugs. I just don't...'

'Ffffk, he's off again!'

'Get him! We can't have this caper!'

The Skipper had taken calculated advantage of a lull in locomotion to make another bolt for it. This time he made a bee-line to the doors of St Nicholas' church and began hammering on them with his fists, demanding sanctuary or a seat in the Commons. This time too, the second car was better prepared. Ten pairs of hands snatched him quickly away, then hoisted him shoulder high back to the roadside. We paused indecisively against the first car as he jostled and fidgeted haplessly.

'Wha-what's going on?'

'He's faced!'

'Eh? How?'

'*Haaahahaaahah*!'

'He can't be.'

'I know when he's faced, and I'm telling you he's fucking faced!'

'He was stone cold, twenty minutes ago!'

'What can he possibly have done since then?'

I racked and racked my brains and the word "bathroom" flashed on, every time. Bathroom. Bathroom? All roads led to bathroom.

'What's in his bathroom?'

'Taps?

'Mould?'

'Spent farts?'

'I'm actually trying to be serious, here! He's due up in one minute and he's fucking faced! What d'you think the syrup's gonna say? Eh? Don't blame you, me old son – quite fancy one meself! Wait while I fetch the car? *Paul*! What's in the bathroom? What've you had?'

'He mentioned the mouthwash.'

'Mouthwash?'

'Uh?' Another rack and then the penny fell. Years before, I used to work in the stock rooms at the mail order distribution centre. There was some old bird I recalled in perfumery – Joyce Duckminton – always sipping at the consignments of Listerene because of its alcohol constituency. Quick half of cider on her lunch break to get the taste, then back to work; belt a couple of bottles with the tackhammer she kept under her desk and then write a whole batch off for herself – 'Received Damaged'. Off her tiny planet by 3.30. Now I feared the worst.

'Oh, fuck!'

'What?'

'Shit. Shit. *Paul*! Slap him – *Paul*!'

'*Aaaahooo*! My mouth is *cleansed*! My breath is *frrreshhhh*! And my *life* is my *own*!'

'What's all this mouthwash hogwash?'

'Paul, listen to me – eh? Paul? Did you spit the mouthwash out? Did you spit the mouthwash out, or did you drink it?'

'Haa-aa-aa-ahem! Mahwosh! Hah! Ad... ad... adrank it, of course – *ha*! S'watcha s'posed to do cos... iz no mahwosh in jail, they say. Hiznit?'

'Oh! Fucking turbo!'

'Uh? So he's necked the gobrinse – so what?'

'So it's at least fifty proof, "so what"!'

'Oh, shit.'

'*Paul! Paul! Paul*! How much? How much did you drink?'

'*Haah*! Hum. *Ahahahah*! Ahum! Rind abite this time, I owe

you a bottle of mife woss – *aaaahahhhahahaaa*!'

'Well that's that, then. He's swilled the lot, he's swilled the jolly fucking job lot. Absolutely fucking turbo!'

'Is that bad... then... is it? Much?'

'What size bottle was it, Curl?'

'Economy seven fifty mil – so, er... pint and a mouthful, at a guess.'

'Economy?'

'Yeah. Sure it was more like sixty proof, though.'

'Glorious – victorious! So in other words then, we're talking a bottle of whisky – minimum!'

'In less than three minutes.'

'Luxury.'

'We've had it.'

'Now what?'

'Right! Get the fucking boot open and get him in. If we're not too late, there'll be a chance for his brief to get a case or two jumped in front of him.'

'But if all this is correct, Buck Rogers'll be back before *he's* sobered up.'

'Got a better idea?'

'Come on, lift!'

'*Liffft*!'

We hoisted his squirming torso into the boot of the car and clammed it shut before he could regain equilibrium and raise resistance; the drone of ambient traffic providing a handy muffle against the hammerings and frequent everberations of 'Bassahhz!'

'Right! Get back in; fast as you like, driver.'

In short time, the convoy was drawing alongside the shoddy sandstone colonnade of the Old Shire Hall. Whilst the Croc paid off the cabs, the rest of us delicately unloaded the livestock and packed tightly around in an arrestive manner to both preclude any further jaunts and to disguise his unsteadfast demeanour. Once fit and hot to trot, we stormed the courthouse steps as if the premises were licensed. Inside, we were immediately set upon by a rather dumpy, stark-faced lady usher with a smoke-grey perm. She was evidently harbouring a manifest fear of some out of hand scenario, making busy inquiries as to who was which, from whence and to whither and why so many. By now we held the gross attention of the foyer, which buzzed in speculation over the obvious high ignobility of the suited patriarch amid the sunglassed and leather-clad human shield. The Skipper had spotted his brief.

'Iss me man!'

'Who? Him? *Oi*! He's here, matey!'

Lee Siddons switched directions, slightly raising his enormous head to better purvey his cheery grin, and ambled towards us.

'Assit! Iss-iss me man!'

Siddons halted abruptly in mid-amble and glared weighingly at his case.

'Oh, dear!' But the grin didn't subside. 'We're in two, if you'd like to take him up to the landing. I'll organise some coffee.'

'Believe it or not, mate, he's accidentally swallowed a load of mouthwash! He's never used it before; didn't realise you have to gob it out. Any chance of getting his case leapfrogged for an hour or so, while we hold hands and summon up his spirit?'

For an hour or so, we all took turns in the great coffee relay from the downstairs dispenser. When he was eventually tiring of the bean, Tinker nipped out and returned with two litres of apple juice, fobbing it on as sweet cider. This bore a much greater acceptability, and after he'd despatched it all, he seemed to settle down into a more subdued and relaxed candidate. Then, shortly before 11.15, as he was emerging for the umpteenth time from the men's washroom under heavy escort, the mountainous presence of Lee Siddons loomed large again.

'Okay? Well, we're on then. I'll try to keep your answers as short as possible... I take it the rest of you wish to be in the gallery?'

'*Bien sûr, mon poulet*!'

'Cock on, cocker!'

'Okay, I'll have a word with the usher! Paul – if we could just have a brief word before we enter...'

By the time we'd all pushed, shuffled and nudged into a block assembly at one end of the gallery pews, a mournfully resolute Skipper had already assumed sedenture in the dock and was haplessly browsing between courtroom features with a trepidation befitting that of the guest of honour at Dante's housewarming bash. Sticky swayed towards my ear.

'Ssst! Do you think he'll be okay? He looks quiet...'

'He'll be alright! Siddons knows his veg!'

Mark Anthony whispered guardedly from the seat behind. 'That's just it! He's quiet. He's *too* fucking quiet! I never trust him when he's quiet...'

'*All rise*!'

'...here's the syrup!'

The court clerk jerked to his feet as if held on wires by some lofty puppeteer.

'Be upstanding for His Honour, the Right Worshipful Judge John Hopkin!'

The Skipper wobbled. Mark cut in again.

'Holy custody! It's 'ang 'em 'igh 'opkin!'

'Set me rabbit on yer tiger – he's fucked!'

'Fucked, fried, cooked, and dried!'

'Yep, he's fucked! Can we go now?'

In veritable earnest, there was very little to be taken away from old Hoppy. He was nothing if not fastidious in his crusade for equity among all. But on the malarky tolerance scale, Hoppy flickered without exception between a one and a one point one; whereas most of yer Happy Shopper circuit syrups might buckle to a seven. Moreover, on the procedural decorum scale, Hoppy demanded an immutable ten from every player in his courtroom and – be ye villain or Chief Constable – say or do something to rev the rev and the outcome would be much akin to that of poking a Smartie up a polar bear's hooter.

After the puppet had barked aloud the interminable array of indiscretions alleged of the ne'er-do-well in prospect, counsels introduced themselves to the forefront and Hoppy popped his maiden delivery to the dock.

'And how do you plead to the first charge of reckless driving, Mr Snowis?'

Lee Siddons rose immediately in interjection.

'M'Lord, my client wishes in the public interest to enter a blanket plea of "guilty" to all of the charges which he faces here today. Quite clearly, as one may detect from the case depositions, a tragic behavioural imbalance emerges. My client is, Milud, currently embroiled in an ongoing personal struggle against what he freely admits to be an acute and morbid addiction to alcohol. At this stage, I would point out to Milud that there is no suggestion or even the remotest of suspicions that my client's unfortunate predicament is, or ever *has* been compounded by drug abuse, and that there now emerges a solemn determination on his part to seek all available help in restoring both a modicum of self-respect and a more healthy quality to his life. Milud, my client is both genuine and unreserved in his desire to atone for these recent and most regrettable antisocial episodes which are palpably fuelled by his affliction; and as the court may well soon observe, he is deeply remorseful of each and every offence perpetrated during this dark and desperate chapter of his life. We might for instance refer to the latter of the offences, where a sparking of conscience and deep-rooted decency infusing Mr Snowis's hindsight would not permit him to evade punishment. Subsequently he reflected, and turned himself in to the Police as part of – in his own words – "a cry for help".

May I additionally inform Milud that, despite their informed awareness of Mr Snowis's illness, he still commands the unquestioning trust and esteem of his work colleagues and forbears, and has so far dedicated some fourteen years of loyal and valuable service to his long-term employers – The People's College of Nottingham, having frequently merited...'

'Sausages!'

All eyes departed from Siddon's delivery and fell instantly upon the dock. A raucous guffaw tumbled down from the packed gallery. The puppet jerked to his feet.

'*Silence*! Order among the gallery members! This isn't a matter for general hilarity!'

As the excitement ebbed back to a loaded silence, I half turned to Mark, breathing through a clench-jaw smile, 'Too late for General Gordon, you fucking maggot.'

'Told you he was too quiet.'

'Silence in the gallery!' Hopkin edged forward, spanning the fingers of both hands across the oaken table.

'I beg your pardon, Mr Snowis?'

'Preposterous, Yer Shoeburyness!'

'Ha ha!'

The puppet grasped another opportunity for obsequiousness.

'*Silence*! You may *stand*, whilst addressing His Honour!'

The attendant jailer, maintaining frontface, hissed sideways at the Skipper, 'On yer feet, Sausages!'

The Skipper clambered to his feet. 'I said preposterous – it's preposterous, Yer Battleship!'

'Ha ha ha!'

'*Silence*!'

Lee Siddons again rose to intercede with grin preservate.

'Ahem, if I may be permitted a brief word with my client, Milud?'

Hopkin edged forward further yet and offered icily, 'I would suggest that you *do* engage your client in a brief word,

Mr Siddons! And I would further suggest that at some point during this engagement you might consider acquainting your client with the rudiments of law pertaining to Contempt of Court!'

'Thank you, Milud.'

The Skipper's expectant goggle tracked Lee Siddons all the way to the dock where, turning up the grin a notch, Siddons directed *two* brief words to the side of his client's head.

'Shut up.'

His client shut up. His staring eyes panned from Siddons to Hopkin to Siddons to Hopkin. Siddons, still warily half-eying the dock, turned to readdress himself to Hopkin.

'Milud, my client can scarcely contain his shame. His reminiscence of the facts continues to plague him with discords of guilt and remorse – he is often given to traumatically recount his misdeeds, which he now considers "preposterous". Albeit at present an inopportune moment to so do...'

'I could have sworn your client's remark was "sausages", Mr Siddons!'

'*Hic*!'

'Ha ha ha!'

Hopkin panned from Siddons to Snowis to gallery to puppet, whose response was as ever indiverse.

'Silence, good heavens! This court demands silence from the gallery!'

Hopkin wheeled around to view his public full on. His steely grey eyebrows hauled a disdainful and searching glare over the top of the narrow, rectangular reading glasses.

'Alright, Mr Farquharson – I'll deal with this! Members of the public gallery! You may view me as a complaining old stickler! You may indeed view me as a stuffy old hat! You may view me as you wish, but I assure you, you *will* view me as a man who expects nothing *less*... than impeccable conduct and propriety in his courtroom – and I will have it! I will have it with or *without* the participation of its public element! Now! If this court is forced to suffer any further interludes of this unruly nature, then I will have no option but to clear the gallery. May I also remind you that Contempt of Court is an imprisonable offence which is not exclusively applicable to the defendant here. Thank you!'

'*Hic*!'

'Ha ha!'

'*Mr Siddons*!'

'Yes, Milud?'

'Would your client perhaps be the better for a drink of water?'

'If Your Honour would permit.'

'Please sit down, Mr Snowis! Usher? Would you fetch the defendant some water?'

'Yes, Milud.' The lady usher from the foyer glided across the room towards a glass pitcher upon a salver, set at one end of the stenographer's table. She turned up one of its matching beakers, half filled it and making haste to the dock, held it to the glazed-eyed inhabitant propped askew in one corner. He gazed at the beaker, he gazed at Hopkin. Then snatching the beaker, he downed the contents immediately, offering it back before she had time to turn away. His gaze returned to the bench, whose custodian had turned to invite the table for the prosecution.

'Mr Henson?'

A tall, black-haired, Latinesque gentleman in a flawlessly tailored flannel grey suit rose to beg to differ.

'Milud, the one thing which *is* palpable in this particular case is that, irrespective of his alleged miscorrections with regard to alcoholic intake, Mr Snowis palpably and beyond all doubt represents a clear and considerable danger at this time. He represents a clear and considerable danger to other road users, a clear and considerable danger to the general public, a clear and considerable danger to common decency

– even a clear and considerable danger to his own self, as long as he is permitted to enjoy the liberty to so represent. If one only *briefly* reviews the evidence, one invariably marks a brash and cavalier disrespect for law and order emerging, if not *leaping* from each and every page; perhaps the most recurrently alarming aspect of all therein being Mr Snowis's vociferously bold and aggressive demeanour when confronted by any instrument of authority – whether it be a police officer or a member of the legal profession – or even a waitress merely trying to provide his table!' He stooped momentarily to prise open his depositions with a keen, ruddy thumb.

'Here, for example, the police inspector "placed an arm in through the side window of Mr Snowis's vehicle and politely requested that Mr Snowis hand over the keys" – whereupon, Mr Snowis, presumably to *evade* punishment for drink driving in a vehicle which was "clearly unsuitable for the public highway", "immediately pulled away at great speed, *drrrrrraggging* the officer alongside the car and putting his life in great jeopardy".'

'Ha ha ha!' Henson's knack of dragging out the drag for some extra mileage provoked a snigger upstairs. Hopkin eyed the gallery. Order restored, Henson went on.

'Milud, suffice for the moment to conclude: the prosecution ventures to contend that a custodial outcome would undoubtedly be in the greater interests of the public – both from a safety view and also to the immense relief of the public coffer, which is in desperate need of a rest from bringing Mr Snowis to court. If, then, his afflictions are as true as he would have us believe, a custodial outcome would be surely not so much punitive as *remedial* to Mr Snowis – although it must, Milud, beg the question of whether Mr Snowis is merely concocting his drink problem as a convenient "safe house" in which to retreat from his responsibilities, and from where to devalue both the severity of his bloodlust for reoffending *and* his avid contempt for the law.'

'Thank you, Mr Henson.' Hopkin viewed the dock.

'Would you stand please, Mr Snowis?'

Once again, the Skipper shuffled reluctantly to his feet. Farquharson leered on with abject disrelish. Hopkin pawed at his deps for a while, then reviewed the dock. Again, brow first, his eyes cleared the reading glasses.

'Mr Snowis. Would you consider it fair to say that you currently have a significantly serious drink problem?'

Silence. The Skipper stared. The puppet jerked.

'His Honour asked you a question!'

The Skipper's traffic-fraught head turned slowly on its axis until, upon contact with Farquharson's now less than easy smirk, a manic stare ignited. The lips pursed. The purse subsided.

'Sorry, dear boy – I have to think before I speak... not being a lawyer.'

'Ha ha ha ha!'

'Silence! Order in the gallery! Silence!' The puppet's fastly reddening complexion now complemented his general aura of consummate wanker for all to see.

'Silence!' The Hopkin boom was ever supercessive.

'I shall not repeat my warning to the members of the gallery! I shall, however repeat my question to Mr Snowis. Mr Snowis! Would you consider it reasonable to say that you have a problem with drink?'

'Yes! It's a bit pricey, Yer Championship!'

'Ha ha ha ha!'

'Silence!' The Hopkin shoulders hunched forwards.

'Mr Snowis! In regard particularly to your motoring offences, it is absolutely imperative that the court establishes both the validity and the severity of your misrecreations with alcohol! You seem to enjoin alcohol, cars and crime as if it were the most natural association on earth! It is my proposal therefore, to defer sentencing you for these offences until the court is in absolute cognisance of the facts surrounding this alleged addiction and its potential motivations. In order to establish these facts you will be bound over to keep the peace until this court reconvenes. You will report in the meantime twice weekly to an allotted probation officer and you will report more directly for assessment by an alcohol addiction clinic, to which you may be obliged to re-attend as and when requested. But be in no doubt, Mr Snowis; this binding over is neither a soft option nor a let off. It is merely a stay of judgement. A custodial sentence still hovers perilously over you, and I assure you that if we meet again before this order is fulfilled you will go to prison. Now, motoring offences aside, have you anything further to say before I pass sentence on you for the charges of theft and using threatening behaviour?'

The thieving threatener's head wobbled detectably. 'I don't recognise this court!'

Lee Siddons leaned back in his seat, sighing profusely. He dropped a large red book carelessly onto his desk and an expensive inkpen onto the floor between himself and the rim of the desk. He smiled resignedly and turned away. Hopkin did neither of these.

'I'm sorry, Mr Snowis, did I hear you correctly? Did I hear you say that you didn't recognise this court?'

'No – I don't recognise this court! You've had it decorated!'

The gallery roared. The puppet squirmed. The jailer bit his lip as his nose flared and a tear welled in his eye. But Hopkin boomed on unbeset.

'Mr Snowis! If you are neither drunk nor insane, then you are evidently a very foolish young man, and though you have elected to spare public time and money by pleading guilty across the board, your asinine conduct in my courtroom this morning has served only to negate any favour or sympathy which I might otherwise have been inclined to consider. I have already made it clear that this court is not in the business of dispensing the soft option, as you will now discover. Your disgraceful behaviour in the pizza restaurant on the third of last month was particularly inexcusable, as there existed no mandate for you to be breathalysed and therefore no clear documentation from which to infer that you may have been drinking at *all*.' Shit – he hadn't thought of *that* one. 'Late night crime in the city centre is an unwelcome old chestnut, and one which I am determined to crack. Bilking is not ingenious, it is not glamorous, it is not hilarious; bilking is theft, and the wanton and calculated derision and menacement which you designed as a precursor to your bilking was both cowardly and distasteful. You caused this young woman great alarm and distress for merely performing her job. For this you will be fined in the sum of one hundred and twenty pounds. For deliberately absenting yourself from the restaurant in order to shirk payment of your bill, I fine you in the further sum of fifty pounds, and since the police have been subsequently unable to ascertain the true identity or whereabouts of your co-offender, whose name you have provided as... what's this? Whose name you have provided as one... "Vanishing Frank McSkanky"...'

'Haaa ha haah!'

'Silence! Silence!'

'...you shall therefore assume "Vanishing" Frank's very real and manifest obligations! I fine you an additional fifty pounds for conspiring to commit a theft – consider it on his vanished behalf...'

'Ha ha ha ha!'

The cobalt blue eyes widened beyond healthy. 'Whu? Two hun... whu?'

'...you will reimburse the restaurant for stolen tableware, which I understand amounts to some eleven pounds fifty pence, and you will pay forty pounds court costs – amounting in total to a sum of two hundred and seventy-one pounds and fifty pence. How do you propose to pay, Mr Snowis?'

'Wha? Wha? Two sev… two sev'ty… *Oi! I had a deep pan pizza, not a bloody deep bath bastard! Right! That's it! Woof! Woof! Woof! Woof! Woof!*'

'Hahaaa-hahaaaa!' The gallery erupted.

'*Silence*! The court demands *silence* from the gallery!'

'Usher! Call security if necessary and clear these people from the gallery! Mr Snowis! How do you propose to pay?'

'*Awooof! Wuff! Awoooo!*'

'*Mr Snowis!*'

'*Erwuff! Ruff! Aahwufff!*'

'*Mr Snowis!*'

'*Ooooohuhoooooawooof! Ooof! Wuff! Owff! Erwowwuff!*'

'Haaaahahahaaaah!'

'Clear the court! Clear the court! Warden! Take the defendant down to a holding cell until he comes to his senses! If by 3.30 this afternoon, he is willing to organise payment…'

'*Woooof! Yip! Awrrrayip! Wufff!*'

'Ha ha hahaaa!'

'…*If* by 3.30 this afternoon, he is willing to organise payment… he may then… collect his summons… to reappear in court and then be released!'

The jailer took the Skipper by the arm. 'Come on, Fido.'

'*Aaooof! Wowrrr-hoof! Eewowcha*!'

'Ha ha ha!'

'*Wuff! Hoof*! And another thing! I resent being referred to as cowardly! I'll have you know that brave men run in my family!'

'Haa hahaaaaa!'

'Clear the court! *Clear the court!*'

EIGHTEEN

'Just shut up and get the helmet on.'

'Why me?'

'Because you're the only one who's never driven in his life.'

'Why's no one else having a go?'

'Get real! At these daft prices we won't have enough cash left to drink our way back to town. So *we* all chip in a quid, and *you* get the go – that way, *we* all get the biggest laugh for the money. Get the helmet on.'

'Cammaan! You gonna stand there camping it up for France or you gonna get in the kart?'

'Do I get a couple of practice laps?'

'Practise as much as you like. Just get in.'

'Tup, he'll pull out a note from his mum, next.'

Seeing no plausible way out of this, Curly clumsily donned the black open-faced crash helmet, which then duly expanded upwards and outwards, being the correct size for his head, but far too small for his hair.

'Ha ha ha!'

'Spooky or what? Now the fuckin' helmet's trying to eject before he gets near the kart!'

He straddled the go-kart and carefully lowered himself into the seat. A rather concerned-looking track official swanned over to volunteer a brief induction governing the subtleties of throttle and brakes; after which, to a tirade of derision from the five flopped against the wooden perimeter barrier, Curly crackled and hummed the tiny kart away at a snail's pace. Sticky was pawing tentatively into a tattered bag of chips with half a gnarl creeping onto his face. Joe was grappling with a rather stubborn carton of milk; the rest of us unloaded cans of budget lager, chished and settled back against the barrier in avid expectancy of lap one. Joe, peering casually around, had clocked Sticky's facial infestivities.

'What's up with *your* juff?'

'Well, either it's the beer or these chips. I'm sure these chips taste a bit funny.'

Joe curtailed the grappling and reached over. 'Let's try one...' He tried a fistful, and gnashed away for a second or two. '*Aaahaaahahahahaaaa*! You're right! They're a fucking scream – *aahaaahaa*!'

'Yeah. Time we found him another girlfriend I think, Shed.'

'Sounds like it. What's he gonna be like after another month of whitewashing his ceiling?'

'Mere thought of it clenches yer buttocks, dear boy.'

'Ooowarr!'

'Tup, what's clenching *my* buttocks at the moment is your big, bright, twelve-pint ideas. When you suggested "'ave-a-go karting", you forgot to mention that it was highly advisable to 'ave-a-go robbing a post office first! I ask you – five quid fifty per 'ave-a-go!'

'Oi! This was Shed's idea!'

'That's because I can't trust *you* to arrive without Sherpa Sentencing in tow.'

'I really don't think we'll clap eyes on *him* again.'

'Really? Don't get too extravagant at Ladbrokes!'

'Tup, *now* what's he doing with the chips?'

'I'm looking for the valve.'

'Valve? What bloody valve?'

'The sign clearly said, "Try our delicious fish 'n' chips and enjoy some *real* valve for money." Right or wrong?'

'Oh dear. Someone get ready to catch my head.'

'Ho ho ho! Let's *all* go Vaudeville! I say, I say, I say – my dog thinks he's an engineer! An engineer? Yes, an engineer! Every time I shout "Cats!" he makes a bolt for the door! Ho ho ho!'

'Hey! And it's the end of the warm-up lap!'

The mighty escargot was jittering back towards us with a look of almost vicious concentration about him; his coiled shoulders imparting erratic jerkings to the steering wheel.

'*Yayy*!'

'And he's into the hairpin... pulling three point seven gees!'

'Gee!'

'Gee!'

'Gee!'

'Juh!'

'Tup. Tup. Tup – these bloody tetrapaks of milk! You ever opened one successfully, without wearing half the sodding produce down yer dicky bow?'

'Just follow the instructions. You grip it firmly...'

'Pull back the wings...'

'And stick yer tongue in!'

'Gruh! I'll just wear it again, then.'

As the buggy swung past into lap two – generously bedecked with two handfuls of freezing cold *pommes frites* – a more austere breeze began to overthrow the mood.

'So, er... all in all, the chips weren't all that recommendable, then, dear boy?'

'Well, dunno... They were about two hundred and seventy-one quid cheaper than *your* last eat-out!'

'Ha, ha!'

'D'you reckon Curly's getting the hang of it out there?'

'Yeah. Relaxed as a wedding fart.'

'Okay, so what's happening in the racket department, eh?'

'Tup, Sticky's sorted something out.'

'Yep. Packed agenda – forthcoming attractions – something for everyone, a facophany tonight!'

'And, er, so by any chance – would these forthcoming attractions be, er... forthcoming in remuneration? By *any* chance?'

'Listen! I spoke to Cueball last night...'

'Yuhh...'

'...no listen, Cueball's fixed it with Peter Kirk...'

'Ohh! The Captain's lad! Good show!'

'Tup, you never actually get to see that Captain Slog, do you? You know – him who chunters away at the beginning of *Star Trek*...'

'Are you all going to gimme a rest? Thank you! Peter Kirk is Shipstones' area manager. Shippo's are sponsoring some charity event in the Square on Saturday and we've been invited to enter two teams in a supermarket trolley race around the Council House...'

'Uuhh? Race? We're struggling to stay with the human one...'

'What the ffff...'

'...ah! So you won't be interested to know that they'll be loading the trolleys half full of Shippo's ale and considering a sponsorship, then?'

'We'll do it.'

'Ooowah!'

'But only under extreme protest, dear boy!'

'No surprises there, then! Next Sunday, as you know, is the open air music festival in the Arboretum. I've got us on at around three o'clock between the Coathangers and Harry Stephenson's mob...'

'For the sum of?'

'...fucksake, Shed! I *am* actually on *your* side here, you know! For the sum of whatever publicity a well-attended major local event generates for us! That's the sum of what for! *Thursday*! Live interview with John Holmes, 9.30 p.m. Radio Nottingham. The Beeb would appreciate us at the rear car park by nine. Any boo-hoo-hoos at that one?' He glanced around us all in turn. 'Amazing! Friday night! Cueball wants us at *his* place. We'll be fresh from the Beeb show and we can name it as the very next gig over the air the night before...'

'Handsome! And so, how much did Cueball offer to cut us for a grand's worth of free publicity and busting our guts in front of a packed out shithole for an hour?'

'Shed – it's nearly two weeks away, yeah? Can't we just talk to him nearer the time?'

'Get fucked! Are you seeing this, *twat*? No, we fucking *can't* talk to him nearer the time! Because "nearer the time" always begins with being the week before, then slithers up to the *day* before, then craftily on to the *morning* before, then – before most of us have even realised it – as usual – "nearer the time" has sneaked through the gig and out the back door five minutes *after* the time! Just what the fuck's *up* in this band? Yeah, yerhoo – we're having a scream! Yeah, yeehaah – we're having a guzzle! Yep, wayhaay – we're having a shag! But does all this mean we don't deserve anything else? Because if it does, then somebody explain it to me. You've heard him: four bookings. Which one opens out its wallet? The fucking "off your trolley" derby!'

'Tup, sorry and all that, Shed. Would it cheer you up if I got us booked on Jacko's next tour?'

'Don't patronise *me*, you fucking cunt! You're always guaranteed to be the *first* whining sound to go off after we've been skanked!'

'For Jeff's sake, hang it up you two – will you? Look – Curly's back!'

'Hey! Just bide with me for a bit, m'man, eh? We'll talk to Cueball.'

'Let's do that, m'man, because I'm beginning to get a little sick of this same old fucking pantomime!'

Curly sailed by, taking in an earful. His head turned briefly towards the barrier.

'Oh no, you're not!'

Two nearly empty lager cans glanced off the back of his helmet as he throttled up to beat a hasty off into lap three. With the tension partially defused, the Star Chamber reconvened in less hostile tones along the barrier.

'Look, Chims. I promise you this is less selfish and more simplistic than it sounds out. Aside of the Band, all four of you work from gerrup till four, five, or six tops. Five days a week. Five and a half when someone's arse needs rubbing, then you put a couple of hundred away, knowing your nights are free to get faced, eat out, or get shagged, or go out and play some toons. And when you do those things, all it takes away is a little bit of your couple of hundred, then it all begins again on Monday. Now! Given that I'm just as entitled to trawl a living as the rest of you, and given that I'll soon be the only one of us trying his best to ignore the patter of little feet and given that I don't particularly want my kid to grow up remembering me as "Whatsizface – y'know? That one who spent his whole life farting banknotes off the window ledge" – given all that, it behoves me now and again to give common sense a little hug, although its breath does stink a bit. And what common sense then often politely reminds me of is that since I'm a taxi driver, and taxis invariably strike more custom and less traffic after six thirty; working *after* six thirty would therefore be the ideal way to avoid growing old on a mixed diet of noodles and banging my head on the wheel.'

'Yeah, but...'

'There's no yebbuts about it! Okay then? Let me put this in even *more* absorbable terms. Monday: average take fifty. Tuesday/Wednesday: average take seventy. Thursday: seventy to one hundred. Friday/Saturday: between ninety and one two five. In other words, I could play for The Chims on one of *those* two nights, blow a hundred and twenty-five, plus whatever I drink, plus curry and wake up around one hundred and sixty quid lighter the next day. That's *one* gig! And Sticky – God save him – he's booked us *four* outings within these seven days! How many of you refused a hundred and sixty quid last week? Roaring fucking silence!'

'Never realised we were blessed with such a fucking breadhead, dear boy!'

'*Again*! You've either completely missed or deliberately ducked the issue. I'll go out tomorrow. I'll give the car a good polish. Dip the oil. Clean the windows, feed the nodding dog, then go and park it face first in the fucking Trent – *just* to be able to play bass – two, four, six, fourteen gigs a week for The Chimneys. All I need to know is whether we *are* The Chimneys. If we are? Then I want for The Chimneys what The Chimneys are entitled to: not half, not some, not most – the fucking *lot*! *Cash! Kife! Liquid! Legend*! Now is that *really* so much to ask? The *best*, remember?'

'Oowah!

'Tup.'

'Sparklin'.'

Chish. The noise of the kart engine had now become long overdue.

'Right. So before we go and pull Curly out from whichever pile of tyres he'll be stuck head first in – here is the news. I'll do the trolley race – I'll do the Arbo. Call it a "publicity weekend" – call it whatever. I'll do Cueball's for the same money as the Westwoods, and no less – and that's *plus* the usual beer allowance that we get. But. I'm not doing anything – anything – unless we get together and work some policy out before the John Holmes broadcast, because we can't *surely* be fucking silly enough to go on the air, announcing gigs and answering questions concerning a band we all seem to know fuck all about. That's my lot.'

'Suppose we'd better go and find him...'

NINETEEN

The Saturday morning trolley race served, if little else, to shape and set the pace for the rest of that weekend. As faithfully promised, two supermarket trolleys stuffed to the gunnels with flagons of Shipstones' Bitter were tail-hoisted down from a brewery wagon and presented to the Chimney 'A' and 'B' teams, along with specific instructions with regard to the race rules, to wit: the sole permissible procedure for reducing this handicap was to drink it. Thenceforth, with instant effect, a pitched battle for liquid levity had ensued well before the event had even been announced over the speakers. The subsequent outcome of this, following an unholy bout of perspiration, transpired to be Chimney 'A', consisting of Sticky, Sergeant and Shedfixman enjoying a glorious last place, whereas ahead of that by at least half the circuit – Chimney 'B', comprising of Croc, Curly and the Skipper – blazed home second to last. Amid the thousands cheering on the event were Peter Kirk and Shippo supremo Edgar Wayne, both guests of the Lord Mayor and his other dignitaries up in the Council House balcony. At last, synchronised drunken decadence had been publicly applauded by all sections of Nottinghamia, and for the time being, there grew a new apple in the eye of the Star Brewery.

Upwards, onwards and downhillwards, that apple's core sustained the theme of bulk imbibement throughout the afternoon and further on into the small hours. I didn't bother to wake Selina after eventually stumbling in at around three the next morning. She didn't need the upset, and I was decidedly dispossessed of the delicate applications imperative to the marital arts; and thus accordingly resolved to suck on lager tins and cuddle up with a bass guitar until around nine thirsty. Around nine thirsty, I freshened, packed and set out on foot for Maples Street, where the collective hangover of Chimneys was due to muster to shift kit at the duly specified time of a.m. In the event, I was stunned upon arrival to discover that the arrangement had been forged compliant with the machinations of BST, and that the only Chim yet to show was Joe, on account of his cab being a touch tardy.

When the remnant overnight surfeit of beer had been murdered off by all, all took turns to lever kit into Sticky's Capri. Thankfully, at the Arboretum, the amplification would be communally catered for, which meant that now Joe had showed up, everything could be packed around Sticky, who could then most kindly ferry the jolly lot down there. Then lug it all onstage and set it up, whilst the rest of us copped the dirty job of buying the Atlantic's weight in beer up at Ranjit's. So it was.

We'd been due to pitch around mid-afternoon, so we were given ample time to craze about or take it easy. Then, shortly before the Coathangers had finished their set, they announced that we were to follow them directly, due to a slight change in order – which shunted things on rather rudely, but at least the buzz was ignited again.

As we began our set, two guys poured out of the woodwork and began probing around with video cameras. One of them, we were never to clap eyes on again. The other, a familiar old hippy named Mole, took a Sunday off from tightly pleating his hair and beard to record – with his customary insouciance – some of the most depictive, enthralling, charming and characteristically hilarious footage extortable of that particular window in time. Mole caught the lot – however unwittingly: the whole preamble; the band interviews; the audience interviews; interviews with Chimney lovers; interviews with Chimney haters; interviews with small babies being carried in papoose slings; interviews with

Rottweilers proudly sporting neatly pressed Barcelona home kit. Up on the bandstand were window cleaners, dusting the windows in the background to the beat of The Chimneys, rocking in the foreground. He caught rosy-cheeked, ice cream-toting youngsters running on stage, politely requesting the Croc's autograph, and the Croc then politely offering to bring yet more rose to their cheeks if they ever laid mit to his beer again or posed any more tiresome interrogatives concerning the rapidly expanding piss patch which he was now indifferently culturing about the lap of his jeans. Mole caught it all happily for ever. But in all of it, Mole caught something which I wouldn't have wanted to believe catchable. He caught the last ever performance of The Chimneys.

TWENTY

Wenckk!

Clenk!

'Shhhuh!'

'Come on, you Vaseline-valleyed little bondage tiger!'

The Sergeant turned away to chug hard on a newly fired Gauloise and calmly circumspected the postcode. He shrugged pitifully at the lapels of his famous liver green leather gig mackintosh.

'Perhaps he's out?'

'He's in. He just don't know it yet.'

'Oi. Look – for ff's sake just give 'em 'ere!' Tallbob skipped sideways then leered down at the Parson as he tried to snatch away the fistful of pebbles.

'Oi! Don't be so comical, Shorty! Just – no! Let's examine the facts here. I'm practically a full storey closer to his window than you...'

'And who broke it in the first place?'

'Be critically honest, now. Is it *my* fault that he insists on going out drinking for France every lunchtime as a preamble to pitching his limp, furry carcass into various pink rinse parlours, looking to poach a hairstyle to go with his lifestyle and asking if he can walk your chihuahua round the nearest puddle before he hops home backwards on a moving bus whilst simultaneously guaranteeing safe sex to the first pensioner who can recite "Aqualung" by Jethro Tull? *Then* he suddenly wakes up four hours later, with one bite out of a fishcake still in his mouth and blissful indifference in his mind and trousers to the fact that he should've been up, dressed and ready to meet us more than two hours since. Well? Is it?'

'I'm struggling hard to disagree with you.'

'Fuck him. Give his window another whack. But just for me – try and go for the melamine board covering your previous little indiscretion, can you? There'll soon be more hole than glass.'

'Hmm.'

Whukk!

'Jer!'

Whokkkat!

'Nearly!'

Wokkit!

Wekkit! Tinkle!

'Oooops!'

'Go on!'

Wrakk!

Wrenc!

'Again.'

Wollk!

'Hellurw!'

'Jackpot, m'boy.'

'Is it going?'

'Yep! You win a case of hiccups and a massage from the Swedish prime minister!'

Inside, on the floor, directly below the wooden board, lay Fig – face up, spread-eagled, apart from the customary right hand stuffed down the underpants, and snoring like a road drill. His melamine visitor teetered half a second, before flopping inwards to crash flat into his blissful countenance.

'Zznnervah – bwuh? Mah? *Oi! What the fff?*'

Via hole, Fig's nightmarish demeanour revealed itself to all below. It appeared somewhat dazed and cheerless. A stream of claret was seeping out of his nose.

'Nope! Seems all you've won is an ugly head!'

'Ha ha ha!'

'What's your fucking game?'

'Hide the saveloy on a Saturday night – what's yours?'

'You've broken me nose, you fucking maniac!'

'*Mister* fucking maniac to you, young fella m'laddio!'

'Look. Just get dressed. We're late enough without your further assistance.'

'Fuckid ndose!'

'Fig, Fig, Fig!'

'Come on, hurry up! The Westwoods are playing Cueball's...'

'Hate der bastards...'

'...yes, exactly! We promised Shed we'd nobble them, remember? We're off to Pilkington's to fetch the nobble...'

'Then we get nobbling...'

'...then we'll just have enough time to find a boozer with a radio and listen to the Chimney interview on the John Holmes programme. Get moving!'

'Wait a second. Abstard dose.'

The door of his twenty-fifth floor Vic Centre flat cautiously opened a few inches and the inquiring, fox-featured apparition of John Pilkington carefully exuded into light from the blackness behind its two shivering brass security chains.

'You bring me kebab?'

'Shish doner mix. Chilli, yoghurt, no lemon, no cucumber, no tomato.'

Pilkington's bony hand clasped the piping hot package.

'Wait.' Clicking shut the door again, he scurried back into the living room and, swiping aside a pair of jaded and threadbare floral cushions, he set about cramming his feast down the back of the sofa, alongside the kebabs from the last four evenings. He snatched a miniature airline bag from the table and returned to the front door, this time removing the security chains. He twisted the catch and flicked on the hallway lights. Once again he confronted the Clergy.

'Okay. It's all here. You know what to do, yeah?'

'Let's just see the goods.'

'Right. As you know, the box is by the coffee machine at the end of the bar. Vol, tone, reject rocker switch in between. Number one. Portable electric screwdriver. Screwdriver off. Diamond bit metal drill on. Fully charged. Keen as you like. You go in vertically – one centimetre in – directly above the rocker. You then use it to countersink the potentiometer stalk after number two: slimline metal saw blades with taped handles, which you use to saw off the volume dial. Remember to take it off while the music's turned down and hold the switch still. The blades are keen, but fragile. You've got three. The countersinking'll automatically crank up the volume, so be quick. Power supply – is behind the juke nearer the left. Number three. One metal shroud. One tube of superglue, one pin for the tube. Take pin. Pierce tube. Glue all six points inside the shroud. Press the shroud firmly and accurately over plug and powerpoint. Hold for thirty seconds. Cueball then has three options. Chop the wire, trash the juke, dig the point out. All cost time and big money. He'll need at least twenty minutes to think – that's nearly half the Westwoods' set time down the dustpipe – meanwhile, number four: miniature transmitter; miniature receiver. Three hundred yards, in optimum conditions. Apart from clarity of vocal/acoustic reception, can also pick up on all proximate police and emergency traffic at the top end. Radio traffic, bottom end. Slip the receiver into any miked up acoustic guitar on this piece of Blu-tack and flick on the switch. Then do what you like. They won't have a fucking clue what's going on, or what's coming on, or where it's coming from – haha-haha-hah! I want the drill and the receiver back. Burn the bag!'

Clank. The door slammed shut in the Clergy's faces. Busy footsteps pattered away inside. The Parson turned to the bulbous-nosed Gherkin.

'All a man needs to nobble with!'

'Ready, neighbours?'

'Let's nobble.'

Over at Maples Street, Curly and the Skipper drew up in a taxi, nursing some two gallons of coping fluid in their bellies and a further two in bottled form, packed into two polythene carriers. The Skipper negotiated the carriage fare whilst Curly stepped out, tripped on the kerb, fell backwards over the bonnet then toppled sideways off it, headbutting the nearside wing mirror clean off into the gutter.

'Ooop! Ahsozz, evybodee!' He hauled himself to his knees and made numerous wavy attempts to re-affix the mirror unit, before they gave it up to the driver and both staggered precariously off towards the front door.

'Okey-chokey!'

'Assat then! Beer, a sandwich and we're off to star as ventriloquisses on t' radio!'

'Hah! We'll knock 'em dead!'

The Skipper tried desperately to find the end of his roll-up with a lighter as Curly trawled the beer into the doorway and made repeated stabs at the Yale with his door key. As it finally clicked home, more through mathematical probability than judgement, the pair of them tumbled inside and onto the hallway floor, guffawing like well-wined pirates.

'Ha, ha, bit – assay – bit dark hereabouts! Lemme get some light on the sitcom...'

'No!'

'Wha?'

Curly snatched the Skipper's arm away from the light switch and then the lighter from his hand.

'Whut? Wot?'

'Gas! Can't you smell it?'

'Uh? Gas? Woss... huck... goin' on?'

'The living room – careful!' Now consumed by a sudden jolt of sobriety, they nudged open the living room door with a beerbag and peered inside.

'Iss gas, alright! Check the fire!'

'Fire's off.'
'Wait. It's bad in the kitchen.'
''Ang on... whoof! Not much!'
'Think it's the cellar?'
'More over here, nearer the boiler.'
'Well, get some bastard windows open, then!'
'We nailed 'em shut, remember? I can throw the furniture through them...?'
'Think we can compromise and just open the back door, dear boy – uff! Quickly!'
Curly slammed open the back door, indenting at least four of its twelve coats of Council gloss against a cupboard unit. He plunged headlong into the yard for a clean breath.
'Curl?'
'Oofyerh! What is it? You leave the cooker on again?'
'Hope not. It's electric. Just come and feast your eyes on this shit!'
Curly slouched back into the kitchen, attaching a precautionary hand to the door frame.
'What?'
'Look.'
Perched guiltily on the Formica worktop in the far corner was a beak-fronted can opener. Running through the worktop, the kitchen gas main. Where the main met the worktop, it displayed a telltale kink where the opener had evidently been utilised to prise a gaping hole in the main.
'Only four people with house keys, dear boy...'
'Me.'
'Me.'
'Tarif...'
'*Billy*! The fucking maniac! Been back to try to do for us!'
'*Basta*!'
'Get to a phone! Gas Board!'
'We'll be late for meeting the others!'
'We'll be late full stop, if the entire show blows!'

'Fuck and bollocks! I'll go – you got the number?'

'I've got *that* fucking nutter's number! Borrow a phone book! While you're at it, you'd better call the Electrissfuckingty Board as well, in case he's rigged the cistern up to the National Grid! Oh, and better get some brandy – for the shock!'

In Russell Road, the umpteenth tin of Guinness had just fallen from Joe's lifeless fist as Joe was entering level four of his coma in front of the evening edition of the Channel Four News. A weighty Chinese meal lay untouched in his lap. A pool of stout slowly perfused the peach-coloured carpet around his feet. Joe's head slowly tilted onto his right shoulder. Joe was not going to see the next five hours.

In his newly-built Bridgford townhouse, the Croc seated himself at the kitchen table and sniffed furtively at the glass of red wine to his foreright. Soon, Frau Croc arrived with a lusciously dressed and tossed salad and bread rolls and tagliatelle carbonara and condiments and specific advice that if he were even to *think* of putting his shoes on afterwards with a view to meeting The Chimneys, then sex wouldn't even be an antipasto for a month...

At The Peacock, across from the Radio Nottingham studios, Sticky and the Shedfixman sat pratting around with beer mats and ashtrays and beer glasses.

'Well? Turbo! Not one of them! Not an arsoul!'

'Can't see them pitching up now, Shed.'

'Academic anyway; we'll soon be late for the interview – fuck the conference!'

'So this is it, then.'

'It's it for me. I've got an evolutionary table to participate in.'

'Can't believe the Skipper...'

'Can't believe the entire bunch of 'em – well?'

'Soddit, Shed! Let's go for a curry – come on! Drink!'

'Or...'

'Ha, ha! Is there an or?'

'There is an or.'

'Name that or.'

'Or. We hit the top shelf like tomorrow's Armageddon, grab a bag of chips next door and march into the studios as if nothing's unusual and be complete drunken nuisances and talk nothing but lies and parp over the airwaves...?'

'Mm...'

'Yeahhh!'

Next, I vaguely recall being led into a rhino-carpeted, air-conditioned corridor, infested with anoraks carting around every kind of radio-interviewable subject matter imaginable, from Schefflera to Jack Russell terriers. I was carrying a quarter-eaten sausage; Sticky was struggling to carry a heavy stammer. I recall seeing a very large speaker with various dials and buttons down the side. It was relaying the current broadcast at the time, and next to it sat the man with the Jack Russell. The next bit I remember quite vividly, because the dial on the speaker – which I *accidentally* cranked up full – turned out to be the volume dial of an immensely powerful system. This caused the man to suddenly twitch and chuck his dog down the corridor, six feet off the ground. The other chap with the Schefflera turned out to be stone deaf and therefore remained completely unruffled by the fracas, until the startled face of a Jack Russell suddenly came anxiously peeking at him through the upper foliage of his seven-foot plant. It seemed a little harsh to then blame the animal for its automatic propensity towards self-preservation as it clasped the plant with all four members – however unfortunate the consequence of which, being the progressive stripping of every leaf and stalk of the plant by the terrier's arse on its swift descent of this floral 'fireman's pole'. The livid botanist, now only endowed with a potted quarterstaff, set off after the dog with it – yet the dog still displayed sufficient testicles to double back to me for a bit of sausage before resuming to bait his hunter into a lung-crushing chase along several walkways and sitting rooms.

'Oh my God!' John Holmes had manifested at the height of the hightime. The disarray in the corridor, however, played second fiddle in his estimation compared to the disarray in our equilibria. Sticky still teetered in hysterics over the dog.

'Er... Shed? Sticky?' He shook our hands as warmly as he professionally dared.

'This way... I think I'll get you both some coffee...'

Meanwhile at Cueball's, the Westwoods were entreating all to some fiercely inane pre-match babbling and nervous twanging of the self-reassuring kind. Some twenty-five minutes earlier, behind his trusty guile of pretend deadpan enthusiasm, Tallbob had marvelled at the intricate workmanship and heavenly resonance of Clive Westwood's £29.95 Happy Shopper guitar and flattered him into accepting a drink. Providing of course that he fetched it himself, and accorded Tallbob the rare privilege of a quick strum whilst he was about it. Tallbob was now poised on tenterhooks at the end of the bar with a sawn-away volume switch under his right foot and the hand drill in his left pocket. He sniggered profusely each time a member of the bar staff respectfully reminded the Parson that he was wasting a fortune in the juke box, as it was already turned right down for the band to begin. Alongside the Parson, Fig was grinning roguishly at the ceiling, muttering away to himself, patting his nose-end and maintaining an ideallic screen for the handiwork being performed behind him by the Sergeant and the superglue.

Then, as fiddles fiddled and grown men yeehaaed and Clive Westwood jiggered in the first few bars of 'Sourmash', the juke saboteurs discreetly wove through the assembly of footstompers to rejoin with Tallbob.

'Got it sorted?'

'Wha? Jeez – what a fucking racket!'

'I said…'

'Wha?'

Tallbob pointed toward the juke.

'Ohh! Yep. Job!' The Parson winked.

'Amma git me serma that 'ol myoonshine!'

'Jeez!'

'How's Pilkington on shotguns?'

'Uh?'

'Forget it, just do it…'

'Arcane b'leeve yer liff me, mawmuh!'

'Wuh?'

'Do it. Please do it.'

'Sep'n furr yew ain't theyrr da cleng tyew!'

'For Jesus Christ's sake, will you fucking just…!'

'Oi! No need to shout!'

Tallbob took a brief cursory. There seemed no obstacles to the caper's furtherance; only the backs of a hundred light heads. He took out the hand drill and waited for a flicker of stage lighting to come his way to quickly eye the drill and confirm that it was still at the clockwise setting. Once again he checked heads. He delicately nuzzled the bit into the realms of his most recent craftwork. Checked heads again. He hit the orange button, pushing hard and horizontally to his right.

'Avoooooooomahwaddayerwanna make those eyes… at me for…'

Even Tallbob was startled into dropping the drill behind the bar. He watched it roll mercifully away to lodge out of sight behind a brown bucket under the sink. Not that it would have been of any interest to the barmaid, who was now in dire and immediate need of dustpan and brush to make a start on the two dozen mixer glasses which she'd just launched against the back wall in shock. Nor would it have been to the barman, looking for at least two dishcloths and a first aid kit – as, unluckily, he'd been under the misconception that it was possible to pour ale whilst leaning over the bar to chew at his girlfriend's ear.

The Parson tapped at the others' forearms in turn.

'Right! Away! Over hereish! Let's have a change!'

They wandered calmly over to the midst of the chaos, where the floorboards were now suddenly becalmed from all stomping. On stage; hands were clear of fretboards, drumsticks were spinning impatiently through fingers and pink painted fingernails fiddled nervously with Celtic auburn tresses.

'Doowop! Bidoowidoowidoowop, bidoowidoowidoowop, bidoowidoowidoo!'

Back at the end of the bar, Cueball was already culturing his steaming purple dome as he wrangled to small avail with the mutilated control box whilst being further antagonised by the cluelessly inappropriate suggestions thrown up by his number two. It seemed prudent to the Clergy that the best way to safely laugh themselves to death at all of this, was to form a loose circle and pretend to tell each other hilarious jokes. Before long, his number two was dispatched out to yank the plug and for two more selections, he toiled convulsively on one knee – if only for the sake of his girlfriend's poorly ear. He eventually threw in the towel after a last ditch attempt at the cable by sticking his rump against the wall and bending over to pull between his legs was beginning to crucify his neatly gelled slickback. He stood motioning over to Cueball, palms up. Cueball, now beginning to hate number two as much as the predicament itself, stormed around the bar and marched grimly over to the juke. He barged the barman aside, and with some inaudible but indubitably profane putrefaction hissing through his grinding incisors, he took the shroud in both hands, stuck his fat arse in reverse then fell swiftly on it, graceless as you like. Now even the Westwoods were beginning to hazard a chortle. The Clergy were mopping away tears and gagging for air. This was Cueball's limit. Bad enough living in an uncontrollable disaster; bad enough making a complete newark of himself with spectators aplenty, but absolutely intolerable that nobody could hear him shout about it.

He swam to his feet, grunted something and stormed off into his kitchen, three paces ahead of himself, to further emerge a few seconds later, bedecked in short green Wellingtons and yellow rubber sink gloves and toting what appeared to be a pair of large red-handled secateurs. As clear as his objective was his express intention to remain unelectrified by it. With a sweep of his arm to clear all immediate bodies, he grasped the juke cable and one simple quick snip gave way to a brief silence before a hearty cheer from his patrons.

Once again the aimless twanging welled up from the stage people, followed by some tenuous topical babble before a brief spell of heated in-bickering over whether or not to begin the set again. The Parson was already cringing at the prospect.

'Think I'm gonna need to go for a shit. Who's carrying number four?' The Sergeant dug into his Mac pocket and discreetly offered the tiny transmitter.

'Know what you're doing?'

'Oooh, I've been shitting nearly as long as I can remember – I'm just hanging on Bob's job!'

'Don't worry – it's rigged *and* he's stuck another mike down for the guitar, so it's going to be happening through *two* channels – just to throw them a bit more!'

In the boys' room, the Parson selected trap one, latched the door, dropped the lid, dusted it for any remnant moisture, sat down and waited for stage racket with transmitter poised. Back onstage the 'once again from the top' faction had had their way in the name of aestheticism and were counting in 'Sourmash' take two. The Clergy could scarcely contain themselves, particularly Fig and the Sergeant to whom Pilkington's industry was a novel experience. The count began.

'A-han, a-hoo, a-handoo-heeforr...'

'I'm a pink toothbrush – you're a blue toothbrush...'

'Pffff!'

'Ha ha ha ha!' The Westwoods gawped frantically around at each other in search of a culprit. The male lead singer pulled up the performance and turned to visually examine his female counterpart.

'Well don't look at mee... I'm a blerdee mezzo-suprahno, iznit?'

The Clergy screamed in all directions before returning to face front, chins on chests, shoulders heaving.

'Sorry, everyone, we've got a bit of a fault. We've obviously got a bad earth and we're picking up something else... can we check the desk inputs back there, please?'

'Tsss! Iss! Iss!'

'Clear? Sure? Okay? We ready? Okay then. A-two, a-hon-tooheehaw...'

'It's fun, just running through... the alphabet with you... but what are we gonna do about – him? Gaw, blimey – A! You're adorable – B! You're a bastard – C! You're a fuc-king cunt...'

'Haaa haaa haaa!'

Once again the customary opener folded into disarray as the Clergy folded into dispossession. In the traps, the Parson was clinging to the roll dispenser to avoid falling off the seat. After three attempts, he successfully composed himself for the next ambush. Fate however, was to decide otherwise. Being consumed with glee, he was blissfully unaware of two concurrent factors. Firstly, he was sitting with the 'transmit' button pressed in. Secondly, there had been a silent occupant in the next-door trap who now, without warning, was flushing the pan. The Parson flinched. He'd always been blessed with a talent for fast thought in adverse conditions which, for a man who provoked most of his own, was pretty lucky. An instant evaluation of his circumstances convinced him of an eighty to ninety per cent likelihood of antipathy from the erstwhile silent crapper, who, if not already, would soon be privy to the machinations of the whole caper. He could've been staff! He was sure to be pro-Westwood; he might even be one of their crew – being so unfussed as to toilet himself during a number with which he might be overly familiar! Now there was a pressing urgency to preserve anonymity and get his slight rump out of there, before the jangling of his neighbour's trouser belt was curtailed.

Leaping at the latch, the Parson whipped aside the door and strode briskly out, without looking back. He was in the clear for now. In the corridor leading back to the bar, he was suddenly forced to hop tentatively aside for the purple-faced Cueball – still equipped with secateurs at the ready and the number of the beast stamped across his forehead. The Parson was not thinking of waiting around to catch the end of this one. He strode on, back into the bar, past the Westwoods – who were now organising a more thorough dig for the source of the nobble – and over to the others. His fist feigned a drinking-up motion as he approached them.

'Out of here! We're about to get bubbled!'

No one argued. They'd done what they came to do, and well. Now it was time to duck the backfire. After a swift volley of glugs, four empty vessels were slammed onto the bar in passing and the Clergy filed out into the street. In the street, the Parson was chuckling all over.

'Pity the poor bastard, when he opens the bog door to a twenty-three stone, hairless nutter in rubber gloves and Wellies, waving a pair of snippers around like some gone bad Rabbi at a fetish gig!'

'Ha ha ha ha ha!'

Tallbob zipped up his jacket and turned to the Sergeant. 'Well. Unqualified success, I think!'

'Apart from the receiver. *And* the drill. What do we tell Pilkington?'

'Any old shit, I suppose. If he still throws a hormone we can always chip in for another – they're only a tenner brand new.'

Fig's nosebleed had returned in his haste to knock back the beer. 'Whoddabout this boozer with a radio, then? I can do with taking the weight off!'

The Parson computed the options. 'The Charles Napier – round the corner. It'll be deader than the grave. They won't mind sticking the wireless on for a highly personable, clean-cut, mild-mannered foursome such as we!'

They set off at a march, Napierwards.

'Or, if they do, we'll saw a few chair legs three-quarters through and put our socks down the pool table pockets.'

'Precisely.'

'Hey! Sounds like they've finally got going back there!'

'Lucky world.'

'Hey – you still got the transmitter?'

'In me pocket.'

'Let's test the distance theory with one last chorus of "A – you're adorable". See if the battery's playing.'

'Yeah, you never know.'

'Unless you try.'

'And we *always* try!'

The Parson plucked out the transmitter and poised to press as the Clergy moved in closer to sing up.

'Ready? A-hon...'

'Ha ha ha ha!'

'...ahoo... a-hon, hoo-heehaw-A!'

'You're adorable!'

'B!'

'You're a b—'

Back at Cueball's, the little receiver was copying them admirably, though unfortunately not copying them at that most paramount of locations where they would have ideally wished to be copied. During the witch-hunt on and around the stage, Clive had unwittingly removed his guitar and gone to set it down upright against an amp, to allow him to properly join the search. As the instrument was grounded, there came a clearly audible knock from inside. Puzzled if not a little worried, he picked it up again and gave it a few cautious shakes. Loud rattle. Holding it then face down, it took but a couple of shakes more to dislodge and spill the incumbent pest out onto his lap. After a brief conferral with the more technically minded of the crew, it was surmised that even if it was *not* the source of their ills, then it was still not worth the risk of having it around, *whatever* it was. The receiver was promptly passed to one of the road crew, who then tossed it out into one of the clusters of rubbish skips in the backyard. After its tiny, scratchy relayal of the Clergy's choral debacle, the battery began to die. There was a brief revival, as a passing police traffic car requested a check on a 'Bravo two zero three, Charley Whisky Golf' and then both power and frequency began to slide down. Somewhere on the way, it caught a few seconds of Radio Nottingham's airwaves.

'Mmm! Like it! It's got – I dunno – ooompf! That's The Chimneys and a song called "Saint Ann's Well Road". With us for a few more minutes and some *more* sounds, two of The Chimneys – drummer Sticky and bassist the Shedfixman! Now guys, you've already mentioned the history of the group...'

'*Buurrp-oop!*'

'I dropped me sausage... I 'ave...'

'Ahem! "Saint Ann's Well Road", then! Does this have some poignant theme, or is it just a Nottingham thing?'

'It's a song about a road...'

'About... how... roads are the best things in the world to take your car on...'

'And come back.'

'...speaking as a Nottingham thing... a thing that lives in Nottingham...'

'So, guys! When can...'

'Dropped me coffee, now.'

'...can we expect to see you next in town? Don't worry about it...'

'Tomorrow morning.'

'...you're playing in the morning?'

'Nah – ha ha – silly billy! *You expect us to play? We expect to drink, Mr Bond!*'

'We only ever visit buildings with lots and lots of glasses inside – huck!'

'Really? That's very...'

TWENTY-ONE

Lincoln Prison
6.30 a.m. Tuesday, 29 October 1991

'Whu! Hrr!' Oh. I remember now. Supreme of all fucks. I'm here. Yeah, I'm here, real enough. Just caught my head in time before it fell again. Breathe. Check neck. Check everything. Quietly. That. All that. Was I dreaming, or remembering a life? And if remembering, then remembering in silence or aloud to the others? The others. Others are here. Shall I ask? Have I asked? Shall I ask whether I've asked? Seems logical in the first – but the others... They don't know you. Don't know them. Last thing you need is rollover Lincoln bird wearing the Headbanger-in-Chief badge. No. Listen, instead. Listen yourself a favour, maybe. To Nev upstairs – snoring. To Bab or Flymo wanking for France. To Flymo or Bab flinching from a bad dream, muttering a tide of sorrys. Calling for his partner. Whining. No. Leave the others. Sense rude dawn pissing through some hole which I can't be fucked to look for. But dawn, though.

If dawn? Then a minute must have passed. Surely. Certainly a minute. If a minute? Probably an hour. If an hour, maybe the night? If the night, then finally its demons.

TWENTY-TWO

Grazing field outside Barton in Fabis, Nottinghamshire
Mid-afternoon, 29 May 1997

> Will I ever go to Appledore?
> 'For aye!' the dream it said,
> A lantern burns at Appledore,
> to gild a stair to bed,
> Today I could've toiled for gain
> afresh, but chose to shy,
> Green eyes repair to drunken bane,
> As Appledore slips bye.

Poetry. Sodding poetry. I never *could* abide the cack and here I am writing poetry. Yeah, but look what I've got: sole mammalian occupancy of a lush grazing field beside the prettiest river on earth and blazing sunshine over my birthday for a change. I've got a freshly baked ciabatta loaf, half-moon of lukewarming Port Salut, jar of anchovy-stuffed queen green olives and a second bottle of Montepulciano D'Abruzzo on the breathe and all heaven's looking back in envy. And what price does the magnificent put on me for this entire sacred array? Simple. A levy of rotten poetry, then afterwards? It's further reward. Drift on to bathe in another warm, dreamy summer night and share the bath with a lazily reclining planet. But such lavish incitement to inspiration provokes a suspicion. Should the poem be the true feast? And good victuals the false frippery? A safeguarding conclusion, then. The good food, the good wine, the poem, the day – all are surely part of a greater verse – all corporate cogs in beauty's tall timepiece, and all requiring earthly witness to be. Halt for a while then and be amazed. Claw off ciabatta, smear a goo of Salut, but first, a neckrinse to up viscosity for comestible conduction. Praise. Feel the sun. Reflect. Recelebrate. A guilt, though. Surely one further wish could only exude from an ingrate or glutton or jackal in the Temple? Then I must be an ingrate and a glutton and jackal to miss that. But on summer nights, I miss that most. The knowing. The knowing there's a stage ready to step onto and belt it out, later tonight. The tingling ears and the dual aromas of Femfresh off the gals, adrenalin off the guys – Sweet Lord! Is it really *ten* years ago? Where did *that* go? Time. The most cruel of abrasives; the grandest and longest-serving larcenist of all. Look at us all then and look at us all now. Jeesh.

Look at the Biffers. They've all flowered into clean, respectable, hard-working girls. Very rare to see them at all these days. Hard-working girls get snapped up by hard-working boys. Raisa has a fine eight-year-old son by the Croc – Joshua. Helen and Dawn settled down and married toy boys. After plenty ado, Selina gave birth by caesarean section to a 5lb 6oz alien with a loud black Mohican. Nadine has since grown – and grown a bloody sight too quickly – into a beautiful and caring young lady with an emergent talent for the violin. Selina and I parted in swift and unfortunate acrimony in '89. She settled with a builder one year later. They had another kid, last I heard.

Tinker, and Steph – his long time girlfriend – run a vegetarian corner shop in Forest Fields. It was the first any of us knew he was vegetarian. These days he's content to sport a sensible haircut, wear catalogue clothes, play Lemmings on the computer all night, weeknights; rugby for the Moderns on Saturday, and Steph on Sunday.

Johnny B enjoys a successful and lucrative career selling and installing computer hardware. Johnny lives with girlfriend Jane and their baby daughter.

Mark and Wendy Anthony remain faithfully and inextricably

married to this day and beyond. They have a charming young son, Stevie – six. Mark's been to death's door and back twice with a serious liver problem, but given his perpetual charisma, joviality and highness of spirit, you'd be pushed to guess it.

Curly Ashmore plumped for a career in pub management. He has since successfully navigated three pubs from bare solvency to irrevocable liquidation. His fourth, The Wheatsheaves, is foundering nicely.

Des Carson the Small Parson decided to cool it, get his nose down and butter his toast on both sides. If anyone could open a pork pie shop in Tel Aviv and retire by Christmas, that would be Des. His extraordinary flair and aptitude for gushing hairy-arsed rhinoceros shit has netted him a veritable harvest of opulence in the world of cold calling. Car on the firm, mobile on the firm, unchallenged plastic on the firm, fax and Internet on the firm – in case he prefers to sell from his bed tomorrow. Designer house, paid for. Soulmate / bedmate in equal status. Wowza.

Tallbob is content in hot pursuance of hermitude, living alone in Forest Fields' bedsit land. From there, he nightly shatters every scrap of mortal peace within a five-street radius between teatime and weetime by ladling out some bobby-dazzling blues guitar, care of his Les Paul Gold Top through an overdriven Vox V120 which is, I swear, the loudest cowin' ladle beknown to hearing man. If Bob goes out at all, it's either to work, or to the offy or to the halal for curry parts, or to the doctor's for more green sink cream, or to another spell in a drying-out clinic, or up to his local to drive the regulars round the twist. If he's skint and out of strings and there isn't much on the telly, he gets his chortles from hanging upside down over his window ledge and caning the downstairs neighbours' windows with a pool cue before rushing down in a bogus panic, convincing them that the whole block's under attack from a horde of stone-throwing hooligans. As a direct result of this, nobody over the age of thirty speaks to anybody under the age of twenty in Forest Fields anymore, and a privately funded neighbourhood vigilante group regularly tramps its streets on the look out for absolutely no sod whatsoever.

Fortune favours Fig frugally. The Iron Gherkin became temporarily composed of more iron than he ever bargained for, whilst operating an angle grinder on site without protective goggles. A sharp sliver of the stuff flew away from a steel lintel he was cutting, piercing through the front of his left eye and lodging in its retina. Bang. Monoscope for ever. The poor get had barely recovered from this, when he was coshed and robbed on his own doorstep, late one night. The attack left him unable to work properly ever again, because it left him saddled with bouts of epilepsy. Pills for epilepsy, pills for migraines, pills for depression after the migraines, pills for stress after the depression, pills for total eczema after the stress. Undaunted, Fig makes his invalidity benefit stretch to a night out, or to a mobile phone which never rings by working a burger stand now and then. But he'd still bail you out with his last coin; even *that's* his downfall now. His last coin usually gets poached by the latest cute slag who collects last coins for beer or drugs and he gives it belly up, just to get a few minutes of their company when the loneliness begins to cook his crust. No more dark bulb weekends. No more canal barges in his kitbag. No more the Gherkin. As for the late night bravehearts? Diarrhoea drips on a dyspeptic llama's dinner plate. As for coinwomankind? Consider the code of the Chu; arrive the day when I need to become a fucking witch-biscuit just to land a tepid shag will arrive the day I finally turn Cliff.

Phil. After Christmas 1987, Cueball's place had budgeted for the expected January slump and used the downtime to close up for renovations. Mindful of the returning polytechnic students, all the surrounding non-Shippo licences lopped prices and threw in various gimmicks in a bid to capture the sudden loose trade. By the spring half-term, mindful that breweries expect prompt and substantive returns on such dramatic refurbs, Cueball still hadn't shown able to drag it back. The Chimneys had split, and the Westwoods had split after the two guitar players had robbed the safe at Jaycees Bar and legged it to Hollywood to paint film sets. Cueball couldn't fill the band bill anymore and the place bombed as a venue. One Saturday that April, as the pub was really beginning to lose it hand over fist, a limousine containing Peter Kirk, Edgar Wayne, and the Sons and Holy Ghosts of Shipstones' Brewery drew up outside, demanding an on-the-spot meeting with his Cueballness. As a result of this ten-minute audience, Cueball was given twenty-four hours to assemble bag and baggage before being summarily exiled to Ilkeston to manage... The Hayloft! He was never to smell the sweet Nottinghamshire air again for the next thirty months.

The Crocodile marriage ran all the way to nine months before Frau Croc – mysteriously to all but the Croc – shoed the boo with yer friendly neighbourhood 'I'll organise the fetish party, you bring your wallet' smarm warehouse. Interviewing the Croc shortly afterwards, he appeared to be vocal of no worldly concern, other than that since The Chimneys' demise, the world had not only come to paying to attend fetish parties, but they were now tending to run out of steam by morning of the next day. Today Croc co-holds the weighty reins of the family jewellery empire, collects Swatches for a laugh and travels frequently far and wide in the world, taking exotic sabbaticals whilst secretly doubling as unofficial cultural ambassador and sex test-pilot for *Marie-Claire* magazine. Ooowah!

The months came, the months went and somewhere in between, Sticky had forgotten that I wouldn't forget the great pizza caper. Past the falling leaves and on into the snows of January did I bide. Then, at that month's end, the advent of first quarterly gas and electricity bills. Two weeks on I sat, knowing that Sticky – being never in a rush to appease such inconveniences – had hung on for a meter reading. Now, Stick's meters sat inside a white plastic wall box, next to the front door on the outside of his domicile. By remarkable coincidence, so did mine! Ergo I possessed an identical triangular-headed box key. It was equipped with this key and a large frozen bag of stir-fry chicken pilaf that I arrived at my good friend's house in the wee hours of one early February morning. Bearing in mind that Sticky was in the habit of leaving his dustbin by the meters, where it was out of the way, and that it would be at least three months before any further readings, the mo was simplicity itself. Meter door open. Generously pierce stir-fry bag. Stand bag inside meter compartment. Close door. Drive home. Wait.

After an unseasonably mild Feb–March and halfway through a rather clammy April, the meter man had again come to visit Sticky's house, and after some two to three short seconds in the performance of his duty, respectfully inquired as to whether Sticky minded if he threw up his breakfast in the downstairs trap *before* attempting to recount of the malodorous and gruesome nature of the post-pupaic menagerie encamped in the wall box thereout – a sight which apparently would pervade his worst nightmares beyond retirement. More sadly, prior to his visit, Sticky had, over several weeks, been forking out hundreds, even thousands of pounds having the drains cleaned professionally, having them twice dug up completely, then the plumbing dismantled; kitchen and bathroom and toilet tiling ripped down and remounted, downstairs carpeting and floorboards pulled up and relaid; and the entire downstairs redecorated. All in all, a fraught and fruitless effort to locate the epicentre of the humongous ming which greeted him from work each evening. Broke my heart to be the first one to grin when he finally stormed the pub to ask who the fucking stir-fry comedian was. Gotcha, m'man!

Today m'man resides deep in the buxom bosom of matrimony with Duty Miss Cutey and their two young daughters. Still the high-flying whizkid on a bowl of cereal. Asides of that, I've honestly never in my life seen a woman peg out two lines of a man's underpants with such regal serenity and aplomb like Miss Cutey on a twice-weekly basis. Sticky says you know you've found the girl of your dreams when you're able – during a piss in the bathroom – to perform an unexpected afterparp or weighty follow-through and yet still grin, as you throw open the window to select instant and ready replacements from the massed buntings of whistle-clean substitutes swaying in salute from the washlines below. At your service for your next bout of sub-pantalonial anarchy – sir!

All along it had been Joe who'd been the secret lemonade drinker – Martini, to be precise. The bottle binner. For more years than we'll ever know and he'll ever admit, he'd been caning between three and six bottles every day, until he spent a couple of years in pub management; then you could add another two to that, due to acceleration, availability and the fact that he no longer had to stash the empties in the pedal bin. No wonder Joe always wore his Marlowe titfer. He had a bit more to keep under one than the rest of us – pissheads as we were. After a series of highly questionable stock-takes, Joe was finally sacked and left to eke out an existence on benefit in a flatshare. His self-esteem hit rock bottom, and by 1992, the boozing had become even worse – if that could be possible. One Friday evening in October of that year whilst dog-sitting for his flatmate who'd gone away for the weekend, Joe was on the way to his bedroom and bed, when his liver failed. He tumbled downstairs and fell onto the floor, unconscious, then into a coma by the front door. Nobody heard the fall. The dog, sensing that something was very up with Joe, trotted downstairs and lay on top of him for the entire forty-eight hours, keeping him warm until its master returned and alerted the emergency services. The dog had saved Joe's life... just. He certainly broke some records down at intensive care. Today, now forcibly teetotal, Joe still enjoys making music and remains a skilful and prolific songwriter and brilliant guitarist. He has released two excellent CDs with his latest band, Echo Park, and in spite of it all, still maintains an upward pecker and a cheery wit. There but for the grace!

The Skipper heartily relishes a proud and dignified bachelorhood at his downtown residence, where most evenings, he's likely to be found doing a massive jigsaw – occasionally under the handicap of a tab of LSD, just to make it interesting. Or alternatively he's often found industriously adding to his home-built collection of World War Two fighter aircraft under the handicap of a crate of wine. Or if wine's temporarily unavailable, then a few glugs of aviation fluid. Among his very impressive and mostly flyable collection, include a four-foot Focke-Wulf and a ruddy great Spitfire, copied to the tee – hydraulics, the lot. Rumour even has it that jet engine test sounds have been reported. He's been known to punctuate this lifestyle with the weekly piss-up alongside Curly, and the odd prowl amongst the local slappery as and when his testosterone achieves brim. But he also regularly visits his mum in north-east Notts, to stay in touch and to work on a Mini Moke which he has garaged out there. He's even been clocked several times returning to Nottingham by way of the River Trent on board a motor torpedo boat. How he's barrelled and continues to barrel away all the ale he has and does without serious physical forfeiture by now remains an enigma to us one and all. The Skipper, it seems, has it all enviably sussed. But then, I think he always did.

Hey, then there's me – the Shedfixman. Or if you like, you can call me by my real name – Tom Hathaway.

Well, I was released from Her Majesty's Pleasure (she never even *once* showed up for some) just in time for Christmas '91. I blew all my coming-out cash on a big bag of food and presents for the Schizo bitch and our baby daughter, Molly, and we patched things up, but not for long.

I had to get away from England... all the badness, all the daily reminders of the gone-by good times being waved under my nose. So I got money together and travelled, just like I did as a teenager: Canada, France, Eastern Europe, Israel – even India for a few months – just to get my head elsewhere; but it was all exactly as Joe Planet once wrote in a song: 'Wherever you go, you take yourself with you as well.' Same reflection, same outlook. But in my case, I took my two deadliest arch-enemies: boredom and thirst. And when you're living in a country where it costs next to nothing to live, it stands to reason that it also costs next to nothing to get faced. By the time I'd returned from the big subcontinent, the seeds of my alcoholism were well in shoot. I'd lost both faith and interest in everything and everyone; I'd lost concern for the fate of the world, for myself. I no longer cared. Work, money, women, never seemed to stay around for long. All I seem to recall of '96 is blowing whatever money I ever got on drink as fast as possible, then suffering the consequences. Depression. Agoraphobia. Cancelling arrangements with the kids, because I was either penniless again, or because I was too low and miserable to even smile. I didn't want the kids to see me messed up like that. From one day to the next, not shaving, not washing, not knowing whose room I'd woken up in... just drifting between personal holocausts. Another day, I'd wake up propped against the dustbins behind a Caribbean takeaway. Another, I'd wake up pissing myself in the garden of a block of private offices on Mansfield Road, then get up before the rush hour to walk off the twin damps on my loins and brain in case some good Samaritan spotted me and called the police. Although I've more or less got myself worked out enough to protect me from absolute zero, it can never be far away, and every day is a battle. It might always be – except for the fact the doctors tell me my liver won't put up with much more. I know I must fight. Some days I'll win. Some days I know I'm losing. I don't know what's to become, but I know I'm still looking for something which I must find before this journey's end. Whatever, I can't complain. I've been lucky. So very lucky.

Did I miss somebody out? I think so. The summer before last; it was early August. A beautiful, warm Sunday evening. I'd been drinking in town with the Radford crew and we'd decided to pop into the Hearty Good Fellow for a quickie. We were barely through the door, when the dry cry of 'Shed, Shed, Shed!' filled the air. From the back of the room, where he'd been entertaining a table of semi-familiars, the Sarge leapt up and came rushing over to greet me, beer in hand. This was a departure. Not too long ago, he'd have let me get to the bar and waited for me to take the first sip before whamming me into throwing it over the barman – but no. He offered to buy me a beer, which I declined, because I was in a round. Then he guided me over to an isolated table; just the two of us, so we could 'talk about the old days'. It seemed something of a peculiar call, even a little inopportune, given that the subject was practically inexhaustible and we only had half an hour and company to resume with. In fact, something was bang off, which I couldn't rest with or put a finger on, but it was nice both to see him again and to see him in such a good mood, whether or not it might have been chemically induced. He seemed to revel in each and every golden memory thrown up from either side of the table, and then when it became pressing that we both rejoin our respective crews and move on, there was a tinge of pity for not having more time together. But, it *had* been great to see him, if only for a brief chat – after all, there'd be plenty more time.

Then, when we got up to shake hands and wish goodnight, Sarge did something which *did* rattle my borders. Just as I was about to walk away, he grabbed my arm and crammed, or began to cram, a third of whisky into my inside pocket: 'Here, Shed! Take this!' he said. I told him I couldn't possibly accept it – I'd long been on a self-imposed spirit ban anyway. 'Take it! Take it anyway! You might change your mind! You can give some to Fig or Tallbob when you see them! Share it! Share it out!' He wasn't going to wear a no, so I just took it, just to please him. We moved on separately, but for a while I was still struggling to put a name to the feeling – telling myself he'd probably just been visiting his brother's offy before going out or something. Old times? Well, he was in a good mood. We hadn't seen each other for a long while; yep, that's it. He was in a good mood, full stop. Nothing more.

It transpired that a few days later, the Sergeant visited his daughter and her mother. He spent the usual three to four hours, catching up with the latest, having a drink, a snack, the odd wisecrack – but more importantly, remaining in touch and reaffirming his deep fatherly affections for his child. Then, when it was getting late, he bade them his goodbyes. He caught the late bus home. At home, he opened a bottle of wine. He drank the wine, then he took his own life. Just because he didn't have a job, just because he was behind with the rent, just because he was being ruthlessly hounded for under- and overpayments by the tax and social security. *Just because he was vulnerable*. The rich man's son who never asked for a thing or complained in his whole life.

The only thing larger than the bitter devastation we all felt, seeing him off on that sun-soaked August morning up at Wilford Hill, was the perplexity and confusion whisked up inside by the question *why*? When he had all of us? Did he miss the good times so much? Did he just get sick of running? Surely I could've done something... I was sure something wasn't right. Tallbob and I talked about it for days. He eventually straightened me out, there. The way Sarge had been in the last weeks; the fact that he'd saved up at least four prescriptions of barbs and done about sixty. He'd made his mind up, alright. One way.

Still, for many months to follow, I racked my brains, trying to decide whether he was a hero or a fool for buckling into the bastards. Then, somewhere in the middle of writing this book, and having weighed up some of our lives more seriously, it finally occurred to me why he was a hero all along. He was a hero – simply because, if he hadn't had the guts to die, then more than one of us wouldn't have had the guts to live. And that's a fact. Strange. Almost reminds you of some other script...

Yet, in the losing days, the days spent lying in physical and mental agony on a bed or on a floor... hallucinating... jumping in fit with panic attacks or graphic nightmares whenever I dare to fall asleep... seeing my children die a hundred times over again... sodden with sweat but freezing cold... rolling over and over and over to ease the pressure under my ribs... tearing my own flesh to pieces... watching the acid from my tears bleaching my shirtsleeves... yelling out for someone, or something to come down and help, or take me. In those losing days, as I near the end, the Sarge will come back to me then, and I can forget myself. My so-called problems. I can wonder how low and desperate and broken-hearted he must have felt during those last moments; then in no time, I'm reminded and replenished of the sheer seething rage and fanatical contempt which I hold aside for the walking cess which contrived to gang up and drive him to that despair. The penny-sucking bullies and despotic cowards and flaccid nescientists who march down your throat behind the Queen's warrant and then cut, run and cower behind labelled doors and bullet screens to preserve that safe and hallowed margin between how it is and how they prefer to see it. Between sympathy and smug. Between consumer and consumed. Not me – not me – never, never me. Again, I'm able to stand and walk and drink water and piss poison. I piss it at you. I piss on your poor system. You'll never know me, and you'll never understand why I'm so grateful to you for the gift of anger. The anger I need to survive.

This is dedicated to his memory.

***

> *Only the one who wears the shoe can tell you where it hurts.*
>
> Siraj Houssain Udin
> 1956–1995

He travelled East for a bit of peace…

…unfortunately, he'd taken *himself* along.

The Shedfixman will return in

FULL CHICKEN JACKET

First up – best dressed

Printed in the United Kingdom
by Lightning Source UK Ltd.
106058UKS00001B/70-93

9 781844 014873